HER COUNTRY

HER

COUNTRY

★ HOW THE ★
WOMEN OF COUNTRY MUSIC
BECAME THE SUCCESS THEY WERE
NEVER SUPPOSED TO BE

MARISSA R. MOSS

Henry Holt and Company

New York

HOLT

Henry Holt and Company
Publishers since 1866
120 Broadway
New York, NY 10271
www.henryholt.com

Henry Holt ® and ⏺ ® are registered trademarks of Macmillan Publishing Group, LLC.

Distributed in Canada by Raincoast Book Distribution Limited

Library of Congress Cataloging-in-Publication Data

Names: Moss, Marissa R., author.
Title: Her country : how the women of country music became the success
they were never supposed to be / Marissa R. Moss.
Description: First edition. | New York : Henry Holt and Company, 2022. |
Includes bibliographical references.
Identifiers: LCCN 2021060818 (print) | LCCN 2021060819 (ebook) |
ISBN 9781250793591 (hardcover) | ISBN 9781250793607 (ebook)
Subjects: LCSH: Women country musicians—United States. | Women
singers—United States. | Country music—2001–2010—History and
criticism. | Country music—2011–2020—History and criticism. | Sex role
in music.
Classification: LCC ML3524 .M67 2022 (print) | LCC ML3524 (ebook) |
DDC 781.64209—dc23
LC record available at https://lccn.loc.gov/2021060818
LC ebook record available at https://lccn.loc.gov/2021060819

Our books may be purchased in bulk for promotional, educational, or business use.
Please contact your local bookseller or the Macmillan Corporate and
Premium Sales Department at (800) 221-7945, extension 5442, or by e-mail at
MacmillanSpecialMarkets@macmillan.com.

First Edition 2022

Designed by Steven Seighman

Printed in the United States of America

1 3 5 7 9 10 8 6 4 2

For anyone who needs to be reminded that it's your country music, too

"I'm trying to burn this good-ol'-boy system down to the ground."

—Mickey Guyton, *Rolling Stone*, 2021

CONTENTS

INTRODUCTION · xi

CHAPTER 1: That Good Ol' Boys Club · 1

CHAPTER 2: Black and Blue · 20

CHAPTER 3: Something Brave from Her Mouth · 37

CHAPTER 4: Fastest Girls in Town · 55

CHAPTER 5: Not Ready to Make Nice · 67

CHAPTER 6: And the Devil Takes the Last Car Down · 78

CHAPTER 7: All Their Favorite People · 95

CHAPTER 8: Butterflies and Wildflowers · 106

CHAPTER 9: It's None of Your Business What Other People Think About You · 117

CHAPTER 10: Can't Remember Shit · 135

CHAPTER 11: It City · 149

CHAPTER 12: Where My Gays At? · 165

CHAPTER 13: Faith in the Heartland · 185

CHAPTER 14: You Say Tomato, I Say Fuck You · 197

CHAPTER 15: Hero, MAGA, and Daddy Lessons · 211

CHAPTER 16: To Look at Country a Different Way · 225

CHAPTER 17: Mama Wants to Change That Nashville Sound   232

CHAPTER 18: We Belong   257

AFTERWORD   277

AUTHOR'S NOTE   283

ACKNOWLEDGMENTS   291

PLAYLIST   295

INTRODUCTION

It's been done so many times, that drive from Texas to Tennessee, that their dreams had just as significant a chance as cars to end up wrecked along the interstate, broken before they even had a shot at getting where they planned to go. That wide expanse of untraveled road; the impatient ticking of traffic signs and mileposts; the long, restless stretches between breaks for a soda or restroom; the twisting of the radio knobs, scanning for something familiar; the guitars that sit awkwardly in the trunk, blocking any decent sight lines out the window—which is fine, because who wants to look back anyway?

They come ready for the world to open up, with a song or a notebook or ten years of toiling away at bars and honky-tonks, down the highways and past the towns of the working people they're supposed to write lyrics about, sometimes filled with singers just like them who never could save up enough money to fill that gas tank for the trip to Nashville—dreams tucked under mattresses like old photos and secret diaries. But Maren Morris, Kacey Musgraves, Mickey Guyton, and so many women like them came ready to play and take a gamble on those dreams: they came because, at one point, it seemed like women were the sun in the center of the country music solar system. And they had something to say to help keep the world turning.

This story begins in 1999, the year that Shania Twain, reigning superstar, took home the Entertainer of the Year trophy at the CMA Awards. The biggest hit on country radio was Faith Hill's "Breathe." Chely Wright, an artist who would later be pushed out of the genre for coming out as lesbian, was enjoying the success of her song "Single White Female." The Chicks (née the Dixie Chicks) were one of the most successful bands not only in country music, but well beyond. They'd just played feminist touring festival Lilith Fair, with fiddle player Martie Maguire fiercely wielding her instrument in a crop top, already angering the Nashville institutions to the point that her trio's eventual expulsion for speaking out against the president would come as a relief to some, not just a surprise.

It felt, for a minute at least, that this was a paradigm that could never shift. And if you were a girl growing up in Texas, Tennessee, or even Pennsylvania, country music didn't seem unattainable. It didn't seem out of reach for Maren, Kacey, or Mickey, or for thousands of young girls who turned on the radio during the car ride home from school, to hear voices like theirs on the speakers as the Texas plains whirled past their windows and their breath fogged the glass, their imaginations anywhere but in that back seat.

And how could you blame them for envisioning a certain kind of path? Back when Maren first started performing as an old soul in Dallas bars, when Mickey fell in love with country stardom while watching LeAnn Rimes at a baseball game and Kacey formed her duo, the Texas Two Bits, and began singing and yodeling in harmony across the Lone Star State, you could wake up as a little girl in Texas, Oklahoma, California, or anywhere in America, and think country music was for you. That's because you could hear the voices of women on the radio, in the kitchen, or in the back seat of the car, and dream as the road unfolded ahead.

It was watching a documentary about Faith Hill, in fact, that propelled Taylor Swift to decide she wanted to pursue a career in country music, and later convince her parents to move to Nashville, where she'd become a trailblazer for a whole new generation. It was listening to the Chicks when Kacey understood that she could take her love of the genre's classics and meld it with something new and different and be unafraid to take chances or draw outside of the boundaries set for her. It was through Shania Twain hollering "Honey, I'm home" to her husband in song that opened up Mickey and Maren to a musical world where women are in charge. It was Patty Griffin and Mindy Smith who taught them that beautiful, important country songwriting didn't even need to belong to "country" at all.

They could do that, too, they thought. They didn't know that as they progressed through their careers they would enter a system rigged against them—but that they would also transform the genre in their wake.

Country music was built on women like Kacey, Maren, and Mickey. The signature guitar sound of the genre originates with the playing of Mother Maybelle Carter (with her foundational finger-picking style known as the "Carter Scratch"), and with so many legends: Dolly Parton, Kitty Wells, Loretta Lynn, Patsy Cline, Bobbie Gentry, Sammi Smith, Tammy Wynette, Tanya Tucker, Linda Martell. But while the "outlaws" get the fame for being renegades, it was Loretta Lynn who wrote lyrics about taking the birth control pill and was subsequently banned from most of country radio; it was Dolly Parton who spoke of poverty and suicide; Tanya Tucker who sang about sex, and dressed like it, too. It was the oft-forgotten Rose Maddox who created a subset of hillbilly Western, and Susanna Clark who inspired the much more famous Townes Van Zandt and her own husband, Guy Clark. It was Linda Martell as the first Black woman to chart a country song and sing at the Grand Ole Opry. It was Reba McEntire who built an empire, Martina McBride who cracked a hit with a song about escaping abuse and became an advocate for domestic abuse survivors in its wake; it was Wynonna Judd who used horns on her solo project and transformed the trajectory for country pop. It was Shania Twain who took her music global. It was Kitty Wells and her Honky Tonk Angels; it was Jeannie C. Riley, who brought a miniskirt to the "Harper Valley P.T.A." It was Priscilla Renea, whose songs were country enough for Carrie Underwood and Miranda Lambert to cut themselves, but considered too R&B when she released an excellent album under her own name. It was all the Black women who we don't have songs to talk about here, because they were never allowed to make them. They were all country and changed country, whether Music Row agreed.

Maren, Mickey, and Kacey sang in church, at the local bars and chili cookouts, dreaming about country stardom in a man's world— after all, Texas country was dirty, brawny, and all about a good mix of whiskey and testosterone. When you think of Texas you might think of Willie Nelson, bandana around his head, chugging away onstage with his trusted Trigger guitar. You think of "Red Dirt" artists, like Robert Earl Keen, who sang of hard living and hard loving, with a pair of jeans or a bit of leather never far out of sight. You think of big cowboy hats and even bigger egos. You think of a land where some of the indisputably greatest country artists are men alone, so much so that you do not think of the women. You think of Willie and Waylon Jennings, but you do not as often think of Jessi Colter or Freda and the Firedogs (if you've even heard of the latter at all) or, more recently, Jamie Lin Wilson and Bri Bagwell.

But soon after women like Mickey fell in love with the genre through the radio, consolidation started hitting stations across the country, forcing programmers to become more risk-averse in their choices, particularly in the wake of the Telecommunications Act of 1996 and resulting layoffs, which then president Bill Clinton signed to allow more "free market" competition to radio and other media properties. As a result, huge conglomerates were allowed to swallow up local radio stations, putting decision-making in the hands of corporate offices, bloated-ego program directors, or even software that can discriminate at the push of a button: advocacy group WOMAN Nashville even unearthed training manuals that explicitly advised programmers to use specially engineered protections to prevent playing female artists back-to-back, which became industry standard. Now, only four companies—iHeartMedia (formerly the less cute and cozy Clear Channel), Cumulus Media, Audacy (formerly known as Entercom), and Townsquare Media—own nearly all the country radio stations in America. And it didn't just impact radio—consolidation became the norm in the music industry, with bigger labels swallowing up independent ones routinely and crushing diversity in the process, if it was even there to begin with. It mattered then and it matters now, because there is no bigger driver to success in country music than radio: it's what propels the entire marketplace and keeps the ecosystem afloat.

Cut to 2021, when women are only played on country radio as little as 10 percent of the time. To when country music went from being synonymous with powerful women to truck-riding "bro country" crooners. To when a rule that you don't play women back-to-back is taken as gospel, or that it's widely—and incorrectly—believed that women don't want to hear other women singers. To a world where artists like Kacey Musgraves sell out arenas but barely score a single second of airplay. To when women are likened by one radio consultant to tomatoes, in a salad of men, which became known in the industry as Tomato-gate. To when Black artists, especially Black women, are virtually nonexistent not just on country radio but in the industry as a whole, and the story of how country's premier and foundational instrument, the banjo, came from Africa is all but buried in history. To when you can be penalized for speaking your truth in a genre that's supposed to be built on it.

But also to a world where these women are infinitely bigger live draws than most male counterparts, having massive pop crossovers like Maren's "The Middle," winning armfuls of Grammys like Kacey, making country music history like Mickey, launching their own passion projects, charities, and clothing lines and taking complete control of their own careers, on their own terms. Women are rarely perceived "country enough," anyway—too pop, too indie, too anything—so they're left with no paths but to continually, in the words of Kacey Musgraves, follow their own arrows.

But this isn't just a story of sexism in music; it's a story of America: of how misogyny and class permeate the most basic of threads, and how power supersedes decency and art in the minds and hearts of those who should know better. It's a story of triumph, and how to pave your own way in an impossible world. It's a story about how politics, corporate greed, and the decisions of our political leaders trickle down to our most precious art forms. Of how the oppressed can also be the oppressor, especially if you're white, and how whiteness became country music's most historical currency. It is a story of how country music has used its gender wars as a cover for its deep, embedded desires to preserve and weaponize that whiteness.

It's the story of a young girl growing up in Texas named Kacey Musgraves, who wore cowboy hats bigger than her body and wrote her first song at the age of nine, who would go on to win Grammy Awards, sell out arenas, and change the face of the genre. With songs like "Follow Your Arrow," she would open the door for LGBTQIA+ artists, going from playing the George W. Bush inaugural as a child to praising weed and psychedelics as a grown woman. But it's also the story of the genre's true queer pioneers, like "Follow Your Arrow" co-writer and Grammy-nominated artist Brandy Clark, who may not be a household name like Kacey but whose work and visibility offers an intergenerational imprint.

It's the story of Maren Morris, who packed soul and grit into her version of country music as early as a preteen, jockeying with men five times her age for space on the Dallas/Fort Worth bar and honky-tonk stages as well as Texas regional radio, who broke the mold in Nashville to speak her mind politically and do things her own way, joining with Brandi Carlile, Amanda Shires, and Natalie Hemby in the Highwomen to mobilize the efforts to get all kinds of women played on country radio into a movement—and simultaneously transforming into a pop star with her breakthrough collaboration "The Middle."

And she did it all with, on occasion, the embrace of country radio, banking three number one singles on Billboard's Country Airplay Chart with "I Could Use a Love Song," "Girl," and "The Bones," none of which adhered to the modes or models of what was supposed to work.

It's the story of Mickey Guyton, who grew up on back roads climbing trees and singing in church, and who finally saw her own definition of success when she stopped trying to get country music to like her as they thought she should be and became the artist she is, singing her truth and opening up the genre to finally include anything but the white norm. Her anthem "Black Like Me," released after the killing of George Floyd at the hands of police in 2020, would earn her accolades and open doors, but her main mission became how she could prop that door open for anyone else who wanted to come through.

It's the story of so many women—and while this book focuses on three major-label country stars, there are countless female artists in this genre who have pioneered, cracked open, and transformed country music with their craft: Miranda Lambert and Carrie Underwood, who have become business moguls in addition to superstars, and Taylor Swift, of course, who all deserve many books focusing on their stories alone. Not to mention Margo Price, Nikki Lane, Rissi Palmer, Ashley McBryde, Hailey Whitters, Miko Marks, Brittney Spencer, Kelsey Waldon, Leah Turner, Carly Pearce, Rhiannon Giddens, Angaleena Presley, Ashley Monroe, Cam, and many, many more.

Yet this is not the story of all women in country music because there are so many of them that never made it to Nashville, never felt welcomed because of the color of their skin or who they loved or the language they were born speaking, or who left the industry because of sexual harassment or abuse. This book should include their stories and their voices, and this book is for them, mostly, to show that there is a place and a world that is trying to shift the paradigm for them, but never by denying the truth.

This book is the story of how country's women fought back against systems designed to keep them down: how women like Kacey, Maren, Mickey, and others reinvented the rules to find their place in an industry stacked against them. About how they've ruled the century when it comes to artistic output. About how women can and do belong in country music, even if their voices aren't dominating the airwaves. Because art, and truth, sings the loudest of all.

HER
COUNTRY

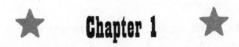

Chapter 1

THAT GOOD OL' BOYS CLUB

There must have been eight thousand glowing cowboy hats. Or at least it felt like there were, clogging up the arteries of the Bridgestone Arena as concertgoers filed in to see Kacey Musgraves, yelping with excitement, swigging expensive beers, and waving pride flags, clutching their ticket stubs like Charlie entering the Chocolate Factory. Not just glowing: blinking neon, aggressive and brash, nearly winking and paired with glitter everywhere, sequins and more sequins, arena lights skipping like rocks from the dipped tops of one to another. Kacey had designed the hat with a company called Neon Cowboys, pink and decked out with a light-up wire around the rim, and it had sold out easily.

There were multicolored sequins and pink denim pants; there were tight white tank tops; there were requisite cowboy boots paired with tucked-in jeans. There were little girls watching their first concert with their friends, their moms or dads pretending to be dutiful escorts but trying to covertly snap a selfie when the kids weren't looking, impressing their children and their friends in one fell swoop, clumsily adding hashtags in the faulty arena Wi-Fi. There were even more sequins: sequin coats, sequins on shirts, sequins glued to faces with mascara adhesive. There were covert puffs of a joint or a vape pen, one girl methodically fanning the smoke away with a limp paper towel from the snack bar, stained with pretzel grease. There were tears that streaked through rainbows drawn on cheeks with face paint crayons that turned to smudged, carefree wadded Kleenexes of color when they were wiped off—dripping rivers diverging at the jawline, hopeful rivers. More sequins, still.

This was country music, somehow. This was country music, thankfully. It may not have been the country music that you know—or that you think you know. But it was. It is.

Yola, a soul singer from England with a voice that could shake the rafters, and the euphoric dance-pop of Maggie Rogers had kicked things off. Unusual for arena shows of this size, most of the crowd was snugly in place for both opening sets, cowboy hats already blinking as if in unison, beers already purchased, little pools of sweat on brows gathering.

It's no easy feat to entertain a room full of this many people, 18,373 to be exact: most artists level up the bombast with giant LED screens running prerecorded videos, while others spin and dance from ropes dangling from the ceiling. All are fair and fun and glorious entertainment, but Kacey had come to the Bridgestone stage from tiny corners of tiny bars, places she played when she first moved to Nashville a decade prior from Golden, Texas. She had graduated from those bars to clubs to auditoriums to, now, an arena, and she wasn't going to leave that feeling behind, the intimacy, the closeness, the conversation with the crowd. When she finally took the stage, it felt like she, armed only with her acoustic guitar and backing band, shrank the room to fit right up there with her, no grandeur at the expense of it all.

Kacey's set ranged through her career, from the beginnings ("Merry Go 'Round") to every pivotal song from *Golden Hour*, which, by this point in October 2019, had already won the Grammy for Album of the Year and transported Kacey to worldwide icon. She brought British pop star Harry Styles onstage, whom she had opened for in the same room not long before—full circle, her in a pink miniskirt and heels and him in crushed velvet. He flew in from London just for this, and a security guard backstage had nearly ruined the surprise by sending a picture of Harry to his daughter, who posted it on Instagram. It was the largest audience a woman had ever drawn to the venue, and Kacey's family and friends were all there in the sea of it. It was a victory lap and a homecoming all at once.

And Kacey's team had a surprise in store, too—for her. When concertgoers arrived, they'd found sheets of colored paper at their seats with instructions to hoist them in the air when Kacey played "Rainbow," her "Imagine" for a new generation of beautiful queer kids who needed to know that something, someone, was looking out for them when times got tough. It was meant to create a rainbow that unfolded all across the seats of the arena, everyone playing a part to make it whole.

The little pieces of paper reflected the light, spiraling that rainbow throughout the venue as one blossomed over her head. "Rainbow," from *Golden Hour*, was a song about remembering that there was kinship and support and love at the end of the storm, and she was going to sing it here at Bridgestone, down the road from the hotel gigs where she used to play for an audience of ten in the early days of arriving in Nashville, to a room that included in-secret country fans who had tears streaming down their faces, holding each other by the shoulders, and probably some of the same executives and radio programmers who had undersold or counted her out long ago, or felt offended when she didn't do something that fit inside the tidy, oppressive Music Row mold. They'd probably begged the label for free tickets, all while knowing they'd never actually play her songs, even after an armful of Grammy Awards.

"This is for you," Kacey said, admiring the ring of color that had exploded across the arena. They believed it, because she meant it.

Grandma Musgraves was not going to have her little dark-haired granddaughter miss out.

It was late in the year 2000 and Texas was about to be the center of the biggest political spotlight in ages: its governor, George W. Bush, was headed to the White House after a massively contentious election, and he had no intentions of leaving his roots, or his cowboy boots, behind. His presidency was going to be Lone Star from the gate, beginning with, but not limited to, his inauguration. The plan was for a "Black Tie & Boots" gala that would highlight people and products from all across the state: Western swing band Asleep at the Wheel (helmed by, hilariously enough, a Jew from Philadelphia named Ray Benson) would play a gig, patriotic garb in Texas style overtook the usual stately decorum, fringy things lingered where formal things usually are, stuffed jalapeño poppers for snacks instead of tartare-filled spoons. It was not lost on anyone that one of the most pervasive rumors about Bush was that he never had really worn boots before he got to his gubernatorial ranch in Midland (he was a Yale graduate after all, born in New Haven), favoring black slippers over the traditional Western wear. But country-ness, like country music, is often a farce of authenticity anyway.

It was a world still adjusting to a new millennium, a way of living after the Y2K fiasco that was supposed to disrupt systems and clocks but mostly prompted everyone to purchase a few extra boxes of dry pasta and batteries for no real good reason. Superstar Garth Brooks had announced his temporary retirement, paving the way for a world driven by the crossover-sensational women of country music (until he eventually made a comeback—even Garth Brooks couldn't resist Garth Brooks), like Faith Hill, Shania Twain, and the Chicks. Bush's election had introduced hanging chads to the lexicon and made nonstop cable news essential: it was one of the most divisive elections in American history, at that point at least. But in Texas, there was nothing divisive about the party that was about to happen, because Texas knows how to do a good party, especially when there is Texas music involved. No politics would get in the way of that, nor would it get in the way of their Texan pride and chance to show everyone in Washington exactly how things were done around those parts, their parts—the parts that those tuning in to cable television would often predictably dismiss as a vague collection of rednecks and/or hillbillies.

Barbara, Kacey's beloved grandma with a lofty white pompadour who would go on to have her own starring role in *The Kacey Musgraves Christmas Show* many years later, had read about the Black Tie & Boots gala in the paper, and thought that her granddaughter's duo, the Texas Two Bits, would be perfect to perform. A trained yodeler, little Kacey Musgraves had formed the group with her friend Alina Tatum, and they were picking up speed around town—they were wholesome, talented, and traditional, which was a jackpot combination. Kacey and Alina could not only yodel, though; they could also harmonize: when they sang "Amazing Grace" on their debut CD, *Little Bit of Texas*, there was a lonesome sort of echo, that joy shrouded in worldly knowledge that seemed to be preternaturally programmed. It sounded, really, happy and sad at the same time, as Kacey herself would sing on *Golden Hour*.

But little girls in Texas (or anywhere) have a hard time being taken seriously, and this was where Barbara could help—with a set of ramshackle PR skills to aid their rise above the rest. "She would sling our press kits and be like, 'I got somebody you need to hire for your event. It's my granddaughter,'" Kacey told the *Fader*. "And it would work."

Barbara set about getting her magic in motion, putting together a clip reel and working tirelessly to make sure that information about the Two Bits got into the hands of whoever was in charge of decisions about that inaugural gala. Texas grandmas were and are often crackerjacks; not stage mothers or pageant hounds, using their daughters as pawns for vicarious fulfillment—many had developed their skills during the war, working as telephone operators or the like until their husbands came back home, if they did at all. Texas grandmothers wanted their daughters and granddaughters to succeed because they were damn good, better than the boys a lot of the time, and they were willing to help them fight in whatever language and manner they chose. In Texas, that language was often music—it was and is built into the soil, something that connected the mariachis to the folk singers to the dance halls and beyond.

Bush was going to build that language into his inauguration. For those reporting in the media hubs of New York and Los Angeles, it was an easy target, a way to jostle the incoming president and the oft-stereotyped genre of country music in one fell swoop. Bush was for ignorant rednecks, they thought, so therefore country music must be, too. Easy peasy—they'd already established that the genre wasn't something that could appear in the canon of a sophisticated music listener—"anything but country" was the common bourgeois intellectual refrain, to the point that it would become commonplace study in sociology classes. It was redneck shit, and Bush was redneck shit.

George W. Bush could have listened to Pearl Jam in his personal time, for all anyone knew, but he homed in on something both important and entirely unoriginal: country music as a political tool, and political capital. Politics has been and was at the fiber of country music all along—no musical form is apolitical, and certainly not a genre that had been born out of segregation. At its inception in the 1920s, it was split into "race records" for a Black audience and "hillbilly music" for whites, intentionally marketed by executive Ralph Peer to uphold racist structures, an original sin it never properly atoned for. "It didn't matter that what [Peer] found in the South were white and black musicians recording the same songs and playing the same music with the same instruments," wrote Elamin Abdelmahmoud in an essay for *Rolling Stone*. "At some point, it became an accepted cultural narrative that country music is the domain of white people."

President Reagan honed a Nixon-era but much longer-stewing blueprint that Bush followed: he saw an electorate—his white electorate, specifically—becoming increasingly nervous about the way America was moving toward progressive ideals and an embrace of equality, in both amorphous and concrete terms. Country music's obsession with the past became a perfect tool in which to express the evolving Republican ideal that America was better *before*, whatever that meant to a country where the before had been slavery, segregation, and pre-suffrage. Any smart strategist who needed a large, conservative white base to make it to the ballot box was certainly taking notes on this phenomenon: in particular, the nefarious political consultant and "Southern Strategy" mastermind Lee Atwater. It even made its way into Reagan's 1980 campaign for president, running with Bush's father, George Sr., as VP: *Are You Better Off Than You Were Four Years Ago?* And the even more specific and amorphous choice all at once, *Make America Great Again*.

Bush had gained some ground in the lead-up to the election by being the goofy cowboy you can have a beer with, who also happened to not believe in full marriage equality under federal law. He also, according to an anonymous source in a newspaper interview, had two favorite kinds of music: "country & western" (why this had to be anonymous is anybody's guess). Loretta Lynn (who both performed for Richard Nixon in 1971 and forged a friendship with Jimmy Carter) had supported him on the campaign trail, along with plenty of other marquee country names: Brooks & Dunn, Wynonna Judd, Ricky Skaggs. As his opponent, Vice President Al Gore certainly could have claimed an ownership on the genre—he lived in Tennessee, after all, having stayed in town after attending Vanderbilt Divinity School and Vanderbilt Law School. And, unlike Bush, whose love of cowboy boots had been heavily disputed and questioned, Gore had been wearing the things as early as 1988 when he first ran for president, to the point that the press had often made fun of him for what they viewed as tacky or hickish wardrobe choices. He even gained the prized endorsement of Johnny Cash. Country "authenticity," as usual, was beside the point.

Gore didn't try to ride his country cred alone to the Oval Office, though. When he announced his choice of running mate, Senator Joe Lieberman, in Nashville, he didn't ask anyone from Music Row to perform, or even from the state itself. Instead, he recruited a singer known for her appearance at feminist music festival Lilith Fair: Jewel.

That left country music almost fully within the GOP domain. "One aspect about country music is, a lot of it makes you feel good about yourself and your country," Bush's Tennessee campaign manager told the Associated Press. "The Republican Party is the one that those who are more patriotic lean toward." Patriotism was political currency, and country music its dealer: and Gore, in one of his biggest upsets, ended up losing his own state.

Naturally, any party celebrating Bush's win was going to contain country music—and a lot of doubling down on those cowboy boots.

"It's over the top this year because of a Texas president," said Barbara Musgraves about the inaugural gala to the local paper, who had also become Kacey's foremost booking agent in addition to public relations advocate. "It's the hottest ticket in town." That was shaping up to be true: tickets were showing up on scalping sites for thousands of dollars.

Kacey and Alina just wanted to go play music, and fly on an airplane for the first time: anything else was a bonus. The Two Bits were unabashedly cute and unabashedly Texas, the perfect kind of act for a celebration meant to signal both that Dubya was going to hold on to his cowboy image and that this was a beginning of a more "wholesome" America, free of whatever those riotous liberals were intent on peddling, or the Clinton era and its love for the jazz saxophone over the banjo or fiddle.

The duo had only been around for about a year when they got that presidential honor, but they had already found a niche after meeting at a show at the Fort Worth Stockyards. Though young singers weren't uncommon in Texas tradition (like most musical cultures, a familial connection to the art form started early), the Two Bits were praised for how professional they were, as young as they were. They got the inaugural planning committee, like almost everyone else, under their trance.

At twelve, Kacey had three years of performance under her belt before she headed to Washington. Born on August 21, 1988, to Craig and Karen Musgraves, Kacey had been singing since age eight. The entire population of the town she was raised in, Golden, Texas, would barely fill one small section of an arena like Bridgestone, if that. It didn't have much, but it did have an annual Sweet Potato Festival that somehow caught the attention of Oprah Winfrey. Kacey emerged a month early, her mother going into labor during her baby shower. Born in a hurry, as she'd sing one day.

Golden had a small grocery store, but if you wanted to do much of anything—go to school, engage in substantial shopping, dine at a chain restaurant—you had to go to Mineola, about ten miles southeast. "Wherever you grow up really shapes you a lot," Kacey told the *Fort Worth Star-Telegram*. "But in a small town, word gets around about who you are. There's something really transparent about living in a place like that." It was the antithesis, Kacey would come to learn, of Nashville, where many things are known but nothing is transparent.

Kacey's parents didn't fit the stereotypes of Texans and that's because they were wrong to begin with. They were of modest means but used art and craftsmanship as an extremely suitable substitute for fancy trappings the other kids might be able to afford. When the girls got bored, Karen told Kacey and Kelly to go figure it out; ride a bike, write a song, make up a poem.

Creativity was in the family on all sides—Kacey's cousin Cathy Pegues owned her own gallery in town, called the Golden Homestead. "We were all raised in a very artistic family," Cathy told the *Fort Worth Star-Telegram*. Karen's paintings hung on the walls, of Willie Nelson and Texas imagery, wide expanses and desert flowers. Her grandpa—Barbara's husband—collected records, and it was in his stash that Kacey had found a Byrds LP in her earliest days, and later snagged a mint copy of the Beatles' *Abbey Road*.

Her first musical foray had been yodeling, which she learned to do at eight. Kacey and Kelly would sing at the Fort Worth Stockyards as members of the Cowtown Opry Buckaroos, before Kacey formed the Two Bits with Alina when Kelly's interests drifted to other pursuits. Kelly, who became a photographer and shot all her sister's album covers, didn't end up following a path to a country music career, and neither did Alina—but in that moment, she and Kacey were about as dedicated as could be, and about to be catapulted to a national stage.

And it was big news for the local paper of record, the *Tyler Morning Telegraph*, that two of their own were going to Washington. A reporter had spent some time watching the girls rehearse, getting a sense of how both families helped keep the ship moving—how Kacey's dad handled the promo materials out of his print shop in Mineola, how Alina's grandmother sewed their Western-style costumes.

The reporter, Jonathan Perry, then editor of the paper, asked who the girls were both most excited to see.

"Clint Black!" the girls said, apparently in unison. "Bush did not immediately spring to mind," Jonathan wrote. After all, he pointed out, the girls were only twelve.

If George W. Bush knew then what we know now—that the little girl his team picked to represent the purest of country music conservatism and traditionalism would kick off her second album release show with a fleet of gorgeous drag queens, or get booted off of country radio for daring to sing about girls kissing girls, he may have choked on a pretzel and scheduled an appearance from a young Kid Rock instead. But at the time, doubling down on his connection to country music told the America he was about to rule that this would be the cultural reset they'd been hoping for—that those uncomfortable with the pace of change around them could still hear traditional sounds on the radio, still have women in traditional roles (be "Pageant Material," if you will, as Kacey once sang), still keep prayer and God in their music and in their homes. They didn't have to fear the loss of Values, with a capital "V." That maybe they could control the paths of girls like little Kacey Musgraves, and that country music could always be a safe and secure place for those conservative beliefs: pure, white, innocent.

There was a lot to be scared of, after all, if you were afraid of women with some power and the agency to show their midriffs, who dared to sing in twang. The Chicks' *Fly*, Faith Hill's *Breathe*, and LeAnn Rimes's self-titled record were the biggest albums on the charts, and Sara Evans, Lee Ann Womack, Chely Wright, and Martina McBride were leading the singles race and dominating video rotation on CMT (Country Music Television)—not to mention one of the biggest record and rule breakers of all time, Shania Twain. Beyond the legendary stardom of Dolly Parton and Loretta Lynn, women were claiming, or reclaiming, a chance to be the faces of the genre—and its cash cows. And they were doing it with songs of true substance, like Martina's "Independence Day," which addressed domestic violence and was written by a woman, Gretchen Peters. They were doing it with wit, like Mindy McCready on "Guys Do It All the Time." They were doing it for other women to listen to, for their feminine worldviews.

Shania was one of the original instigators when it came to late 1990s and early twenty-first-century country music disruption. She came from rural Canada, cowrote most of her own songs, partnered up with rock producer Mutt Lange, and burst on the scene in 1995 with "Any Man of Mine," which flew to number one on the country charts and entered the *Billboard* Hot 100. Her 1997 album, *Come on Over*, was the biggest-selling album by a woman of all time (over forty million copies worldwide), and she made even more waves when she took her sound international, with multiple remixes. She played with feminism, ownership, and authority and brought countless "never country" fans over to the genre. Naturally, it was often Mutt who got the credit for her inventiveness while Shania drew the ire for exposing her navel too much—the public eye loved to strip her of agency when it was time for accolades, but fully rewarded it when it came to criticism.

Country music history looks back on this period of the late 1990s and into the very early 2000s as its golden era for women—but also, depending on who you ask, as a blip in the trends or a tidal wave that was cut short by sinister intentions. Shania had won the CMA Award for Entertainer of the Year in 1999, followed by the Chicks, a title that has only been taken by one woman in the years since (Taylor Swift in 2009 and 2011, which captures both the slow progress of the CMAs and the lack of imagination when it comes to nominees). Even more traditionally songwriter-oriented acts like Mary Chapin Carpenter and Nanci Griffith were doing well commercially, forcing a "crisis of credibility," as some around town called it. It started to scare the suits on Music Row, the center of the Nashville country music industrial complex.

"We had Martina with 'Independence Day,'" songwriter Brandi Carlile said, reflecting on the women in country music who fed her youth and, eventually, her band the Highwomen. "We had Sara Evans, and we had Lee Ann Womack, these narratives for young girls and women, and how empowering that was, because those songs weren't just there for us; they were also huge hits. And they told us what we could be when we went off into the world."

For every moment of the Chicks' ascension or success for women like them, there were checks and balances—little ways to keep women in line (artists of color, meanwhile, were never allowed to acquire enough power to ascend to begin with) and keep them from getting too big for their britches. LeAnn was embroiled in a legal battle with her father and label since 2000, Faith Hill saw the industry support wane after her album *Cry* failed to generate what the industry viewed as radio "hits." The Chicks were downright banned from country radio. Music Row was never going to let women be its bread and butter— that was for pop music, if anywhere, and its "feminist" music festivals like Lilith Fair.

But one perfect example of the crushing duality of that country music industrial complex—the one Kacey would grow up to try to tear down—and the way it prioritizes comfort, or even lies, over truth is the story of Chely Wright. Thirteen years later, Kacey and Chely would meet at an event for GLAAD (Gay and Lesbian Alliance Against Defamation), the organization's first one headlined by a country singer. But in 2000, on the eve of the Bush presidency—an administration that would work backward when it came to gay rights—a closeted lesbian was telling the story of a single white straight woman.

A gifted singer and intuitive writer, Chely worked her way to Nashville via the Opry circuit before hitting number one with the song "Single White Female." She was also a lesbian and had lived her entire initial success in the closet and afraid. Nashville in the late 1990s and early 2000s was an unfriendly if not an unsafe place to be openly gay, to the degree that it was nearly unheard of for an artist to come out beyond the periphery. When Kacey won the CMA Award for "Follow Your Arrow" in 2014, it would be the first time that two openly gay songwriters, Shane McAnally and Brandy Clark, would stand on that stage as winners.

But for the duration of "Single White Female" as Chely's breakout hit, she was in the closet, singing as a straight woman pining for a man—all the way to the top of the country charts. She dated men, including the artist Brad Paisley. Kacey heard her on the radio like any girl in Texas or elsewhere would. And what better metaphor for country music success than success that was built on a lie, in a genre that preaches three chords and the truth?

The boom (or farce) of the late nineties was good for women like Chely, if you were willing to hide the parts of you that might rock the boat. And, being white, that option was readily available. "A lot of us women were, for the first time, writing songs," Chely said. "There were always some women who did, but for the most part it was understood that the songwriters write the songs, and they are men, and the women sing those songs. When I got signed there were just a few women who were doing both." Loretta Lynn, Dolly Parton, as far back as Mother Maybelle Carter, and brilliant but somewhat lesser-known writers like Sammi Smith had driven so many songs and their own careers through their lyrical craft. Bobbie Gentry was one of the first to demand that she write and record her own songs on her breakthrough album, *Ode to Billie Joe*, as well as "Fancy," which she considered her "strongest statement for women's lib . . . and the serious issues that they stand for—equality, equal pay, day care centers, and abortion rights." But in the machine of the eighties and nineties, women were expected to simply select what was available.

At Polygram, where she was signed as a writer, Chely had been trying to get a bigger demo budget for her upcoming work when she noticed that there was a new male singer—one who had not yet scored a record deal—who had a loftier allowance than she had, an artist with a label and an established future on the table.

"Why is he getting that?" Chely demanded to know. "I have a major record deal and you are telling me I don't have a demo budget?"

"'Well, your chance of having a hit is slimmer,'" they told her. A man without a record deal, in their eyes, was still somehow a better gamble than a woman like Chely, who could write, sing, and perform. When Kacey was signed, labels did a similar calculus: How many women were already on the roster? Could they have another? Was there room?

If Chely didn't already know that she was going to need to figure out some ways to subvert the usual process, that was a clue. Music videos on networks like CMT became key to how young girls like Kacey were able to access country music idols, and they gave women a new place to be heard and gain support outside the web of terrestrial radio—and their videos tended to say something new, push boundaries that couldn't be pushed elsewhere. Women had a platform to distinguish themselves and, sometimes, cause a bit of controversy: Shania's navel—shimmying without apologies in all leopard print, Faith's steamy, PG-13 sensuality. They had sex and heat and mischief: The Chicks even hid their fictional murder victims in the trunks of cars (Earl deserved it).

"The way we were saying it, how we were saying it, and how we looked in those videos, it was just enough magic in the tank at the time," reflected Chely. "The thing that took us down was those hard-and-fast rules about how many women could be played on the radio."

Those rules that Chely talked about were real—in country radio, women were intentionally programmed not to be played back-to-back, one woman an hour, if that: and programmed by software that turns bias, racism, and sexism into computer commands, if not by the estimated 90 percent of radio executives and program directors who were male and white, kept that way and doubled down on since the institution of the Telecommunications Act of 1996, which allowed consolidation to run rampant when it loosened regulations on how many stations a single company could own and allowed the purchase of multiple stations in a single market, depending on that market's size. Country music is not only a boys club, but it's a boys club with political, technological, and institutional support.

This approach even made its way into programming manuals and became such a pervasive part of training that it changed every aspect of decision-making. "It is important to orient the announcers about the general preferences I have about music flow, the formatting rules I want them to follow," one programmer named Steve Warren noted in his guidebook, *The Programming Operations Manual*, which he claims has been purchased by more than four thousand broadcasters. "For example, I don't want more than two ballads in a row. *I want to avoid having more than two female singers in a row.*" It was also assumed, and then accepted, that "women didn't want to hear women," which was a complete fabrication with no data to support any of these assumptions.

The "one woman an hour rule" was also, naturally, a convenient tool to keep whiteness, and straightness, preserved. If white women were already put in the minority, they certainly weren't going to be willing, or be in a place, to fight a larger power structure at play. They were battling for scraps as it was. "Classic union busting," said Dr. Tressie McMillan Cottom. "If you think about white artists and white women artists as a collective, not necessarily a union, but as a collective, their position in the labor market is both so fragile, and so conditioned on what white male country stars allow them to have, that they become accommodationist. And therefore, we're never going to form an alliance with the Black country stars." Keep the white women oppressed, who then in turn oppress the Black women: everybody wins (if everybody is the straight white male establishment).

It was a trend that would continue for the next decade and a half with barely any public interrogation until May 2015, with an incident now called "Tomato-gate."

Industry trade publication *Country Aircheck* ran an interview with a radio consultant named Keith Hill, who claimed that women were the tomatoes in the salad of country music airplay—in other words, men were the lettuce, which you want a lot of, and tomatoes were for sprinkling sparingly.

"If you want to make ratings in country radio, take females out," Hill told *Country Aircheck*. "The reason is mainstream country radio generates more quarter hours from female listeners at the rate of 70 to 75 percent, and women like male artists. . . . The expectation is we're principally a male format with a smaller female component. I've got about 40 music databases in front of me, and the percentage of females in the one with the most is 19 percent. Trust me, I play great female records, and we've got some right now; they're just not the lettuce in our salad. The lettuce is Luke Bryan and Blake Shelton, Keith Urban and artists like that. The tomatoes of our salad are the females."

Public reaction was swift and fierce, but what was even louder was the incessant hum of an industry that had always believed exactly what Keith Hill said, even banked on it, only behind closed doors. Women were speaking out about the ghastly tomato analogy: everyone from independent country artist Margo Price, who came out with a shirt that said YOU SAY TOMATO, I SAY FUCK YOU, to Martina McBride, who led her own campaign with red shirts featuring the word "tomato" drawn across the front that benefited her charity. Martina had seen the impact of the Keith Hill logic play out in real time throughout her career, and even when she was having chart success she was still aware of the limitations placed on women, encouraged to pick potential "hits" over songs of substance like "Independence Day," which grew a life of its own despite programmers' fears.

So even when elevated songwriting, crossover success, and innovative videos were actually forcing a change in the usual practices, the women knew it wasn't going to last—the genre's gatekeeper groupthink was always going to win out in the end. "When we started to get a little traction, it was fun," Chely said, "and it was exciting, but I think we all knew our days were numbered. I remember hearing all the men complaining: 'Aw, women are getting all the sponsorship deals!'"

Chely also remembers hearing men talk about how the women

were catty with each other, or "difficult." Hearing that women were "bitchy" and tough to be around, or that all the success and the fame was going to their heads. It plagued the Chicks, and would later be a predictable through line across the narrative of everyone who came next: Maren. Miranda. Kacey. Mickey. They were often viewed as bitchy or cold or intolerable, because that was how the well-trained public translated their ambition or desire to push against subserviency. Wanting too much, giving too little. The men? Reserved. Thankful. Loved God. Didn't abuse their power and took it with grace. Bless their hearts.

It didn't take much thinking for the women to figure out that this had been a farce. Staci Kirpach, who worked in promotions at several radio stations in Texas, including those in Texas and Red Dirt Country, Mainstream Country, and Americana, heard those complaints all the time. "I remember being told other women were bitchy or high maintenance or slutty, by men in power," she said. "It's not until later that I was like, 'were they?' Or did he just hit on her, and she said no? Or did he talk over her in the studio and she pushed back?"

And since country music's entire brand was built on preserving a sense of "family," anyone trying to disrupt the status quo, speak up, or change the climate was swiftly dismissed from the Thanksgiving buffet. Country music was a family that only lets certain people in through the door; a family that only lets certain conversations happen over the dinner table. A family that will bend over backward to keep uncouth arguments from breaking out. A table with a fixed number of assigned seats. A family that will just as easily hug you as disown you if you say the wrong things about the beloved patriarch or step too far out of the industry's approved gate.

And to stay in the family, to be a part of it, you had to behave. Kacey would come to understand this as she progressed through her career and started to chip at the barriers that kept people like Chely Wright from passing through, as would Maren Morris and Mickey Guyton, two other artists who happened to grow up a short drive from where Kacey was born.

Kacey got a taste of how good the life could be in 2001 at that inauguration—how cozy the existence of a country musician can be if you agree to play by the rules. And then she never chased comfort again.

"I thought it would be real bumpy and that we'd go straight up and I'd get sick," Kacey told a writer for the *Fort Worth Star-Telegram* about the flight to Washington, DC, for the inaugural ball. It was the same flight where Kacey and Alina ended up singing for the passengers, one of whom was a teacher who'd had the Bush twins, Jenna and Barbara, in her class back home in Texas. Kacey was wearing a Polo Jeans top, her haircut with fresh bangs across her forehead. She was prepared for what was to come.

The families had worked around the clock to make sure they had several hundred CDs in tow to sell, as well as plenty of merch (Barbara had been a little worried because everything came in later than planned). It was a family hustle, everyone attending the rehearsals the girls would hold leading up to the departure in downtown Mineola. As seventh graders, they had to miss a little school. They were not upset about that.

The scene in DC for the gala at the Marriott was Western-themed chaos. People trying to look Texas with Western bolo ties and shiny, unbroken boots, real Texans trying to make sure everyone knew they were exactly that, and every crime of decorum imaginable, down to an older white male guest sporting a full Native headdress while clutching a cocktail. "If you're from Texas," a guest from Forney, a town outside of Dallas, told C-SPAN, who had asked about a dress code, "you just dress like a Texan." He was, of course: hat, bolo tie, Texan.

When the girls finally took the stage to perform, they didn't even make it through the entire set—their mic was cut to open up a line for the Secret Service. They kept singing anyway. It would be the first and last time that Kacey would appear at an inauguration, but not the last time a woman in country music—and one from Texas—would interact meaningfully with George W. Bush. Two short years later, Natalie Maines of the Chicks proclaimed onstage in London that she was ashamed that the president, on the cusp of launching a war with Iraq, was from her home state. Over a decade after that, Kacey herself would be slammed by Fox News for supporting gun control after back-to-back mass shootings occurred in the lead-up to her performance at a Chicago festival. "She's the modern-day Dixie Chick," Fox anchor Ainsley Earhardt insisted. Maren Morris would receive the same reception after featuring an immigrant family in her video for "Better Than We Found It," and Mickey Guyton would receive the most incessant and brutal brunt for singing a song called "Black Like Me," among numerous other reasons they were targeted for rocking the boat a little too far—remember, country music is a *family*. A nice, obedient family.

As Kacey sang on her 2015 album, *Pageant Material*, she had no desire to be a part of the good ol' boys club.

She didn't then, she doesn't now.

Chapter 2

BLACK AND BLUE

"Oh, what a cute little girl," someone whispered. It was a crowded night in September 2001 at the Texana Grill in Arlington, Texas, and Maren Morris, eleven years old and wearing a grommeted outfit fresh from the local mall, had been invited to sing onstage with the band. This was her sixth performance of the year already, and Maren belted alongside the group that was supposed to be the main focus that night: a trio aptly called 3 Fools on 3 Stools, helmed by Tommy Alverson, one of the "fools" and a respected focal point of the Texas honky-tonk and dancehall scene. Maren wasn't anywhere near drinking age (well, legally anyway), but she had become a regular at local venues by this point. In the summer past, she'd also racked up her biggest audience yet over the Fourth of July weekend at the annual jam at a ranch in Hico, where her crowd was somewhere in the thousands, sprawled out on mats with picnic baskets and coolers, baking gleefully in the Texas heat. The performance became a bit of local Texas legend; talk of the talented girl who sang over the campfire: *"Have you seen her? The little one?"*

Maren may have looked like a cute little girl to the crowd at the Texana Grill but, as usual, anything to do with her age swiftly went out the window as soon as she started to sing. She'd gotten in the habit of reciting a little prayer beforehand with her parents, and then swallowing any sort of remaining nerves once she was actually out on that stage, ready to go. Somehow, she carried the weight of these shows with a nearly uncanny aplomb, as if she'd been made for it—not with the precociousness of a little kid proudly belting at a school recital, but with a relaxed demeanor of a seasoned professional. While Kacey was known for her yodeling and Western approach, Maren was just trying to kick it with the band—only half the size you were accustomed to seeing.

Tommy Alverson had met Maren before at his notorious occasionally roaming and beloved annual gathering in Glen Rose, Texas, at the Tres Rios Campground—the "three rivers" resort where the Brazos, Squaw Creek, and Paluxy converge at a pretty and lyrical bluff known for its spectacular sunsets. "After the show, everyone stayed up most of the night and picked and sang at someone's campfire," remembered Tommy. "Everyone was asking me if I'd heard this little girl sing. I think she was eleven at the time. She was belting out 'Angel from Montgomery' at someone's camp and they brought her over to where we were. I was blown away. We added her to our schedule the next year and she was on the bill for years, until she got too big for us." "Angel from Montgomery" was a John Prine song made famous by Bonnie Raitt, two musical legends who, nonetheless, weren't always on the radar of eleven-year-olds in a world obsessed with pop groups, but Maren, like Kacey, was not every eleven-year-old kid.

Maren had always been an old soul, anyway: she came out of the gate not trying to perform like a kid with a guitar but a small adult, just sitting side by side with the band, another player in another honky-tonk on any given night of the week. She'd even write about it some years later with the Highwomen on "Old Soul," because old souls start young.

Her home—Arlington, Texas—was an area between Dallas and Fort Worth that now houses the newer home of the Dallas Cowboys, the Texas Rangers (a team co-owned by George W. Bush, who often appeared in the stands for games as an ever-present force in many area childhoods), and a couple of theme parks, as well as a university. It's where Maren was born on April 10, 1990, and though it didn't have a substantial downtown, it was a bit grittier than many middle-class suburbs and managed to both be unclaimed and claimed all at once, as the home of many childhood memories at Six Flags park or hours in traffic from the football games. It was about ninety minutes from where Kacey lived, a drive on the flatlands and plains and road signs blown out by storms. "I was a suburban kid," Maren said.

Maren's parents, Kellie and Scott Morris, were known as being ambitious and kind; Maren also had a younger sister, Karsen. Kellie and Scott, both from the Dallas area, weren't "stage parents" so much as supportive, creative folks—their business rotated mostly around the Maren Karsen salon, which was named after both of their children. Kellie had a knack for maximizing the salon's usage, transforming it beyond a spot for locals to get their hair cut and colored into a community space. They'd have parties or bands come and play, any way to expand outside the walls (Kellie wasn't a musician, but she had a love of karaoke and would often tackle songs like the Chicks' "Sin Wagon" when given the mic). Maren and Karsen would work odd jobs around the place to help out, greeting guests or learning the register and then would occupy themselves at home or in the back when the adults mingled. For Maren, that was often on the karaoke machine that her godfather had gifted the family.

"Any time they would throw a party, I would sneak out of my room and monopolize the karaoke machine," Maren said. "I would sing *Wizard of Oz*, LeAnn Rimes. My parents just realized that wow, she can actually carry a tune."

It was at age nine, at that particular party, when her parents really took notice of how serious this little habit might actually be. Maren had been singing those LeAnn songs in her room, working to hit the notes, massaging her way around the yodel. Her parents heard something above and beyond the usual kid's capabilities, beyond the cute wisps of a childhood tune. It reminded them a lot of LeAnn herself, who, at the time, was one of country music's biggest success stories, and one of Texas's biggest exports. Though she was born in Mississippi, LeAnn was raised in Garland, another relative suburb of the Dallas metro area, and had completely rocked the Texas machine. Everyone was looking for the next LeAnn Rimes, while Music Row was already growing frustrated with her assertiveness, and most young women rising in the genre were growing tired of having to be compared to her.

Maren, like many young aspiring singers in Texas and elsewhere, had become "obsessed" with LeAnn. She was proof that a little girl with talent could break through and sing with an otherworldly maturity—she was a favorite of Kacey's, too, and a big reason she formed the Texas Two Bits. LeAnn didn't just sing, she yodeled, and her debut single "Blue" had shown the world that a twangy warble like that could compete with the glossy pop-tinged tracks that were dominating the turn of the century (that yodel was also a flourish that LeAnn had pushed for by herself at the wise old age of eleven). It had motivated Kacey to work with a woman known as "the yodeling queen," named Janet McBride, honing her own warbly skills, and eventually go on to win accolades for it, in 2001, at the International Youth Yodeling Championship in Tucson, Arizona, and the Patsy Montana National Yodeling Championship in 2002.

"I really looked up to her because she was only a few years older than me," Maren said of LeAnn to the *Dallas Observer*. "The era we came from was really dominated by women in country music, and I think I felt a personal connection to her because she was so young and it made it seem possible. She just sounded like an adult woman."

One of Maren's first real concerts was a LeAnn show, at a local venue called Trail Dust Steakhouse, where she and her mom had a front-row seat. She was wearing out her album *Blue*, and once her parents realized that she could sing, they helped her work her way toward performing at the same place where LeAnn got her start: Johnnie High's Country Music Revue.

Johnnie High's Country Music Revue was the heartbeat of country life in Arlington, and anywhere in the vicinity. Since its inception in 1974, its namesake Mr. High had made it a mission to recruit the best young talent to his stage at the center of town, which was a mini-Opry under a bright-lights marquee at a former movie theater. It nurtured LeAnn, as well as the Chicks, Lee Ann Womack, Miranda Lambert, and both Maren and Kacey in their youth—Johnnie High himself was a showman, often in a candy cane red jacket and semicircle pompadour somewhere between Hank Williams and Elvis Presley, and he had an ear for talent. It's the kind of place that someone outside of Texas couldn't quite comprehend: it had been driven by a devoted fan base who viewed it as a social center, with active members who paid, in 1999, twenty bucks a year for a newsletter, invitations to an ice cream social, a chili supper, and other perks.

It wasn't only a platform for women, though it did provide a certain unique jumping-off point for young girls who didn't quite see a road in outlaw-type music. You didn't necessarily have to play an instrument—you just had to be able to sing your face off. For some, like LeAnn, Johnnie High's was a springboard to Nashville. For others, like Maren, it was a place to kick things off in the early stages and unlock the local honky-tonk floors, and to hone her craft.

When Friday mornings crept up, Maren would wrestle out of bed and wait in line at Johnnie High's, which was located right across the street from her parents' salon, to audition—all covers, singing with the house band. One particular morning, Maren decided to try a new song: LeAnn's "Blue." She stood on the stage playing with real musicians for the first time, marching up the semicircle steps and belting in front of a twinkling curtain of lights.

Johnnie was sold—he moved her to the Saturday show: "the big one," Maren said. After making her debut performance in September 2000, she played at Johnnie High's frequently enough that she got enough steam to go to the honky-tonks, where the real action was, which is how she ended up with those 3 Fools on 3 Stools on that September night in 2001 at that crowded bar. It felt, for Kacey and Maren, that there could be a path to country music success, in whatever version they shaped it: whether it was yodeling at the inauguration, for Kacey, or hanging out in honky-tonks, like Maren.

For LeAnn herself, though, things felt different. Curb Records, her label, was dead set on keeping her in one box—while the rest of the world was content to place her in another—a pattern that would never fade as she released album after album proving her talent. It would become nearly predictable: anyone who seemed in a position to ruffle the comfortable status quo would eventually meet some sort of inevitable end point. When *Blue* was released in 1996, the title track had become one of the biggest-selling singles in the past decade, and it shot LeAnn, then thirteen, from local Texas singing sensation to the CMA Awards and, the following year, to become the youngest solo artist to win a Grammy and the first country one to win Best New Artist. "The question is," Tony Thomas, the musical director at Seattle's KMPS Radio, asked in an interview with a reporter at the time, "is this the dawn of a career for a new artist, or is it just a novelty? I believe, in the end, Rimes's talent will win out."

Tony Thomas was both right and wrong. LeAnn's immense talent did emerge to match the promise of her debut. But it also wasn't always enough to "win out" against an industry that has undervalued, and continues to undervalue, the legacy of both *Blue* and LeAnn herself, an artist who helped to birth an entire generation of country singers, most of whom were barely years her junior, if that.

As with Tony Thomas's interview, the bulk of LeAnn's early press speculated if she would be able to withstand the windfall of success while simultaneously helping to create the vehicle to swallow her whole. LeAnn spent most of 2000 and into 2001, at only eighteen, embroiled in various lawsuits—with Curb and against her father, Wilbur Rimes, who also filed his own countersuit. "Stepmom Says Leann Rimes Tapes Reveal 'Spoiled Person'" was a headline that the *Tennessean* ran on the front page in 2001, alongside a photo of LeAnn biting back tears. Somehow she, the victim at eighteen years old, was being positioned as the villain while adults, and the willing media, delighted in her as the scapegoat for their own shortcomings and fears. Media scandals involving young women were bankable anyway, as the Bill Clinton-Monica Lewinsky affair demonstrated.

After all, pop culture loves embracing young women and then eventually digesting them (just look at Britney Spears), chewing them up, leaving only the toughest bits to try to gasp for air, a tired dog toy that was once a daily companion. This is not particular to country music, but the feigned innocence and familial nature of the genre makes it predisposed to it: LeAnn, child star Tanya Tucker, Wynonna Judd, seen as the "problem child" of the Judds in the press, then Taylor Swift (it was honestly rare to find a young woman in country music who wasn't portrayed as being completely abhorrent, actually, as soon as they showed any signs of maturation into womanhood, grew opinions, "misbehaved," or desired the touch of another). Culture set them up for it, and almost anyone progressing through the awkward pains of early adulthood would make mistakes and trip over themselves more than once or twice. For women, it was a scarlet letter; for men, it was outlaw cred. Taylor Swift was not immune when she came to Nashville as the youngest artist to ever be signed to a publishing deal, expected to carry herself with the pristine demeanor and choices of an adult robot while possessing the sexual maturity of a child—and she eventually left country music altogether.

"There's a way that country music places women on this pedestal— like I was this otherworldly angel child, the way people perceived me," LeAnn said. "And anything outside of that, any kind of humanity or sexuality or rowdiness or just being a woman, would never have been welcomed in country music."

And even though Shania and the Chicks were the biggest things in popular music, they still weren't getting significant or serious coverage in mainstream media: at the height of their popularity, the Chicks were never able to secure a *Rolling Stone* cover, let alone consideration from anything that skewed indie or "cool" like *Spin*. So if you were a girl growing up in Texas, you had to do some digging to find those photos to tack up on your wall, tracking down the *Country Weekly*s or an issue of *People* magazine that probably was more interested in tackling the gossip around whatever "drama" they had chased down in the young life of LeAnn Rimes that week. Luckily, you could hear some of those women on the radio, the saving grace and where Maren found her church in the back of her parents' car—one that would come to life years later in her debut single, "My Church."

Only Waylon Jennings or Willie Nelson seemed to capture the public imagination in a way that demanded real serious critical thought—Dolly Parton, in 2001, was still mostly fodder for boob jokes, over a decade away from her proper critical recontextualizing. Coverage of women often relegated them to tabloids: LeAnn Rimes's relationships, LeAnn Rimes's clothes or weight or new home in Los Angeles, or the degree to which LeAnn Rimes was annoying anyone in that given moment in time, because women with agency were inevitably found annoying. "There's just always been some way to keep us down or check us a bit. It's not something you can directly point to and say, 'Oh yeah, this is the exact thing that they did in order to do that.' But I can definitely tell you I felt that along the way," LeAnn explained.

It was a model already designed and manufactured for Tanya Tucker, who became famous as a young girl for her song "Delta Dawn," and then watched as her "bad boy" colleagues, friends, and boyfriends got a glamorized treatment in the press while she was turned into a witchy, rebellious floozy instead of a brilliant artist. Tanya became a star in 1972 at thirteen as "Delta Dawn" blossomed into a huge hit that transformed her into a country sensation but then rapidly threw her into the washing machine of fame that would befall LeAnn Rimes later: public adoration and obsession, intense and unrelenting scrutiny, and then active attempts to exile her from life. Thankfully Brandi Carlile stepped in to help correct the narrative that Tanya was nothing but washed up and wrung out when she co-produced, alongside Shooter Jennings, her Grammy-winning comeback record, 2019's *While I'm Livin'*, that also worked as historical redo, but far too many women never find that lifeboat to ferry them to shore (Mindy McCready, who died by suicide at thirty-seven, comes to mind).

Maren's parents surely knew that all these outcomes could be an option, but they wanted to support their daughter, who seemed to have unusual talent and unusual drive. They became her managers, a way to keep it in the family—which, if you watched LeAnn and Britney Spears, could still be a risky move. When Maren was twelve, Greg bought her a guitar so she could learn to have control over the music she was making. "It was like a family project, too," Maren said. "And then it just kick-started ten years working and playing in clubs and bars. My parents were always present. But it was a weird childhood."

In Arlington, Maren was surrounded by future collaborators in the fertile lands of Texas. She didn't yet know Mickey or Miranda Lambert, who lived not far from Kacey in Lindale. She didn't know Lee Ann Womack, though she knew and lived with her music as one of the area's other preeminent exports—"I Hope You Dance," after all, was the hit of 2000, and more proof that the Texas women of country were seemingly unstoppable. Lee Ann, who evolved into a brilliant writer later in her artistic career, had undeniably set herself apart as one of the best vocalists in the genre, if not beyond, and continues to zig and zag at her own will even after mainstream success.

It was at one particular festival on the Brazos River called Raz on the Braz, organized by local artist Terry Rasor, where Maren met one future collaborator—Amanda Shires. A young fiddle prodigy from farther outside the sphere in Mineral Wells, Amanda had picked up the instrument when she saw one sitting in a Texas pawn shop and asked her father if she could take it home: his condition was that she learn to play it. Those sixty dollars, after all, were quite a bit of money for the family, and it couldn't be a toy that sat unloved in the closet.

Amanda's father had explained the instrument briefly, as his daughter took it all in. "Well, that's awesome," a young Amanda said, looking up at her dad and holding the then foreign thing in her hands. "I'm gonna do that!" She brought the fiddle home, playing so hard that most of the strings popped off at first—she had about two left for the rest of the summer, and had to make do. At school, her orchestra teacher encouraged her to get private lessons, and she and her mother concocted ways to get scholarships that would allow her to pursue what was clearly becoming an incredible, unusual talent. Soon, she was playing as a side person in famed western swing group the Texas Playboys—and getting fired from her job at Jason's Deli for taking off time to go see the Chicks when they came through town on tour.

Festivals and chili cookouts were always on the agenda for Amanda, and Raz on the Braz was a music and campout event with tents, tons of kids zooming around, and vendors dishing out turkey legs. "Dirty camping and music," Amanda said, who had by then been backing up the late, great Billy Joe Shaver—a man who would encourage her to step out beyond her role as a fiddle player and move to Nashville to pursue her songwriting talents. "Texas country, but also troubadour country."

Amanda had shown up to play Raz on the Braz and spotted a young girl going from campfire to campfire with her mother. It was Maren, no guitar player, singing as loud as she could songs like Kris Kristofferson's "Me and Bobby McGee." Amanda was floored, if not a little concerned that she was up past her bedtime, and never forgot her name—she'd see her at a few festivals over the years, making the same rounds. "I wish I could sing like that," Amanda thought. Years later, they would form the Highwomen together, reuniting for the first time since their teens.

It's hard to say what exactly it is about Texas that breeds such talent, such give-no-shits, but it's there. Texas has something built from its rich pantheon of music history and its inextricable link to Mexico. "Something in the water," Maren said. Part of it is due to its size, and ability to house so many cultures and points of view under one roof. "Austin has its own music culture, Dallas and Fort Worth have their own, and it's really deeply embedded, and there's tons of clubs and venues that allow children to play in, which I did," said Maren. "So I just feel like it is a breeding ground for performers. And then the song-writing elements, Willie, and Waylon Jennings and Jerry Jeff Walker, all these incredible songwriters and storytellers come from there."

Establishing yourself on the Texas scene was as crucial as anything else (in addition to being an influential hub, it's also a major media market), but it's not the most ideal world for a little kid—late nights in loud bars, smoke and cheap beer, men who smell like they drank their whiskey yesterday and were still sweating it out. The path from Johnnie High's to the club scene was pretty brisk, and any young performer had to grow up fast enough to do their time in the honky-tonks while reserving enough youthful innocence to pull off a stint at a local Opry. And, if you were a woman, you had to do it all while constantly trying to be one of the boys. Because of that, women were taught to compete with each other for the limited spots: not become friends or peers, but believe in a "scarcity complex" mindset.

Still, women were doing well when it came to the radio charts, to the point that this became enough of an anomaly that the national media began to notice a pattern, some even finding themselves slightly perplexed that suddenly a female voice was popular in country music: "Why the vogue for female singers?" wrote the *New York Times* in an article called "In Country, Women's Turf Widens." "Why" the vogue, as if female singers in country music were a new breed of animal, or a particular purse style—or that "women's music" was a trend in and of itself, and just as easy to dismiss. But it did expose a growing weakness in that sort of eternal question: if there were more women at the top of the charts than men (or anywhere, really), it must be some sort of quirky trend, some blip in the radar that needed in-depth exploring?

"One answer might be that women," the article said, "particularly within the relatively circumscribed borders of Nashville, are still discovering fresh voices and identities in a way that is harder for men. The Dixie Chicks, after all, are the most interesting thing to come out of mainstream Nashville in years, and the current crop of country babes—part Nashville, part Cosmo—are tapping into real changes in women's lives. A more cynical explanation might be a simpler one: sex sells, and the alt-country babes are benefiting from the same sexual friction that works for the mainstream ones. In a world in which looks and sex appeal seem to matter more all the time, it doesn't hurt to look like Allison Moorer, who poses seductively on her CD cover as if she were auditioning for an update of something out of Tennessee Williams."

Allison Moorer had emerged from Mobile, Alabama, writing and belonging more in what was then loosely referred to as alt-country, and eventually known as Americana. But she had made the occasional foray into mainstream country, especially when watching the success of her sister, Shelby Lynne. Allison, however, didn't see her cover as sexual (and she certainly didn't want to be called an "alt-country babe")—this was an album about serious loss and serious pain, but somehow the focus was on her appearance, not the depth of her artistry.

Maren always knew that Nashville was a major foe for the Texas scene—mentioning any desire to go to Nashville and break through to Music Row was like a kid from the DIY punk world going after corporate sponsorships in the eyes of lifer Lone Star musicians. There was a popular shirt she began to notice at the local festivals: NUCK FASHVILLE, it read. In other words, Texas was Texas and nothing was going to mess with that, especially not the suits over in Nashville. It was also the primary fodder of Texas artists themselves. Pat Green, Ray Wylie Hubbard, and others had all made careers off singing about how Nashville was the evil one—and that anyone who made a move to Music City was selling out their roots and succumbing to the machine. At that point, Maren didn't have real designs to go anywhere anyway—she just wanted to sing, play, and get better.

"There was always a sort of 'fuck you' if you went to Nashville. I don't know why they hated it so much, I guess it was the commercial sellout of country music," Maren said. "Texans are very prideful about their own brand." Maren was prideful, too—years later, she'd ink a longhorn topped with roses on the inside of her upper arm. "Little bit Texan sass, little bit feminine," she described it.

"Please rise as a 10-year-old LeAnn Rimes sings the national anthem," the announcer said.

Mickey Guyton—born Candace Mycale Guyton—slapped her hand on her heart two seconds before her jaw dropped to the sticky bleacher seats. Here, at a Texas Rangers game in the nosebleeds with her church group, she saw her future in a little blond girl with a massive voice.

It was Mickeys's father who discovered that his daughter, in the Angel Choir at their church, could hit the notes far better than the other kids. And even the choir had been joined by default. "You needed to be an usher or in the choir," Mickey said, "but the last thing I was going to do was stand there in an aisle and hand out envelopes and fans for the congregation."

That evening at the baseball game, though, changed everything. It was early in LeAnn's career, but for Mickey, it burst open the myth that little girls had to be just that—little girls. She sang with the confidence and range of a grown woman, and Mickey wanted it, too. "You see it, you can be it," Mickey reflected. "That rang true to me then." As with Maren, watching LeAnn go from little local girl to massive superstar shrank the world around her just enough.

Mickey was born in Arlington, too, on June 17, 1983, not far from Maren, but she had moved around a lot due to her father's job as an engineer, living in Waco and Tyler and finally back to the Arlington area by the time she got to high school. At one point, her parents enrolled her at a private school, in search of a (costly) reprieve from the racism that had been so prominent in her public school experience. "Anywhere in Texas, it's home for me," she said, even though that home didn't always make her feel as though she, or the rest of her Black family, belonged.

One day, at her public school, the teacher pulled down a map of Africa during instruction. "You saw Niger, and you saw Nigeria," Mickey told *People*. "I will never forget Micah, a little redheaded kid, was laughing and giggling and saying Niger a different way—we know exactly how that was said. I didn't even really understand what that word meant, but I knew it was a word that wasn't supposed to be said. My teacher never said anything. She never corrected him and said, 'You don't say that word.'"

Childhood was church—her parents, Phyllis Ann Roddy and Michael Eugene Guyton, were deaconess and deacon at the local Southern Baptist worship, and time off was spent at vacation bible school if not outside, riding her bike through the gravel roads and ditches and storm drains, climbing trees to find a quiet place to chat with her friends. Her aunt called her "ladybug" because of that propensity to be outdoors, a propensity that didn't last as she grew older. Mickey's childhood, as she says, was country with an emphasis—country, country, the kind of country that men with number one songs and Florida beach houses sing about. She lived it, though, dirt-under-the-fingernails style.

But she also loved to sing, usually the gospel songs that dominated her experience in church—and soon it was country songs, too, which caused a bit of a rift with her mother, who didn't want her to sing secular music. "Church is where I learned how to harmonize," she said. "I learned how to sing with a group of people. It was a major influence on me. My parents loved BeBe and CeCe Winans and Yolanda Adams and so many different gospel artists. That was a huge part of my life. My parents were very religious and before I even really could listen to country music, I was listening to gospel music."

As with Kacey, Mickey had started to spend a lot of time with her grandmother, Mary Lee Roddy, who lived out in the country—the far, deep country of Texas where the streets didn't have names, just numbers—in Riesel, a town with a population of a little bit less than a thousand at any given point in time. It was tiny and flat with not much to do except go outside, ride bikes, get dirty, and then come home and watch videos, which is what Mickey would do: spend time outside and then retreat to the television to pop in copies of *Steel Magnolias* or Dolly Parton and Kenny Rogers VHS tapes. Mickey would find them slung over the back door handle in plastic bags and watch for hours, dreaming.

"My grandmother just loved Dolly Parton. She just loved her so much. And so that's when I found my love for her," Mickey said. "And it's crazy how music finds you, your destiny finds you."

Mary also sewed imperfect quilts—patchwork ones—that Mickey would find around the house. Mary had twelve children including Phyllis, and Mickey would come to learn that she had made them to keep her family warm, out of her own clothes. If it all sounds like a Dolly Parton song, that's because it nearly is: Mary Roddy lived Dolly's "Coat of Many Colors," taking the clothes off her back. The quilts, like Dolly's jacket, weren't conventionally beautiful, but they shone with the fabric of sacrifice. Dolly Parton had always known that "Coat of Many Colors" wouldn't just relate to her experience as a rural white woman growing up in East Tennessee—what made the song so successful and so resonant is that it was the story of so much of America, from a Black family in Texas to a white one in Appalachia.

The music sure resonated with Mickey. Despite the fact that she was often at odds with her parents over what kind of material she'd sing, she kept at it, and kept getting better, though she never did the rounds at Johnnie High's or the honky-tonks—her parents moved around too much to make that possible, and young Black artists weren't exactly commonplace in the local Opry houses, anyway.

"I started doing solos in the church choir or when the school had a talent show," Mickey said. "I'd bring my boom box, and I'd sing Whitney Houston's 'I Will Always Love You.' I was just mesmerized by big-voiced women." That song had been written by Dolly Parton in 1973, covered by Whitney in 1992 for the *Bodyguard* soundtrack. This melding of both worlds made Mickey think that maybe it wasn't so necessary to gatekeep these genres in their own corners. Good songwriting was good songwriting, and good voices helped them transcend.

Mickey, too, loved music videos on CMT, especially the cutting-edge ones—Shania Twain in "From This Moment On," a massive ballad from her hit album that had her walking slowly down a white corridor in a velour dress, eventually joining up with a string orchestra. It sounds simple, but for country it was imagery that no one else was matching. Shania was pushing country music to an uncomfortable place for some—primarily into pop, but also right into sex and power.

But mainstream country fans in Texas, and anywhere, loved Shania—and pop fans did, too. If you watched Shania take the stage for her special after the Dallas Cowboys football game in 1999, you would think that this would be the forever plan—everyone was singing Shania in their living rooms, including Mickey. As with Garth Brooks, the genre's male barrier-crossing superstar, she was becoming country's monoculture offering, drifting in both overt and more subtle ways.

Mickey loved Shania, and made a habit to tune into Waco 100 to get her fix, and, at one point, her mom acquiesced and let her buy a few secular country mixtapes—Patsy Cline, Patty Loveless, Reba McEntire, Faith Hill, Martina McBride, Shania, Lee Ann, and LeAnn all made the rotation. By high school in 2001, Mickey was blending covers of their songs with her love for the big pop ballads, like those sung by Whitney Houston, or even the saccharine fun of the Spice Girls.

In Texas in 2001, you could actually see these women in concert, and you could hear them on the radio, too. You didn't have to actively search. Women were decreasing, as programmers weighed their own internal biases and the golden "no two women back-to-back rule" against the sheer power and pull of women like Shania, and consolidation drastically reduced the number of radio stations—eventually transitioning programming choices to automated devices or major city hubs.

Mickey couldn't glance at CMT or turn on the radio to readily hear or see someone who looked like her, though. LeAnn always represented a dream with an asterisk. Though there had been one well-known modern Black country artist in Charley Pride (yes, at that point, it was still just one, despite the fact that the first performer to be introduced at the Grand Ole Opry was a Black man and harmonica master, DeFord Bailey), country music had never let a Black woman artist reach any kind of substantial fame, or even reasonable success. There was Frankie Staton, who led an organization called the Black Country Music Association (it disbanded in 2003) before being pushed out of the industry soon after, and Linda Martell, the first Black woman country singer to play the Grand Ole Opry and to chart with her song "Color Him Father," and in 2001, Miko Marks was about to consider doing her own pilgrimage to Nashville, which she'd finally make two years later—it, like those before her, never progressed as she had hoped or deserved, leaving her dreams and heart shattered until she finally started doing things on her own terms and far outside Music Row. While Chely was able to hide her sexuality—not without consequence—Black artists coming into country were left to navigate a genre that since inception had been built on keeping walls as high as possible.

She saw LeAnn, she saw Shania. But Mickey didn't see anyone Black like her.

Chapter 3

SOMETHING BRAVE FROM HER MOUTH

Valentine's Day, Los Angeles, 2019. Crimson shine dress, black boots that went past her knees, and a high ponytail at the Ace Hotel, where Kacey was performing two sold-out shows after winning the Grammy for Album of the Year days earlier. She played a cover of *NSYNC's "Tearin' Up My Heart" with opener Soccer Mommy for the occasion and sang a duet with her husband at the time, the venerable songwriter Ruston Kelly. "Let's celebrate together," Kacey told the crowd, periodically tilting the microphone in their direction, though their resounding voices barely needed any amplification at all.

Valentine's Day, Salt Lake City, Utah, 2002. Kacey Musgraves, thirteen, was a little bummed.

After the inertia of the inauguration, Kacey had been moving steadily along in her own music—her first CD, *Movin' On*, had been named Teen Album of the Year by the Lone Star Music Association, and opportunities to perform were flooding in, not limited to an appearance at the 2002 Olympics in Salt Lake City. It was exciting, but, being only thirteen, Kacey was a little upset that she was missing the annual Valentine's Day card exchange back in school in Mineola (even though, on the positive side, she was getting to miss a whole three weeks of classes). "Kind of disappointing," she told a reporter for the *Tyler Courier-Times*. Hard to blame her.

A member of the Olympic planning committee, Dick Bailey, had spotted Kacey on *Good Morning America* the year prior, an appearance tied to her Black Tie & Boots gala performance. "I'm from Texas," he told the *Courier-Times*, "and yodeling in harmony was something I had never heard before."

Kacey's mother wrote her a song specifically for the occasion, called "Olympic Yodel," which made it onto *Movin' On*, and the rest of the year was her busiest yet—after the Olympics it was the Cattle Baron's Ball in May, and other appearances across Texas and beyond. She and Alina had split up the Two Bits because it was "logistically" difficult—the girls lived about an hour away from each other, with Alina in Sulphur Springs, and to thirteen-year-olds, that might as well have been ten. Kacey was gaining notoriety for her title as International Yodel Champion, but smart ears on the scene could recognize a tone and storyteller's mind far beyond the ordinary—and Kacey's own smart ears were always on to new music, especially the Chicks, on frequent rotation around the house. In September 2002, she appeared at a dinner-concert at the Winnsboro Bakery & Café with one of the region's biggest rising stars: Miranda Lambert, with whom she started performing on bills often. She was also, as a teenager, equally eager to gain her own independence in all of the cracks between—the local paper ran an article previewing the event with the headline "Lambert & The Yodeler."

Maren, too, was playing gigs around the state, often billed as the "twelve-year-old singing sensation." She had finished sixth grade at West Elementary School by the summer of 2002, and the family had a dog named Nikko. Days were both normal and not, or as normal as could be for a young kid so incredibly driven to succeed. Maren had been routinely hanging at a listening room called Poor David's Pub, a regular spot for a lot of locals like her, but very few stood out in the way that the tiny Texan did, or held the same sort of vocal promise and self-assuredness that made grown men a little bit uncomfortable (as if a woman, especially a young one with confidence, was some kind of subversive personal assault—a pattern that would continue throughout her career). She had been picking along on the guitar her father bought her, learning to play by ear.

Maren was still a young kid, and behaved as such. She made a magazine with her sixth-grade friends called the Preteen Press, doing teenage things when she wasn't onstage. There was advice on fashion (Limited Too, Rainbow, and Hot Topic were some of the "Totally 2002" picks, pretty reflective of the prevalence of MTV's *Total Request Live* and pop-punk princess Avril Lavigne), but there was also a section about what was in the news: Maren, specifically, on terrorist Osama bin Laden and the soldiers who had raided some of his caves. Being a young teen at the time was juggling the reality of what had recently transpired and caused their parents to whisper in the kitchen while watching the local news: September 11, the economic recession, and the approaching war in Iraq, to be more specific. It changed everything, and country music was no exception.

In the days after 9/11, country music sought to comfort: it was good at that sort of thing, coddling people like a grandmother, reconnecting with shared values. Those days turned into months, as America was thrust into a recession, and then the eve of war. The contrasting mood of excess patriotism combined with sheer economic panic could be felt in every tentative industry party over in Nashville on Music Row, where people moved around rooms with reservation, wondering if their friend, or themselves, might be swallowed up in the increasing layoffs. Radio soaked up its role as the patriot and the consoler: and if it could sidle up with President Bush, that avowed fan and Texan, it might get through this stress alive. Bush returned the admiration. Ballads and pop-leaning songs were shifting out, and America-first ones were in. Nationalism, y'all.

The drastic change in programming was not good for women like Reba and Faith, who had rolled in with songs that should have been massive crossover country-pop hits—big ballads that no longer "felt right" in a climate of impending war. "That now seemed out of step because the country was in super patriotic mode, and also the bottom's fallen out of the economy," said Hunter Kelly, a country music journalist and broadcaster who moved to Nashville in the nineties and, as a gay man, found solace in the women of country music. He saw a direct line from the shift post-9/11 to the downturn that fast befell the women of country. "The women had these big dramatic and sweeping videos and then after 9/11 it was suddenly, 'oh, we're not doing that anymore.'" "Cry," Faith Hill's 2002 ballad, bombed at country radio by her scale—a trauma, according to Hunter, that she never recovered from. The Chicks, miraculously, were still doing well—"Travelin' Soldier," popular in their live set, was actually potently timely for the impending war. Of course, that would not last long.

Radio stations were actively looking for patriotic songs, even "tagging" them on the playlists as such so the programming software could make sure to slot them in in ample numbers—they got more patriotic songs than they could keep up with, and the demand seemed to never wane. Stations reported intentionally slotting in one patriotic song for every ten. You had to program around jingoism, and they didn't think that introspective songs or touching ballads were what they needed—instead, it was stuff that went down easy, like the emerging trend of what they called "Sippy Cup" songs, like "Mr. Mom" by Lonestar, which not only foiled the patriotic tones but took up stories that had previously been told by women.

In a span of a few months, women went from being expected to record soaring ballads and huge crossover hits, like "Born to Fly" by Sara Evans and "When I Think About Angels" by Jamie O'Neal, to being excluded for not having lyrics that, for lack of a better example, encouraged anyone to put a boot in a terrorist's ass—you can thank Toby Keith's "Courtesy of the Red, White and Blue (The Angry American)" for that bit of poetry. Darryl Worley's "Have You Forgotten?"

was incredibly popular, while others, like a song from the artist Pat Garrett called "The Saddam Stomp," seemed to be too on-the-nose even for country radio.

This kind of music wasn't everything that outfitted a playlist, but if you're already limiting spots for women, one more category to compete with just narrowed the options further. The patriotic obsession in country music also gave the coastal press a chance to dismiss the listeners, who they already assumed were poor and uneducated and simply did not know any better—an excuse that would come in handy later to explain the rise of Donald Trump and his Make America Great Again base, which was actually driven predominantly by middle-class white men and women.

Nashville wasn't only pumping out music that paid blind tribute to the flag. Outside of Music Row, starting in Hollywood, Joel and Ethan Coen had written a movie about an old-time band of fugitives, called *O Brother, Where Art Thou?*, their madcap comedy loosely based on Homer's *Odyssey* that helped make George Clooney a movie star and banjos fit for the mainstream. The soundtrack was a smash, full of Gillian Welch, Alison Krauss, and Emmylou Harris and "I Am a Man of Constant Sorrow," though country radio didn't play that, either.

For Maren, Kacey, and Mickey, it wasn't just traditional country music or Nashville feeding them. They loved Patty Griffin and the Chicks, Shania and the Spice Girls. Sheryl Crow, in particular, was a uniting force among them all. Maren learned about Sheryl from her mother, who had made sure to have copies of her albums stocked around the house and get lost in; Maren would leaf through the lyrics and liner notes as most kids would their baskets of Halloween candy, taking stock of syllables and rhymes instead of Snickers and Rolos. These records weren't country, per se, nor was she courting that audience any more than she was just courting ones who loved a story and a good hook. But there was something that resonated strongly, especially the way the lyrics and melody met in a mischievous but introspective place. "Sheryl Crow is what you want your hero to be, which is nothing that will shatter your illusions of them," Maren later wrote in a piece for *Rolling Stone*.

None of this set a tone for Mickey that made any sort of success or career path in country music seem viable—if things were difficult for white women, how on earth would they open up to her? So after high school graduation, she packed up her life and moved to Los Angeles. She'd managed to convince herself that life as an actress would be easier than a future in country music—there were role models, at least, in Hollywood for a young Black girl with talent, though Hollywood wasn't nearly a bastion of inclusivity, either. But at the very least, there were some women to look up to. Still, those audition rooms—once she got the headshots and enrolled in the acting classes—weren't much better than she imagined things could be in Nashville. Casting directors were cynical, if not dismissive.

Culturally, the tides were turning everywhere—post-9/11 tensions spiraled into racial and political fuel, especially as the country geared up for war. And there was no better incubator to watch this happen than Texas. In February 2003, Maren sang the national anthem at a Texas United rally hosted by Darrell Ankarlo of news-talk station KLIF/570 AM at the Harris Methodist HEB Hospital. This was not, as KLIF insisted in a news release (and, presumably, to Maren), a pro-war rally, but instead "pro-America." Still, it was aired before the ABC News radio broadcast about preparations for the war in Iraq—an intentionally chosen contrast.

Things were different, though, at the actual rally. "Pro-America" became pretty clearly "pro-war": BOYCOTT LIBERAL HOLLYWOOD and GOOD JOB GEORGE were on the signs held by attendees, and Darrell hoped that the gathering would serve as a counter to the three hundred peace activists who had gathered in nearby Dallas for their own anti-war protest two weeks earlier. He wanted to send a message, he said, to anti-war celebrities like Susan Sarandon, Spike Lee, and Janeane Garofalo. Clearly a coalition was building within Texas and beyond to consolidate the power to try to silence certain points of view, especially famous people with opinions that they didn't like.

Maren sang her song—most American kids her age had not been around long enough to understand the consequences of war or the circumstances that Bush was using to advocate for it.

There was anger and distrust in the air, spiraling around, looking for somewhere, anywhere, to land. "I think there is going to be more to come," said one attendee, named Chad Cochran, twenty-two at the time. "I think it's going to ignite."

It didn't just ignite: it exploded.

It was hard to concentrate in choir practice when there was a new Chicks album coming out. It was 1998, and Mickey, singing her runs alongside the white girls at private school Trinity Lutheran, was eager to get down to the local Walmart and grab a copy of the Chicks' *Wide Open Spaces*. Everyone was, gathering allowance and Dairy Queen dollars to afford their own piece of the biggest band in country music, if not beyond. Mickey had been excelling at choir, a clear standout, but sharing her love for the Chicks—most certainly secular music that sometimes alluded to sex and mischief—was something that she couldn't do over at the Mount Olive Baptist Church where she would spend her Sundays in scratchy pantyhose. Mickey and her friends piled into a car when the school bell rang, snatching the CD off the rack down the aisle from the groceries and the home goods, trying to shimmy the shrink-wrap off with a nail.

The albums that came next, *Fly* and *Home*, were all equally massive successes: nearly every single they released until 2003 went to number one or close. Mickey had them all. "They were just so cutting-edge," she said. As Maren put it, three girls from "up the street" had become the biggest thing in country music. Three girls from Texas turned old melodies into new things, into cool and clean country tension. They loved hard, got hard revenge, and could outplay almost anyone. Kacey,

Maren, Mickey, any woman from Texas and beyond—it was fair to say that almost all of them loved the Chicks and what they represented.

The Chicks started out as a quartet from the Dallas area in 1989—the same year that Taylor Swift was born. Natalie Maines, the group's lead singer, had not yet joined. Instead the band was founded by Texans Laura Lynch, Robin Lynn Macy, and sisters Martie Maguire and Emily Strayer (both born Erwin), eventually transitioning to the current lineup when Lloyd Maines, Natalie's dad and local steel guitar legend, recommended her for the job. The Erwin sisters wanted to take things more commercial, appeal to more people, and reach more hearts and minds. That move is occasionally marked by history as "bitchy," which is secret code for "women with ambition."

The Chicks had grabbed hold of the country music machine and were steering it exactly in their image—freethinking, jagging left and right, curious about how they could take their version of the genre to any kind of fan who enjoyed a banjo here, a harmony there, some infectious pop construction there. They sounded like country, they sounded like church and bluegrass, they sounded like freedom to anyone tired of prepackaged, glossed-over versions of whatever femininity in the genre was actually supposed to look like. They were huge stars and crossover sensations, and they also were mind-bogglingly talented. And they were a little wild, too. They covered songs by Patty Griffin, who would become one of Maren's favorites, or esteemed writers like Darrell Scott and Matraca Berg. They played Lilith Fair, breaking country music's stance on feminism, which was to never join the club, even if actions demonstrated otherwise.

"The Chicks have always stood up for themselves," Lloyd Maines said. "They would decide, between the three of them, what they wanted and how they wanted it presented. They would not be swayed from that. And they were always spot on with the decisions. They were very in tune with their fans. When the Chicks came on the scene, they gave the country music business a well-needed shot in the arm and a kick in the ass. They breathed life into a genre that had become bogged down with the same old dull subject matter without any edge. I think they probably intimidated a lot of the male artists. I played all the festivals with them during that time period and nobody ever wanted to follow them in the scheduled lineup. The girls hit the stage and took no prisoners."

To Maren, they were a means not only to bring country music into the mainstream fold, but into the future in a powerful way. "They were just so good," she said. "And kind of like Shania at the same time, they modernized the whole aesthetic of country music and the way it sees women in it. They were wearing short skirts and had trendy hairdos and highlights—they weren't wearing rhinestones and prairie skirts. It was hot, the aesthetic in their videos. But the music was undeniably about the songwriting, the musicianship, and the fun." It's an approach Maren would mirror and meld in her own blueprint, never quite feeling the need to dabble in traditional "country" iconography, cowboy hats, or big belt buckles. She would show as much or as little skin as she chose, despite often aggressive backlash for the way a delicate bra top signaled her "impurity" to those who prefer women in long-sleeved dresses, or sing about sex and desire. She'd even do an interview with *Playboy*, as Dolly Parton once did.

They were on top of the world, the Chicks. And they were making everyone extremely uncomfortable. Natalie was simply getting too loud, too fast. So it was bound to happen, what came next.

"The Chicks didn't leave country music," as Lloyd Maines put it. "Country music left the Chicks."

Programmers had already been nervous about them. First, it was "Goodbye Earl," which they claimed glorified murder (as if country music never played a murder ballad before). Then there was the lawsuit against Sony, where the Chicks openly lobbied for a fair contract after claiming that their label had siphoned millions of dollars away through small print and red tape, a shrewd move that would later be echoed by Taylor Swift that was less, perhaps, about their own personal financial interests and more about setting a standard for the female artists of tomorrow to show that their earnings are exactly that—theirs. Like LeAnn, too, they were made to look like the vindictive greedy ones while men with deep, deep pockets stuffed them deeper.

Then there was "Sin Wagon," which spoke of "mattress dancing," and the time that Natalie Maines commented on Toby Keith's "Courtesy of the Red, White and Blue." "I hate it. It's ignorant, and it makes country music sound ignorant," Natalie told the *Los Angeles Daily News*. Toby Keith escalated the feud as much as he possibly could, and Natalie was depicted in the country tabloids and publications as the one who ran her mouth perhaps a little too much.

Maybe they were getting a little too mouthy. Maybe what happened next was the tipping point, and not the first domino at all.

There was already a deep distrust growing against the Chicks. Showing up at Lilith Fair? Speaking out against Toby Keith, like they had? The Chicks were not good at press, and they didn't have any desire, it seemed, to get much better. "On her first day at media school, the Dixie Chicks' lead singer Natalie Maines told her instructor an oral-sex joke. The Dixie Chicks flunked media school," wrote *Time* magazine.

"Everyone in the country industry kept telling us, 'Keep your mouths shut. Why don't you appreciate what you have?'" said Martie Maguire in a 2002 interview—well before they were asked to officially shut up and sing after the incident in England. *Country Weekly* was already running cartoons touting Toby Keith's perspective on Natalie—showing Natalie with a giant, obnoxious mouth.

"Johnny Cash can sing about shooting a man just to watch him die in 1955. When Dixie Chicks release 'Goodbye Earl' in 1999? We can't have a song about a woman who's tried every way of escaping an abusive husband except finally killing him. Banned from radio. Their label almost wouldn't let them release it as a single, only allowing it after the girls played the song at the Grammy Awards without the world ending," said Tyler Coe in his podcast *Cocaine and Rhinestones*.

Part of the Chicks' external success was how they countered this model—they were well aware of the patriarchy and the polite ways to smash and toy with it. They were the rare and unique stars starting to see an overt crossover between coastal critics and Music Row, and the propulsive trajectory of a post–Lilith Fair life had landed them squarely in the middle. While Shania, Reba, Faith, the Judds and the like were known as mostly being vocalists, the Chicks were dynamite players who took the fiddle mainstream. It's no wonder that the good ol' boys of Nashville and some fans, nervous to see the world rapidly changing around them, were scared of this thrust toward progress.

"Just so you know," Natalie Maines said, standing onstage at the Shepherd's Bush Empire theater in London in March 2003, "we're on the good side with y'all. We do not want this war, this violence, and we're ashamed the president of the United States is from Texas." It was just casual banter between songs, and Natalie, with a teased ponytail and acoustic guitar, didn't seem to realize that anything she said might be considered controversial—she didn't cover her mouth or mutter an "oops" to the crowd, who roared in agreement. Instead, she flashed out a huge smile.

There was no Twitter when the Chicks made their statement onstage in London, so the reaction to Natalie's comment wouldn't be instantaneous. In fact, the only reason the comment was reported at all was because a *Guardian* reporter seemed to have a bone to pick with what she perceived as the trio's excess arrogance. "They don't know when to stop," the paper's reviewer wrote. "It gets the audience cheering—at a time when country stars are rushing to release pro-war anthems, this is practically punk rock." The same review also managed to lob a bit of sexism Dolly Parton's way, referring to her as "Country Barbie." It ran in the paper two days later, another write-up of hundreds, maybe thousands, they'd gotten in their lifetime.

In a different timeline, that story could have stayed exactly where it was. News traveled slower but this particular bit made its way back to the States when the American media, thanks to some early-stage right-wing chat rooms already aflame, realized how juicy a comment it was—the Chicks were so popular at the time that their cover of "Landslide" was sitting on the Hot 100 between Missy Elliott and Eminem, and "Travelin' Soldier" was topping Billboard's Hot Country. By the end of the week, Natalie had issued an apology through the group's PR firm, but the damage had been done: country musicians could sing all they wanted about forgiveness and repentance, but no one was willing to offer the same grace to the Chicks (as if apologizing was even necessary).

Suddenly fans were lining up to smash their albums in protest, organized thanks to those conservative chat rooms—and "Landslide" plummeted from the airwaves in record time, from 10 to 43 on the *Billboard* chart and then off completely. KRMD in Shreveport, Louisiana, held a "Chicks Bash," where they rode over the band's CDs with a tractor—the station's program director, Bob Shannon, billed the event as a pro-America rally. Natalie's hometown station in Lubbock banned the group altogether, and Fox News's Bill O'Reilly suggested they deserved to be "slapped around." The vice president and general manager of Cumulus Radio, which had an increasingly strong hold on the market thanks to consolidation, told his forty-two country stations not to play any of the Chicks' music for a month and that Natalie "owes it to that fan base to make her position clear—not through a press release that was crafted to stem the tide of negative publicity."

"[The Chicks'] CDs were destroyed at protests ('Chick Tosses'), and they received hate mail and death threats," Dr. Jada Watson and Dr. Lori Burns wrote in their essay, "Resisting Exile and Asserting Musical Voice: The Dixie Chicks Are 'Not Ready to Make Nice.' "Metal detectors and bomb-sniffing dogs were brought to some of their American concert venues. Two radio DJs were fired for playing the Dixie Chicks' music. Strong supporters of the Bush presidency branded the Chicks 'traitors,' 'un-American,' 'Saddam's Angels' and the 'Dixie Sluts.'" It made it worse, their critics claimed, that they said this not on American soil.

That little comment onstage—that they weren't proud that George W. Bush was from Texas because of his choice to go to war with Iraq without any evidence, then or now, bolstering his desires—led to their being expelled from radio and an involuntary career reinvention. Like the crowd at that rally Maren sang at in Texas, there was a group simply waiting for someone in a position of power to slip up.

"Country music has a really subtle way of intimidating people that don't exist within a certain framework," said Brandi Carlile. "And I remember at the age that I was, I was super political but still living in a small town amongst people that thought that was adequate punishment for them, and they shouldn't be heard from again. That they can have that opinion, but they shouldn't have talked about it outside of this country. Like it was a 'don't tell family secrets' thing. It was so shocking."

Maren was only a teenager, so it's not exactly like she understood the full complexities of why the Chicks were being politically ostracized. But it still left an impression. The fearlessness of the Chicks had always been part of their undying appeal to kids, and especially women—that was the Texas in them, the stuff that got their blood churning. It was never supposed to go this far, and when it did, it sent a resounding message, even if it was one internalized rather than fully digested.

"I remember not fully grasping what it meant," Maren told *Rolling Stone*. "But even at thirteen or fourteen, I knew it was really gross that people were running over their CDs and making bonfires of them. It just didn't feel right. It was completely unfair treatment of a group of women just voicing an opinion, like any dude has in the history of time. They just happened to be in a genre where it's not cool to even air an opinion."

The whole thing horrified Mickey. It was hard to imagine a sterner warning to an artist than that, to stay quiet. As is always the case, but quite specifically often the case in country music, what might be an exciting, empowering moment—and one embraced by the coastal media contingent—is most likely one that sends its true marginalized class even deeper into the well. Mickey was already repressing her desire to be in country music—whether it was a surface-level type of understanding, or deeply embedded, it was abundantly clear that the genre would not be a welcoming place for her. In California, though, as she worked odd jobs while going on auditions, people seemed confused at the swift rate that country music was willing to expunge a massive cash cow because of one offhand comment.

In Texas, "people were appalled," Mickey said. "That was it—bye! You don't matter anymore. Everything was so foggy at that time, but I just remember thinking that if you speak your mind in country music you'd get 'Chicked.' Everybody is allowed to have an opinion in the country music world about a president they don't like, but God forbid you have that opinion about a president they do. You're just forced to shut your mouth and fear that those people are going to come after you like the Chicks—or burn your jersey."

The reaction was different when she would bring the Chicks up in Los Angeles. In some groups, they were cult heroes. But to others, it was a true mystery—an entire genre could really dispose of one of their best, most bankable acts, because of an offhand stage comment?

"'You guys just dropped them, like that?'" she'd be asked by friends, as if she represented all of Texas, or even country music in general. All Mickey could do was shrug.

The summer of 2003 in Nashville was hot, humid, and confused.

No one expected it to look the way it did—the Chicks in country music radio exile, but still on an extremely successful tour, and Shania and company starting to slip from the charts—but no one really connecting the dots between the two, either.

And though getting "Dixie Chicked" would eventually become one of country's most used and nearly cliché terms, was it even accurate? The place where their expulsion was real and tangible was on country radio, which wasn't even necessarily the result of angry fans: just angry people in general. Programmers noticed people were calling in to demand that their songs be removed from playlists who admittedly didn't have skin in the game to begin with—some of the same people burning their CDs and running over piles with tractors. RJ Curtis, who worked as a program director in California at the time, remembers taking some of those angry calls: after listening patiently, he would often discover that those behind the phone barely knew the band to begin with. They were just . . . mad.

"Will Other Artists Worry About Speaking Out?" radio trade publication *R&R* wondered, asking Nashville executives their opinion on the possible fallout—or were they giving orders?

Capitol Nashville executive vice president Bill Catino told the magazine that he tried to guide his artists away from certain subjects. "We do try to convince our acts to stay away from this arena," he said at the time. "I never talk about politics and religion to anyone I don't know well, and if the conversation gets too heavy, I change the subject. You can't win; there are too many differences of opinion." Interestingly, it was never discouraged when artists like Brooks & Dunn supported Bush at election time.

That had always been a subtle order in Nashville, especially if you were a woman—the same laws didn't seem to apply so stringently, at least with penalties, to the men of the genre. But what happened with the Chicks was almost a secret relief to some within Music Row— finally, there was something to point to when trying to explain to a new artist why it was vital for them to conform, to not speak up: "You don't want to get Dixie Chicked!" Later in their careers, Mickey, Maren, and Kacey would hear it constantly. Everyone would. It was a neat and easy way to say "Shut up."

Laura Ingraham had turned this into a best-selling book: *Shut Up & Sing: How Elites from Hollywood, Politics, and the Media Are Subverting America.* In a critique of American "elites" who "hate our country," the Fox News host made a case for the subversion of the entertainment industry and the horror of liberal entertainers—that they should keep their opinions to themselves unless those opinions were better for the purity of the nation. With the stranglehold that hosts like Laura Ingraham were starting to exert over radio itself, it seemed like a doctrine. Already conservative by public view and already white by fact, it was an easy approach. Laura Ingraham would not be done with country music after this—as recently as 2019, she would target Kacey for speaking out about gun control.

It made things in Nashville downright weird and verging on constant panic (mixed, in a traditional Music Row way, with so much denial in the glass that you couldn't taste the other ingredients), and by summer, things had plunged into strange crisis mode. The 2003 Fan Fair, the annual country music fan festival, had somehow plunged into an even deeper jingoistic state than usual—with the backdrop of the Chicks' expulsion, everything felt more essentially "patriotic." Suddenly, this was not only a meeting place for fans of country music but also a center point for American Pride (and Chicks hate). Alan Jackson was there to showcase "Where Were You (When the World Stopped Turning)," and it was a highlight of the rainy weekend, where red, white, and blue ponchos were as commonplace as cowboy boots.

While Toby Keith's songs became the most emblematic of country's more grotesque toxic masculinity posing as patriotic mode, Alan Jackson's song was treated as the sentimental alternative, the foil to the boot-in-your-ass nature of Toby Keith. Still, Alan's saccharine ignorance made it normal to admit in a song that you couldn't tell the difference between Iraq and Iran. And if he didn't try, why should anyone else bother? The Chicks knew the difference and wanted their fans to, and maybe that was part of the problem.

It was also the last year that the summer ritual would be dubbed Fan Fair—the next time the annual festival rolled around was as CMA Fest, having been absorbed by the genre's most powerful trade organization in town, the Country Music Association. But it wasn't a change greeted with open arms by fans who were especially tense given the events around the Chicks in March. Country music was programmed to bank on nostalgia, no matter what, and this was no exception.

"This is the nightmare that everyone feared," someone posted on the International Fan Club Organization message board, and later reported by the *Chicago Tribune*. As had become custom, they were mad that tradition was being squandered and heritage lost. "I am so livid, I'm almost speechless. These bozos obviously have no idea what visitors want out of Fan Fair, and if they think this is going to increase attendance, are they in for a surprise. Attendees love and are proud of Fan Fair's country roots. . . . Another country music institution has died, once again at the hands of suits who have no idea what fans want."

Tensions about change in country music were particularly high this summer, but they always had been high. Though there never was really a "pure" country to begin with, the very nature of country fandom seemed to demand that a reliance on "authenticity" be held dear. The author Richard A. Peterson used the phrase "fabricating authenticity" in a landmark book on the subject called *Creating Country Music*: there was never any real authenticity in country music, just a construct of what it should be. Authenticity always changed, too, morphing to be more effective or more exclusionary over time.

Billboard, meanwhile, seemed to already be focusing on the cooling of country music's taste for women, per an article written by Phyllis Stark. The issue that ran about a month after Fan Fair featured Shania on the front with the headline: "Country Women Lose Hit Magic." The men's club, Stark asserted, seemed to be "making a comeback." But was this organic or was it by design? It seems absurd that articles were analyzing the disappearance of women from country radio with barely any acknowledgment of the Chicks and the bad taste they may have left in the mouths of programmers, worried if they built up another female star she might equally misbehave. Instead of tracing through whether or not the shift in taste post-9/11 carried any influence, or if the

Chicks had made substantial ripples, it placed blame on the women directly: there must be something wrong with the type of music they were making. Did they lose their hit magic, or did country music stop seeing it?

Music Row loves talking about "familiarity," and how radio can only play what's familiar. But if you don't play something it can't be familiar, and it can't be familiar if it doesn't get played. So when not playing patriotic songs, 2003 made familiar a lot of easy listening by a lot of white men: Blake Shelton, Lonestar, Brooks & Dunn, Kenny Chesney, Dierks Bentley, Keith Urban, and Mark Wills all had number one songs on Hot Country that year.

And the Chicks, as Lloyd Maines said, set out on a future without country music—not leaving it behind but being left. When they chose the Patty Griffin song "Truth No. 2" for *Home*, they didn't know it would be a premonition: too many people didn't like the sound of the truth coming from their mouths, as the lyrics said.

"They ended up paying a price," Maren said, "that a man never would have to."

Chapter 4

FASTEST GIRLS IN TOWN

Texas, in case you haven't heard, is famous for big hair. It's a point of pride: rollers and hair spray, coil, fluff, and texturize. The higher the hair, the closer to God. But Kacey, by 2004, had cut hers square off. Her dark brown hair, halfway down her back, had been chopped even shorter than a bob—she had driven to the hair salon in Mineola without much direction, other than the fact that she was looking for a little bit of freedom anywhere she could find it. Freedom from the pageantry of yodeling and the Opry circuit, from the carbon copies of girls up on the Texas stages with their blond curls and heavy pouted lips. Not freedom from music—not for one second. But from rules. "It was 'Who am I? What am I?'" Kacey said, speaking at the opening of her exhibit, *All of the Colors*, at the Country Music Hall of Fame in 2019. She was having a bit of an existential crisis. "I just know I wanted to connect with what I am doing."

Maybe the defiance of the Chicks had given her some power— while getting "Chicked" wasn't anything to aspire to, there was a part of her that maybe seemed to warm to the defiance, the commitment to figuring out who you are and sticking to it, no matter what. The hair, short in the back and long in the front, was a bit swoopy and a bit emo—she later would describe it as a "Kate Gosselin" style, speaking about the reality television star with a similar crop—was a small way of physically expressing that. Kacey wasn't even sure she wanted to do country music anymore—she was listening to a lot of late-nineties and early-aughts indie rock. She wanted to leave yodeling behind, but she had some interest in playing the mandolin, which she was working on in lessons, along with songwriting. She had become a bit of a troublemaker in school, like many restlessly creative kids. She was cited for "continuous classroom disruption"—perhaps she just had too much to say and no way to say it yet, but had started to channel that into songwriting more seriously. Kacey had always been a writer, born a writer (her first song, "Notice Me," came at only nine), but studying the specifics of it gave her a new power in her arsenal.

She was still working with famed local coach Janet McBride the Yodeling Queen, and making appearances at the Rodeo City Music Hall, Janet's home base, not abandoning that altogether. She showed up to one Opry Reunion event in her signature fringe and rhinestones, a Western shirt with silky white threads and stars, and a glistening blue belt, but the short hair and lack of cowboy hat showed that maybe there was a different fire in her eyes now. She didn't want to be a novelty, a word that had been tacked onto LeAnn as soon as she emerged on the scene, despite the authoritative confidence in her voice—a young woman performing traditional country music was a novelty; a young man doing it was refreshingly novel. Kacey started writing more "emo" kinds of songs and paddling away from the traditional music that had always grounded her.

But there was one friend who helped make country music seem a little more interesting: Miranda Lambert. Miranda lived in Lindale, not too far from Golden, and had come up with Kacey in the local scene, at just a few years older. They took guitar lessons from the same instructor, and Kacey's newest record, *Wanted: One Good Cowboy*, contained a song they wrote together called "The Life of the Old Cowhand."

Miranda had always envisioned that she would come up through the honky-tonk circuit with her own songs in tow, but she did agree to audition for *Nashville Star* in 2003, mostly to please her mother. She made the cut, and even if Miranda herself wasn't too keen on it, everyone in the Mineola/Lindale/Dallas area was talking about it. *American Idol* may have been the headline grabber, but *Nashville Star* was the driver for everything else country, and a safe place from the rapidly changing culture, away from what was happening in the mainstream: away from "loudmouthed" Chicks and Britney Spears kissing Madonna at the 2003 MTV Awards.

You're supposed to want to win a competition show like *Nashville Star*, and ride the wave of newfound stardom to the top of the charts and your name in neon, on every marquee you can touch from coast to coast. But Miranda did not want to win. It would have been a cushier ride to do so, as she spent years playing those bars across Texas, pumping out marathon sets and shrugging it off when the drunk patrons asked for yet another waltz or a George Strait cover. But Miranda didn't like cushy. She liked real.

So she didn't cry when it was announced on the finale that she'd come in third. Instead, she mouthed to her parents, sitting in the audience, a hearty, excited "yes!" Losing meant that Miranda didn't have to be beholden to the record label that came with the top slot, or the requirements to work with a certain producer, a certain mixer, a certain engineer. It meant that no one owned her choices but her gut, and that she could mold her career exactly how she wanted to. And that's precisely what she did. She breathed a huge, deep sigh of relief when the judges (including Tracy Gershon, who would go on to sign her to a record deal at Sony Nashville) didn't say her name. It was that moment when Miranda began to form the mantra she would keep with her throughout her career: "If it's a maybe, it's a no."

Though she had spotted Miranda's promise from the moment she laid eyes on her through the camera, Tracy wasn't exactly mad, either, that she hadn't won the show—because she knew immediately that she was going to sign her to a record deal. Tracy had come to Nashville in the late eighties with her husband, a steel guitar player for Emmy-lou Harris. Her sister, Gina, was an actress, but Tracy found her specific talents rested in spotting musical promise in others—it had always come easily, as an effortless gift. The South, however, wasn't exactly a hip destination for coastal entertainment folk, especially Jewish ones. Tracy wasn't programmed to hide her religion as much as she was her opinions, and it was always a road, in her new town, to figuring out how to balance both—that kind of personality, though, made her a good fit for reality television. She talked fast, moved faster, and made people outside of the Nashville sphere feel more comfortable.

Because there wasn't much of a model for working mothers in the business, Tracy had figured it out along the way. With family back in Los Angeles and not nearly enough money yet for a full-time nanny, she would strap her son to her chest in a little carrier, and do her work up and down Music Row that way. "I'd show up pitching songs with him on my arm," she said, "and the A&R people would be like, 'Are you kidding me?'" She shrugged off Jewish jokes and mom jokes and kept on her way most days and, as the first woman song plugger at Sony, learned that sometimes she had to crack a dirty joke to make the very delicate men in the room relax. "I was like, 'I'm one of the guys,'" she would say to them, secretly rolling her eyes and easing their physical discomfort in the same way you might with a group of toddlers who chuckle at the word "penis." "Don't be nervous," she'd assure them.

It made her a good partner for Miranda as she headed in to negotiate her deal at Sony, to help massage the terms under which she would make her first record—along with Simon Renshaw, who worked with the Chicks as their manager. Simon had clearly been through it in this past year, but he had also very specifically stuck by the trio of women with, to Nashville's disappointment, opinions. That might have been a deterrent for some, but it was a selling point for Miranda, regardless of where she landed personally on the political spectrum, because she loved how musically steadfast and secure they were, going against the grain while also being faithful to Texas and country roots.

"She was ready to not make a record if she couldn't make it on her own terms," Tracy said. "And she said it right to the head of the label, John Grady: 'I'd rather not make a record at all.' It was the ballsiest thing I'd ever see an artist do. She was just like, this is how I want to make my records, and this is who I want to make my records with."

"I told everybody, 'I'd rather spend another decade in honky-tonks and do it my way than be the pretty girl for you,'" Miranda explained to NPR.

New artists, especially on a major label, rarely had that sort of capital, and certainly not a voice to direct their career so specifically. That didn't matter to Miranda much, because she could have just as easily gone back to Texas with a loser title, a ripped-up contract, and her boots as long as she was able to preserve her artistry. The label had already homed in on who they were pushing for to have a hand in the record, but Miranda wanted Frank Liddell, married to Lee Ann Womack, to produce. Usually those are the kinds of negotiations made by managers on behalf of their artists, but Tracy encouraged Miranda to start the conversation herself. Which, naturally, Miranda had little problem with.

"Listen," Miranda told John Grady, "I don't want to make a typical Nashville record with all the Nashville guys. I want to make my own. I want to make the record I want to make, I want Frank Liddell to produce it, and I need to do it on my terms."

John Grady was dumbfounded. Tracy just laughed. "He just said, 'OK.'"

Executive Tommy Mottola had wanted to manage Miranda, too, and had even gone to the lengths of flying her out to Los Angeles, sending the limo, rolling out the whole parade. Miranda showed up in flip-flops and plopped herself down on the couch in his office. She wasn't swayed by the L.A. glitz, the showboating, nor did she feel the need to present some glamorized version of herself so she could be more broadly appealing. Some folks on the West Coast thought they could seduce country stars with visions of crossovers and Chanel but not Miranda, who felt that her individuality was her currency. "I don't want to be no Mariah Carey," she said. "I'm a country artist." Needless to say, she didn't sign with him. She focused on writing *Kerosene* and doubled down on her country roots by buying a home in Lindale, Texas, close to her parents, hunting in her spare time and picking on the guitar.

By the time RCA and Sony had merged in 2004, Tracy gave one piece of advice to president Joe Galante: "The best thing you can do with Miranda Lambert is stay out of the way," she said.

It was advice Tracy would give again in her career, in 2011—about her newest signing to Warner Chappell: Kacey Musgraves.

Miranda making headway was, by all means, an encouraging signal to send back home to Texas—as was the success of Gretchen Wilson's sudden hit "Redneck Woman," the first number one country hit by a woman in over a year. Gretchen felt like the women in country music had gotten too "pretty," and that song was her rebuttal. "The reason why I became successful in the first place is I think women—and maybe some men—they accepted me because I was a voice that was speaking to them about them," she told *Taste of Country*. "For a long time, I feel like in country music, women had gotten so slick and soft and pretty. So being authentic and being real, that is what got me to this dance."

But, on the whole, the real-time environment for women was just as limiting: Maren was still working the Dallas-area club scene as hard as ever, trying to break past assumptions that even her local press had settled into.

"Female singer-songwriters always get a bad rap, with their corny sincerity and dear-diary lyrics, but it's nice to sit down and listen to an artist who can just plain sing," wrote the *Dallas Observer*, as the paper embarked on a multiple-band marathon as part of the fifteenth annual singer-songwriter competition at Poor David's Pub. Maren was in the running that year, and had taken the stage at nine p.m. in an orange baseball cap and jeans: "out past her curfew," a reporter wrote before noting that a man sitting next to her, spotting Maren at just fourteen years old, had muttered, "God, I hate kids today" during her set. Young female ambition, as with LeAnn, was rarely looked at kindly.

Even less kind was an assumption that women had to be either pop stars or solemn singer-songwriters. "Female performers tend toward one of two camps: those, like Britney Spears and Christina Aguilera, who can sing but not write; and those, like Liz Phair and Courtney Love, who can write but not sing," the reporter wrote. "Rare is the woman who manages both."

That reporter was not only wrong about that but also about both the songwriting capabilities of pop artists and the pop capabilities of rock artists—even beyond music, it always seemed to be one or the other. Women are pretty but not smart, smart but definitely not also pretty, intellectual but unhappy—and if you were young, pretty (per the culture's preset standards, naturally), opinionated, talented, and a woman, well, then you were veering on a novelty.

"Sometimes people don't take me seriously because of my age or are skeptical about booking a young girl to play their club," Maren told the journalist Alan Cackett in 2006. "Some places are more like bars, and some places they will listen to you and acknowledge that you're there, but at other times, you're background music. There are people talking or whatever. All I ask is to be given a chance to prove myself."

"Prove yourself." Women always had to. Men entered with expectations met already—women always had to work from the ground up. Mickey, especially, would encounter this for her entire career: prove yourself. Or, really, prove to the white establishment that she not only deserved a place among them, and was "country enough," even though she was damn well born for it.

Miranda's first major-label record, *Kerosene*, was her chance to prove that she was more than a reality show sensation—which it did, in spades, even though the LP produced zero number one singles. She had been cultivating an image—as a "crazy ex-girlfriend"—or, rather, the media had been cultivating it for Miranda even before she released a follow-up album under that title. Yes, her music did seem to encourage indulging in a little cleansing anger ("Betty Rocker . . . with a side of rage," she told the *Nashville Scene*), but it was also meticulously crafted and steeped in country music tradition, and a hungry, encyclopedic knowledge both of new artists and underappreciated ones.

In rock, women were allowed to be angry, or at least given a bit of a runway to express some anger. Rage was a dangerous game for country music's women in 2004—it was both a bait and a roadblock. "I struggle to think of women who lost their tempers in public and didn't face ridicule, temporary ruin, or both," Lindy West wrote in the *New York Times* in 2017, reflecting on the Chicks, Uma Thurman, and other women who have allowed their palpable anger to be released in public. When Miranda opened her studio debut album with "Kerosene," burning down the things of a lover who scorned her, she was not going to hide her particular rage. She took the model of the don'ts—losing your temper, getting angry, saying things a little too loud or a little too brash—and turned it all into song. Eventually, rageful women became country music currency—Carrie Underwood taking a baseball bat to a boyfriend's car in "Before He Cheats"—while also being limited enough that Kacey actively pushed against that expectation.

A culture of rageful women, though, didn't leave any room at all for Mickey. God forbid a Black female artist in country music—or anywhere for that matter—show anger, and it didn't exactly compare to how pop stars used rage to spur a larger discourse about feminism. Dolly Parton never called herself a feminist, and neither did Loretta Lynn, and although these conversations were far more complex than just a precise word, they were often used as convenient ways to dismiss the need to participate in any discussion around it. It wasn't that these women didn't relate to feminist principles: it's that they didn't embrace the way they had been defined and, at times, weaponized on the coasts. "I suppose I am a feminist if I believe that women should be able to do anything they want to," Dolly said at a *Time* 100 event. "And when I say a feminist, I just mean I don't have to, for myself, get out and carry signs . . . I just really feel I can live my femininity and actually show that you can be a woman and you can still do whatever you want to do."

Feminism as it was known in Nashville, and in the South, was already undergoing a public awakening and simultaneous crisis, anyway. When a *New York Times* reporter went to the fourth annual Southern Girls Convention in 2002, she found a group of southern belles ready to reckon with the propriety they had been served—albeit in an extremely white form.

The reporting, as it often was, was condescending: "What would Scarlett O'Hara do?" the article opened, interviewing some of the participants. "Some of my best friends, at twenty-two, cannot see how patriarchy has affected their lives," said Ricci Justis, twenty-four, a student at Georgia State University. "They will die if they don't get married and have kids. Being from the South, they think that's what it's all about: the guy being the say-so, the girl being whimsical and getting her validation through him. I have to say, I love the South, but it's there." It never viewed southern women as full humans, and much of southern feminism wasn't able to bring feminism farther into a version that sought freedom for everyone, not just white women.

In the puritanical world of Nashville that had independence confused for aggressiveness, Miranda wouldn't have a number one song until her third album. But with women dwindling from country radio, Shania in Switzerland, where she moved to escape the crushing nature of celebrity, and the Chicks in exile, Miranda herself had no one to give her a helping hand up. "I grew up on the classics, with Dolly and Loretta and Tammy and Patsy," Miranda told *Entertainment Weekly*. "And then there was Reba, and then there was Faith and Martina and

Shania. And then . . . there was a gap—and it was a big gap. I didn't really have a lot of help—like, no one."

Instead, Miranda had to look for partnership in her collaborators and friends. In 2005, Miranda met a woman who would be integral to her creative life: future Highwoman and songwriter Natalie Hemby.

Natalie had grown up in Nashville with a musical family, singing in church. Like many in town, her story was familiar—a promise dangled with a recording contract (with producer Jay Joyce on deck) that eventually fell apart in the consolidation of the late nineties. Instead, she started writing and singing demos, becoming a coveted commodity in town for both. Natalie's husband, Mike Wrucke, started telling her about this contestant on *Nashville Star*, Miranda Lambert, who might need some background vocals. Soon Natalie started lending her voice to Miranda's recordings.

"I was growing up listening to artists like Alanis Morissette and rock artists who are just in your face about stuff," said Natalie, reflecting. "Gretchen Wilson had come out at the time and Gretchen was kicking ass. And Gretchen's always been very in your face. But Miranda was different. Gretchen's like your buddy, but she could kick your ass in a bar. But Miranda probably secretly burned down your house."

By the summer of 2005 Natalie's voice was all over Miranda's music, but they hadn't even met yet. Mike decided to break that pattern at country music's annual parade of song and sweat, CMA Fest.

It was a typically hot summer day—"hot as balls," as Natalie put it—and Miranda was there, in ripped jeans, waiting for a ride to her stage in a different part of downtown. CMA Fest was the ultimate opportunity for new country artists to connect directly with the fans themselves, something the genre was always nicely queued up to do.

Natalie piled onto a golf cart with Miranda to get to her stage. Downtown Nashville in 2005 was but a shadow of what it looks like now, where the honky-tonks are surrounded by high-rises, bachelorette party buses, and multilevel dining establishments where you can get oysters on one floor and a drunken fight on another, riding a pedal tavern from one place to the next.

Miranda turned to Natalie as they zoomed around the crowd. "Sorry," she said, "my ass is taking up the whole back seat." And then she started talking about Merle Haggard.

Unlike the Texas crew, Natalie had been born and raised in Nashville, so she had already seen the city change, along with her own perception of it. She had even tried to run away to Los Angeles at one point, but came blazing back—she remembers running around like George in *It's a Wonderful Life* when she returned, and that stuck: Miranda would forever call her "George" after that.

Their friendship, once Natalie had earned Miranda's trust, grew from there. They started not only singing together but writing together, too. About a decade later, Natalie would write a song with another Texan, Kacey Musgraves. It was called "Rainbow." Natalie would join Maren, Amanda, and Brandi in the Highwomen in 2019.

"They're free, Miranda and Maren and Kacey," said Natalie. "They have to say what they say and do what they do because they are almost incapable of lying about who they are as artists. They just can't help it. They don't know any other way than to be themselves, even if it's uncomfortable for everybody else."

Things had already gotten much more complex back in the winter of 2004 when Justin Timberlake apparently ripped the cup off Janet Jackson's corset during the Super Bowl halftime show. In Nashville, it didn't matter to anyone if Janet meant to show her breast or not—all they knew was that this is absolutely not the kind of content that God-fearing Super Bowl watchers had expected. If there was ever a time for country music to double down on virginity and purity, this was it. And there was no way you were going to get an errant flashing from Alan Jackson onstage. He was safe. Country music could never. *Could never.* If a nipple appeared on Music Row, it might be the nipple to topple the whole thing down—showing skin was a thing that people in pop music did, and Shania's belly button was about as risqué as things were going to get. Until, that is, Maren arrived, completely unafraid to dress exactly as she liked, even if it wasn't conservative enough for traditional tastes, or even a little bit scandalous.

Neither Janet Jackson nor Justin Timberlake was country (though Justin would make somewhat of a transition into the genre later with a Chris Stapleton collaboration), but one year past the Chicks debacle was another powerful woman in music, most importantly a powerful Black woman, pushing the limits of "acceptability" when it came to the public sphere. It would be seven years before another woman played the halftime show.

"When Janet Jackson and the Dixie Chicks are cultural rebels," wrote Martin Johnson in *Newsday* that April, "you know you're in an era of extreme conformity."

Everything buttoned up after the Super Bowl. The Grammys made sure to get extra clean, and country music was a perfect antidote, because it was always the tamest of the genres. Evangelicals and conservative outlets seized the moment. "People are hurting, both economically and morally, and as a broadcaster I feel we have a chance to offer them hope," said Carol Jones Saint in the *Johnson City Press*. This wasn't country radio, but country, too, saw a window—they could be the alternative to the boob-flashing and moral waffling, and especially if you could keep anyone with breasts away from radios and televisions to begin with.

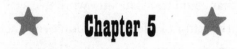

Chapter 5

NOT READY TO MAKE NICE

Maren had brought her mother as her date.

It was the fifty-ninth annual Grammy Awards in 2017, and Maren was in the running in several categories, including Best New Artist, Best Country Album, and Country Solo Performance for "My Church." Another Texas woman, Beyoncé, led in nominations, and Maren was up against Keith Urban, whom she had opened for on tour, as well as Brandy Clark, Miranda Lambert, and Carrie Underwood. Maren wore a purple dress that swept the floor, and had performed with Alicia Keys a tender, emotional version of "Once," off her debut album, *Hero*. Thomas Rhett and Camila Cabello were on tap to announce the winner, and Camila said her name when the envelope was ripped open: *Maren Morris*. Maren Morris, who only two years before had been without a label, watching awards shows at home on the couch or with her friends at local bars, dreaming. "Eleven years ago I went to the first ever Grammy Camp," she told the audience, choking back tears. "It was the first time I ever flew by myself on a plane to LA, and it's crazy to be here."

A decade prior, Maren had arrived at the Dallas–Fort Worth Airport, her ponytail tight and guitar in tow. She hadn't ever flown alone before, but she was ready for what lay ahead and generally unafraid to make the two-hour trip from home with her precious acoustic guitar snugged in its travel case and notebooks full of lyrics in her bag. It was the first year for Grammy Camp "career track," designed by industry consultant Patrick Bolek, and the idea was to provide students with real-world tools that could translate into workable skills—a boot camp for serious kids, the kind of place that didn't see their young talents as "novelty" but rather a hotbed of fertile soil for the future industry.

Maren had been working on her admissions packet for weeks, and the local association Texas Music Project had even raised the money to send her. She was routinely being referred to as an area wunderkind and was more focused on taking her skills to the next professional level than riding whatever sort of momentum she had already built. Grammy Camp gave her that rare chance.

"She was this young, demure, but fiercely gifted writer," Patrick remembered. A lot of the students came in with aspirations to be pop stars: photo shoots with white backgrounds and bright lipstick, trying to sell an image along with the talent. "For her, it was about the music. The one thing I could say about Maren from then to now is that she was authentic. She was such a standout."

Maren's entry packet was "robust and serious"—a step ahead of the other young musicians not just in her abilities but her drive. "I don't mean that in any diminutive way, but there was this subtle simmering underneath the surface, polite, thoughtful, thankful, in every sense of the word," Patrick said. "But also she was just this beautiful powerhouse that was completely confident in what she was communicating. And if you were to look at all of the kids that maybe had more presence, or that were more communicative, or had a more boisterous personality, those are kids that kind of faded away or just decided they were going to move in different directions. But here is a kid that was not immediately front and center, but had something that was definitely unique and special."

Even before she got to L.A., Maren was prepping for her arrival. She even started a song to workshop. "I wrote half of it because I was like, 'I'm gonna come in with something already done and finish really quickly in the class and impress everybody,'" Maren said, laughing at her own early ambition.

Once she arrived, Maren was often by herself, huddled in a corner working on a song or chugging out a riff on the guitar. Most of the classes included real-world contact with the industry: Grammy Award–winning producers David Foster and Jimmy Jam, and Cheryl Bentyne of vocal jazz group the Manhattan Transfer all came in to talk and work with the students, and they also got to visit Capitol Records and meet with the rock band INXS. Maren was in awe, and paying strict attention. This was before young musicians like Billie Eilish could grow organically in their own bedrooms through the power of social media. "Everyone was going to go to Berklee afterwards," Maren said. "It was just like real musicians that are kids."

News of Maren attending the Grammy Camp made the local paper—it was no small thing to have someone from Texas once again becoming more than a blip on the national radar, and more than one reporter was interested in following Maren's career. Maren was the only Texan in the singer-songwriter cohort, in an overall group that comprised forty-seven students from around the country. "I am the only kid I know around where I live who does this professionally, so it was neat to meet people who are doing similar things and learn their perspective," Maren said in 2006. "Though the other kids are going in a different direction than I'm going in, we still had a lot in common."

"Bowie High School sophomore Maren Morris definitely has soul," Elaine Marsilio wrote in the *Star-Telegram* in a lengthy profile. That "soul" is what made Maren different—it was something that stood out in the character of her voice, her approach. She wasn't trying to sound super twangy or emulate Dolly Parton all the time: she was aiming for unique over traditional.

It's not like playing country music made Maren cool, though. Among her peers, the genre was anything but. Sometimes she just wanted to be normal—it was her parents who kept her focused and on track. That was, until things changed with a blond teen from Pennsylvania, Taylor Swift.

"[Country music] wasn't trendy yet," Maren said. "And it wasn't, I think, honestly, until Taylor Swift came along and really modernized the genre, and she was so young. I'm sure so many people looked up to her the way I did with LeAnn. Like she's made it possible. She made country cool to people my age."

Taylor had signed with Sony/ATV Publishing in 2005, as well as Big Machine as her label (a label she would leave in 2018 and enter into a battle with over ownership of her master recordings). She released her self-titled debut album, led by the single "Tim McGraw," the following year, which was cowritten with Liz Rose. Taylor took what Shania had done in merging the worlds of pop and country one step farther—she not only made it accessible to fans outside the genre, she made it relevant for young kids by being young herself and speaking not to some imagined experience but the foibles of daily life. Country hadn't been great at reaching the youth market: that was never really the target audience. Taylor spoke to them in a way Faith Hill could not—she could express youthful fears and insecurities, all while making female ambition, as LeAnn did before her, an acceptable and covetable norm. She was also a generational songwriting talent at the root of it all, singing from a deeply female perspective, and one who fought early for her own agency: she rejected a development deal from a major label at fifteen because she wanted to be able to write her own songs.

"You don't walk away from a big record deal like that when you're an unsigned artist," Taylor told Nekesa Mumbi Moody in the book *Women Who Rock*. "But I had a gut feeling about it, and some of the best decisions I've made in my career have been based on solely gut feelings and my instinct."

The year 2005 was also when another country legend was crowned: Carrie Underwood. Mickey's future labelmate in 2011, Carrie had taken first place on *American Idol* and was seeing success off her first single, "Jesus, Take the Wheel." Though she had already started college and was planning on giving up singing, she decided to give a career in country music one more shot at twenty-one—judge Simon Cowell predicted that she would be the most successful contestant ever. He was right.

The emergence of these women on the scene changed the climate that Kacey, Maren, and Mickey were running into headfirst—or shying away from, temporarily, as Mickey was at least. Mickey, in Los Angeles, had started to make some small acting breakthroughs—an episode of the show *Shark*, where she shared a kiss with actress Caitlin Wachs, and a singing part in Nick Cannon's *Underclassman*. She'd given up trying to pursue acting as the only future, though, and had enrolled in classes at Santa Monica College, all while taking vocal lessons and working at a cigar bar in Beverly Hills: she'd finish up class and then do the daily drudge in traffic only to work until midnight every day, Monday through Friday. She'd sing country songs in her car on the commute, a safe place to pop in a Patty Loveless CD and remind herself where she came from and who she really was.

She was taking vocal lessons and doing background work for artists like Patti LaBelle and Babyface, sharing a one-bedroom apartment with a roommate. But it still felt like nothing was falling into place musically. "I gotta figure out a plan," Mickey thought to herself. "Because this ain't good."

One day at school between classes and before heading back to her car for the long drive home, she decided to pop in and visit with a guidance counselor.

"Maybe I could do speech pathology?" Mickey asked. "Or the business end of things? I could do something with music if I study business," she added, trying to convince herself in the process. They talked through options, looked at pamphlets, made Mona Lisa smiles. She knew it wasn't what she wanted, but it's what she thought she had to do if country music didn't have a place for someone like her.

* * *

At the same time the Grammy camp was changing Maren's future, the Grammy Awards were changing country—or at least forging an even deeper line between critical perception of the genre outside of the industry itself and the folks who turned the knobs and pushed the buttons at country radio. While options were becoming available to other genres—Spotify, for one, was founded in 2006 and would usurp radio for pop, hip-hop, and beyond—country radio remained the biggest driver of market share and control for any artist who wanted to make it in mainstream Nashville.

And after everything the Chicks had endured, they were not ready to apologize to anyone—and they were very intent on making that clear with their new song, "Not Ready to Make Nice." When they won the Grammys for Record of the Year, Song of the Year, Album of the Year, Best Country Performance by a Duo or Group, and Best Country Album at the beginning of 2007, it was a landmark moment for artists like Kacey: the Chicks had broken all the rules of decorum you're supposed to follow on Music Row, and the sheer mention of their names could send shock waves and shivers through Texas and beyond. But it also was a lesson in artistic defiance: the song didn't get played on country radio, but it did become the trio's biggest pop hit, certified platinum two times over and winning three Grammy Awards.

What that meant to women who grew up watching them was that a country act could follow a different sort of path outside of the Music Row confines. They weren't appearing at country events, but they were talking to Oprah. They were no longer accepted among the conservative hobnobbers, but they were finding a place for their music to be heard by new audiences, or audiences that had been pushed out of country music along with them. Maybe it would crack things open, reset the scales. Maybe.

The success of "Not Ready to Make Nice," which the trio wrote with Dan Wilson about their unwillingness to shut up, say sorry, and stop singing, did turn the fault line running through Nashville into a gaping canyon. On one side, there were those who would actually play and make nice: the future Luke Bryans of the world. On the other, the Chicks were creating a new formula that could exist without country radio and the need to constantly appease the powers that be on Music Row. Though they didn't know it yet, women like Kacey, Maren, and Mickey would serve as an exception to what was thought to be a rule. Kacey would win Grammys while never getting a number one hit. Maren would get radio play despite speaking her mind freely and singing from a distinctly female perspective. Mickey would make history without even being let in the door. Corporate country radio would continue to express their say when it came to any of them, but a clear path and footprint around this world was becoming not only viable, but necessary.

The *New York Times* called the song a "vindication," but not for country music: for censorship. "I think it says that, by and large, the creative community sees what has happened to the Dixie Chicks as unfair and unjust," Mike Dungan told the *Times*. Dungan, whose liberal politics are viewed as an open secret in conservative Nashville, would go on to work with Kacey as chairman and CEO of Universal Music Group Nashville, but was, at the time, president and chief executive of Capitol Nashville. Mike Dungan wasn't alone—a good percentage of label heads, managers, and publicists in Nashville all fell on the liberal side of the political scale (as evidenced by their campaign donations), but were happy to work under the perception that the town was conservative, because that's what made radio most comfortable.

The Chicks were barely making a go at country radio anyway. RJ Curtis, who now heads up CRS—Country Radio Seminar, the hugely important and influential yearly trade show for the industry—remembers gathering one day at an industry listening party, during CRS, of all places: he was working as a journalist for industry trade *R&R* at the time. The reaction in the room was mostly positive: this felt like country music after all, and the genre at the time was a strange place, full of mixed identities and a sound grasping for grounding. It wasn't too dissimilar from a usual type of event that happens during the industry conference, and RJ noticed that the room full of program directors seemed open to some new Chicks music. Or so he thought.

When "Not Ready to Make Nice" came on, everyone in the room looked at one another. "Please don't make this the single," the programmers moaned. They could only really sell apologetic Chicks, if they could sell the Chicks at all. "And it was like the worst thing that anybody could have said, because, you know, it's like telling your children to not touch the hot stove," RJ said.

Because if the Chicks were going to commit the sin of speaking out, they would at least have to be incredibly repentant—which they clearly were not. They meant what they said—they weren't ready to make nice and forgive an industry that had exorcised its own demons through their expulsion. For a male artist, though, what could the marketing have looked like? Waylon Jennings, Willie Nelson, Johnny Cash—they had become known and made legends for the degree to which they pissed people off, broke laws, and then turned around and floored everyone with music that reminded people of the sheer humanity within us all. *Wanted: The Outlaws* was a best-selling album in the seventies, the first country platinum record, and created a marketing event out of a subculture (or a subculture out of a marketing event? Who could say, really?). Like Johnny Cash before on his comeback album *American Recordings*, the Chicks worked with superproducer Rick Rubin. This was their outlaw double-down, and if country music was really willing to embrace "outlaws," it would embrace them again.

Thinking like that, though, was a luxury that Black country singers didn't quite have. It didn't matter what you were singing or where you were planning on coming from—if you were a Black woman, you had to continually prove yourself to be as country as you possibly could be ("prove yourself," there's that phrase again, as common for women in country music as "three chords and the truth"). Maren could be praised for that "soul," and someone like Rissi Palmer would be damned for it. Rissi was born in Pennsylvania and was the odd kid in her school who loved "uncool" country music, so much so that she sang and listened to it in secret.

But her talent was too strong to deny, and by nineteen she'd signed a publishing deal, ready to give making it in Nashville a shot. She would be one of three solo Black women in the history of the genre to break into the top 50 country *Billboard* chart, with her single "Country Girl," alongside Linda Martell and, eventually, Mickey.

"You're a good singer, but I'm not sure you are believable," Rissi would hear ad nauseam as she talked to labels and executives on Music Row, continually being told that her songs—pretty straightforward country by all accounts, in tune with the sonic textures of the time—would not work. "'I just don't know how we would market you. I don't know how we would find songs for someone like you.' It was eight years of that. I started to internalize it," she said. "Clearly it was me who was the problem."

Rissi had signed a record deal with a small company called 1720 Entertainment and had managers who were eager to encourage her to either fit a country mold or become some kind of amalgam between hip-hop and country. She had photos taken wearing wigs, with mermaid locks, trying to shape her into a Carrie Underwood hybrid. She found herself in a boardroom, listening to a whole table full of people discussing her hair—could her natural hair be on the cover of a country album? Would it be relatable? There was one person who fought for her, a woman named Donna Lisa, who headed PR at the label. "Let's just do a photo shoot with Rissi's natural hair," she suggested, and that became the one they kept.

Some of the progression of her career was "normal"—the same two cities a day for weeks at a time, the same radio tour schedule all the other country artists were doing. She'd see Taylor Swift in the Southwest terminal, doing the same routes. She'd do the same dinners with program directors at radio stations, trying to win them over. "A lot of times it was fun, taking shots, cracking up. A lot of my battles were won over those dinners," she said. "'Oh, you're so funny, Rissi! You're so cool, I didn't realize you were cool!' And it would go from that to inappropriate stuff." One time, one of the men tried to take a guess at her breast size. "What are you, a D?" Rissi remembered him saying. "You try to laugh it off because you don't want to be an asshole. It was always little microaggressions: you're pretty for a black girl. Rissi, you're not *black* black."

She found allies in women like Joanna Cotten, who was trying to get a solo career off the ground but now tours with Eric Church, Jamie O'Neal, and Ashton Shepherd. And when her self-titled record came out in October 2007, she did all the usual stops: CMT, the Opry, *CBS This Morning*, *Fox & Friends*. "The only nut we couldn't crack is radio," she said. Mickey, still in Los Angeles, paid close attention: seeing Rissi on CMT and hearing her music fascinated and delighted her. *Finally*, she thought, *someone like me, packaged between blond after blond after blond*. Like Rissi's, her music was more straight-ahead mainstream country than Maren's or Kacey's. And while Maren and Kacey would take political actions at different stages in their careers, Mickey and Rissi's mere existence was political.

"I've said it before, I'll say it again, I would not have moved to Nashville had I not Googled Black female country singers and saw your face and saw you singing at a show, nervous, holding your heart and your guitar," Mickey said later, appearing on Rissi's Apple Radio Show, *Color Me Country*. "Had I never seen that, I would have never made the move to Nashville. So you are the head majorette. I'm just following your lead."

Rissi both followed and feared the road map set by the Chicks, who had been a seminal influence ever since college, when she walked in on her first day to hear her new roommate blasting the trio. It struck her immediately—the harmonies, the musicianship. Who was on the radio, she immediately wanted to know?

"Girl, these are the Dixie Chicks!" her roommate replied.

"I just always admired the musicianship," Rissi said. "Super feisty, and smart, and funny. You see them and you know they're having a good time. And you know they're in on any of the jokes that anyone would ever make about them. I just thought they were a breath of fresh air, because they're just young, and fun."

Rissi paid close attention to what happened in 2003 to the Chicks—it haunted her all the way to her radio tours in 2006 and 2007 behind "Country Girl," especially when she would arrive to a station that had made the bold move of trying to work a song like "Travelin' Soldier" into the day's playlist.

"People would call in and for five minutes, just rail about the Chicks," Rissi said. "And just talk about how awful they were and don't play them and they're traitors. And I just remember thinking, I hope that I never do anything that pushes people off this ledge. I remember thinking to myself that politically, I totally agreed with them, but knowing I wasn't willing, in this particular place in my career, to stand up and do that. Because I really just wanted to get along."

Rissi, Mickey, Maren, and Kacey all heard the same refrain at every step along the way: any woman coming to Nashville with an opinion and something to say was going to put everyone on high alert.

"It was like a warning. The industry, the other artists who were threatening [the Chicks] and saying things about them—I think they knew exactly what they were doing," Rissi said. "I got the message loud and clear."

Chapter 6

AND THE DEVIL TAKES THE LAST CAR DOWN

The DeFoore Music Institute sits at the center of small-town Mineola, in a building that John DeFoore bought when he retired from the road—an old red brick former hotel on Commerce Street across from the railroad stop. Kacey insisted that it was haunted, and she's probably right, far too much crushed velvet for a non-paranormal type of existence, the sort of place Hollywood set directors can only dream of re-creating. John had been on tour since the sixties as an accomplished guitarist and sideman, but he found himself bored in his downtime, and eager for a little more consistency than the life of a road dog could ever promise. He was the kind of Lone Star intellectual that most on the coasts can't quite understand: Dylan Thomas with tumbleweeds and spurs.

John had a horseshoe-shaped gray mustache and a triangle goatee, a bit like a combination of Santa Claus and David Crosby. He wrote poetry and fiction books he self-published, talked slowly, and didn't like leaving his spot in Texas unless the circumstances dictated. After his last tour in the nineties, he decided to hang up his road gear for good and purchased an antique hotel in downtown Mineola in 1993 that he converted into his teaching studio. He later sold the place, but it was still his ground zero for lessons until he passed away in 2021, mostly in a wood-paneled "creepy, art deco" room, as Kacey put it, with the walls painted a diluted mint green, if you could actually see the walls through all the guitars hanging on them, and windows that rattled when the train rode through town. He took a small group of promising students each day—mostly women, just by chance—and then went home to tend to his own words and to comb through the papers or the news for inspiring anecdotes that could spur an idea for a song.

It was at his local church where John met Rick Lambert, who started to tell him about his twelve-year-old daughter, who could really, really sing. Eventually he went to their house to share a meal, and ultimately took Miranda on as a student: Rick was a songwriter, too, and a good salesman when it came to talent, and John could only imagine what could happen if the lyrical abilities of that young girl matched her vocal ones. Both Rick and his wife, Bev, seemed to have an uncanny sense for music (they were also private investigators who had worked on the Clinton impeachment case, so sniffing out leads must have come naturally), so while John would normally proceed with a bit of cautious reserve and care, he paid more attention this time. Those Lamberts seemed to know what they were talking about, after all.

John Defoore had his first success story with Michelle Shocked, a singer-songwriter, with Miranda and his next student not far behind: Kacey. A solid track record, maybe because his particular method of guitar instruction included something that others didn't, which was practice writing lyrics, not just massaging out chords. Not Berklee educated or anything of the sort, John never thought too much about wading his students exclusively in theory, and he evolved to be a different sort of guitar instructor, one who made sure to focus on the art of integrating storytelling into the learning process. This wasn't the usual method for a music teacher, but John made it mandatory. He still didn't bill his classes as songwriting, but it became known around

town that he was the sort of guy intent on developing careers and artists, encouraging his students to cultivate the tools that would let them
head to Nashville if they chose. John wanted to develop real talent, not
just machines that could execute a sound.

"Early on in my career, it occurred to me if you taught someone to
play guitar and that's all, what did you help them with?" he said. "I had
taken creative writing in college. I started insisting everybody write a
song. I made them write a song a week." John grew up in a musical
family where the radio was always on and instruments were always
being played—his mother, the violin and piano, and his father singing
in the church choir. After some years in London, where he ended up
staying after a stint in the U.S. Air Force, he returned to Texas and
started studying music theory at McMurry University, playing lead in
a country band and eventually opening the DeFoore Music Institute
in the center of town.

So for students like Miranda, Kacey, and Michelle Shocked, the
assignment wasn't just to play guitar—there was that, too, and their
fingers bled and calloused until those chords came swift and easy—
but to take to their rooms with a pad and paper and create a song from
nothing. And not trying to capture what was already on the radio, but
to go one step beyond—to be ahead of the dial, never chasing it.

"He was a very special teacher and he thought outside the box,"
Kacey said during a speech at *Variety*'s Power of Women event in 2019.
"He dared me to go home and write a song. I did that week after week
and he would critique it. Songwriting became this outlet for what I
was going through. Without realizing it he prepared me with the tools
I needed to move to Nashville and become a songwriter for a living."

For John, ever practical, artists didn't jump out with glitter and
glory. They worked. They worked hard, they honed their art, and they
keep plugging ahead even when it could feel easier to take another
turn, follow a different road to a more steady career path. They had no
plan B. He'd had students with as much promise as those who went
on to become big stars, and sometimes more, but they didn't have the

same belief, he said, that this was the be-all and end-all. For women in particular, he knew this mattered even more: he listened to the radio and recognized that these artists didn't just have to be good, they had to be great, spectacular even, scores above the casual dudes who didn't have to do much but hit a few notes and tuck themselves into tight jeans.

Like Miranda, Kacey had no plan B. Sure, she didn't do her homework from time to time, but she always kept her eyes set exactly on what was ahead of her. John had his students learn theory but also to be flexible: he knew that to limit a student to the confines of a rigid instructional box would end up pushing them out the other side and losing interest. That had happened with Kacey before, when a piano teacher chided her for trying to play something by ear and not by the book—and Kacey did not want to play by the book.

Though John didn't believe artists walked in with a spark, he did know that there's always a turning point—a light switch, where an artist goes from someone who might just have casual talent to someone with true promise. It's not something you're ever able to see on first glance because it takes time: it's not a reality show. "I'd like to tell you people spark from their first lesson," John said. "But they don't."

John spent his days combing the news for captivating subjects, and had stumbled across a story about six coal miners who had been trapped in a Utah mine after a 4.0 earthquake. It was a heartbreaking kind of American tale: blue-collar workers risking it all on a daily basis to do the most difficult of tasks, ending up losing their lives to something as unusual as an earthquake in the middle of a state that rarely saw such acts of nature. He flagged it for a story prompt for his students, and assigned it to Kacey one day at class.

"House your imagination to empathize with the miners," he told her.

Kacey knew about coal miners—she'd heard no shortage of Loretta Lynn songs (aka the Coal Miner's Daughter), and the coal miner had been an embedded metaphor in the country music mindset. She'd always loved Loretta, and saw a lot of herself in the brash and direct nature of her lyrics—Loretta was a southern woman, but she was eager to reshape the bounds of what that could mean, particularly when it came to ownership of her own femininity and force. Kacey would go on to be compared to Loretta many times over, sharing the stage on multiple occasions—Loretta's songs, she said, were ingrained in her brain. And she, like Loretta, wasn't scared to tackle subjects that might not be embraced by country radio, like sex or the pill, and see her songs downright banned, nor to have a nuanced approach to conservative issues: despite her religious foundation Loretta was firmly for abortion rights, writing in her memoir, "All the poor girls who get pregnant when they don't want to be . . . I believe they should be able to have an abortion." And, as she praised in her song "The Pill," she was equally enthusiastic about accessible birth control.

"When Loretta is touted on Music Row these days, the sequined side of her history tends to overshadow the fact that she's probably had more songs banned than any other artist in country music history," Kacey said at the Country Music Hall of Fame. "This is proof that when anyone in the music business—label heads, radio promotion teams, artists, managers, media, songwriters—choose to stay within known, successful lanes, avoiding creative risk and watering down content for easy consumption in hopes of financial gain, they're not only damaging themselves, but they're definitely damaging the rest of us too."

Thinking about coal miners, singing with empathy—that was something that Kacey could do. That would become who she is. The empathy is what existed in the space between the good and the bad, the party songs and the heartbreak songs, the songs that made country music the genre that it is, the safe place for fears and tears and memories.

Kacey took the article home and mulled it over. She returned the next lesson with a completed piece of work, and sang and played it for John, strumming quietly on her guitar. He sat and listened as the Texas heat tapped on the windows, the dust collecting on sills.

"And the devil takes the last car down" was the last lyric.

And in that moment, John knew. He just knew.

"That," John said, "was my aha moment."

John had also been watching the success of his other student, Miranda, come to fruition: an album that she fought for with so much grit and fervor, 2007's *Crazy Ex-Girlfriend*, was getting critical praise but little radio airplay (just like *Kerosene*). Regardless of the trends, Miranda was going to say exactly what she meant in her songs, and that approach was continuing to do little to maintain friendships in the arena of the country airwaves. The press and radio were already settling into her "hellacious" image: burning, shooting, and tearing shit up. In other words, all the stuff that made Waylon Jennings and the Outlaws idols, but Miranda a liability, as if engaging with her too much might make your actual house catch fire. She didn't seem to be particularly interested in talking about politics the way the Chicks were, but the hesitancy and imprinting about what could happen when women in country music didn't feel shy about airing their power and opinions had, nonetheless, remained steadfast. Miranda seemed dangerously close to the promise of the Chicks—fearless, stubborn, adhering to her vision like a gnat on flypaper.

It didn't faze her much, the way she was written about in the press, though, or even the industry's hesitancy to bank the future of the genre on her. "There is no bad publicity," Miranda told the *Dallas Morning News*. "Talk about me any way you want to. If you hate me, tell people. Just say my name."

There was no shortage of saying her name, and Miranda worried little about whether or not her "fiery" edge was too much of a liability. Miranda had a hand in writing most of her songs, but when she did pick an outside track, she didn't just put a quarter in the Music Row vending machine—she was careful and specific, landing on a Gillian Welch and Dave Rawlings track, "Dry Town," on *Crazy Ex-Girlfriend*. That sense would eventually lead her to Kacey's "Mama's

Broken Heart" in four years, giving Kacey her first big breakout cut and also her first taste of how cruel it can feel when someone else ends up living in a song that you poured your heart and soul into.

Miranda was becoming the blueprint so many would follow, not just those riding the Texas-to-Nashville route, but even beyond: she started to rack up endless awards, and by the time she got to 2021, she would break records left and right, without the assured support of radio like her male peers. Sure, sometimes she'd score a single, throwing the airwaves a bone, that would scratch toward number one, or even hit it. Few were doing things like Miranda, of any gender, though—that combination of serious songwriter with mainstream star with generational leader.

And like Miranda, Kacey decided to attempt a shot at *Nashville Star*—Tracy Gershon had been speaking to Miranda's mother, who had recommended that she look into this promising songwriter from the same area of Texas as her daughter. For Tracy, Bev was her ear to the ground to cover anywhere from Amarillo to the coast, but especially the new artists bubbling up around Dallas.

"Miranda's mother was my best talent scout in Texas," Tracy said. "She was really musical and she would always call me. I was helping talent and she sent me Kacey Musgraves. I loved her vibe."

Kacey had to make a video for her *Nashville Star* audition, and she made sure to feature the Beckham Hotel, where she studied with John, taking the crew on a tour of the town: the Golden grocery store, the home where her grandmother was born, the photos of her first appearances in little red boots. Memaw the art teacher made an appearance, as did Wes Hendrix, Kacey's old guitar player. "Anything can inspire me to write," she told the camera, her cool Texas drawl coming through. "A breakup, or a cool word." She showed off the old car she drove, a '67 Mustang with a 351 Windsor, and the print shop, Imprints, where she worked making copies and sending faxes, one of many behind-the-desk kinds of gigs she held in the early years just to make enough change to keep her on the road.

Her stint on *Nashville Star* lasted only three weeks, even though the song she wrote with Miranda's father, "Halfway to Memphis," showed her strength and nuance as a writer. There's a line that hit strongest in that one: "Take it or leave it, boy," she sang. She made herself as known as she could, with her grandma working the PR machine back home. On her artist bio page for the show, she spelled out her goals: "To have a good, long-lasting music career, to stay in shape and to learn to play the [resonator guitar] Dobro."

For her first performance on *Nashville Star*, clad in a blue plaid and bedazzled shirt with the word "western" on the back, she played a song of someone else's: "Leave the Pieces" by the Wreckers, the country duo helmed by Michelle Branch and Jessica Harp. Blake Shelton, Alabama's Randy Owen, and Anastasia Brown, a music supervisor and a rare female manager in Nashville in the nineties, were judging, along with Cowboy Troy and Jewel as hosts.

The Wreckers' debut LP, *Stand Still, Look Pretty*, had been released the year prior. Jessica Harp was known more in songwriting circles, but Michelle Branch had had a slew of early-2000s hits on her own, beginning with the infectious "Everywhere." By 2007, "Leave the Pieces" was still an echoing success, but the Wreckers themselves were starting to understand the dynamic that existed within the Music Row landscape, especially when it came to taking "stand still, look pretty" even more literally than they could have ever thought possible—and they broke up before they could make a second album, fatally wounded by the industry around them. "That's the theme in country music," Jessica said. "Men trying to make decisions about everything, what music you are recording, what you're wearing, to how much you weigh. The whole package, constantly nudging you into the direction they think you need to be in."

The idea for the Wreckers had started out as a joke between friends, and blossomed into a full-on project after a furious two-week writing session at Michelle's house in Los Angeles. The duo had left with a near album's worth of material in tow, but the Nashville wing of their label, Warner Brothers, had insisted that they include a few "outside" songs: songs, Jessica said, "that were much more in the Nashville box." One of those songs was "Leave the Pieces," which became their first single. When it hit number one, it was the first song by a debut female duo to do so since 1953—there was hunger for the type of honesty and authority they put forward, and for the way their female voices rang out in harmony.

"The one thing we heard continuously in the build-up to releasing the album was how everyone missed the Chicks on the radio," said Jessica. Everyone missed the Chicks—but no one was willing to actually play them. Jessica and Michelle knew instinctively and immediately that they were expected to behave in obedient ways so they didn't end up where the Chicks did, something they felt deeply during a few early shows opening up for the trio when Jessica was singing backup for Michelle pre-Wreckers, watching as the venue was swept for bombs beforehand, a necessity after all of the threats the group would routinely receive on their lives. "It was a wake-up call," Jessica said.

Music Row in general had been a wake-up call. "You were very much made to feel like you had to kiss the ass of anybody in radio, labels, and publishing," said Jessica. "To make them feel like they are your friends, your family. My manager always said, 'We're family here in Nashville.'" Somehow, though, it seemed like "being a family" never applied to the relationship of Michelle and Jessica themselves. They were constantly pitted against each other by their own teams with that very "family," Jessica said, even telling them that it was okay if they didn't get along—neither did Brooks & Dunn, so the rumors said. The tensions grew too big to ignore.

"The industry and the people around us hugely contributed to us breaking up in the first place," Jessica said. "Being so young and having so many men around us in our ears and telling us how to feel was a huge contribution to why we went our separate ways." When they both went to release their own music, it felt like they were being "punished" for breaking up the Wreckers: Michelle would eventually go on to attempt to launch a solo country career, with her record getting completely stuck in the Music Row machine and never released. Jessica's 2010 album, *A Woman Needs*, never got ample promotional support to spur hits, with radio stations telling her that a lyric about "makin' love and drinkin'" was too edgy for the radio.

But the Wreckers had appealed deeply to artists like Kacey who existed in a land between strong country roots and indie rock inclinations, making "Leave the Pieces" a perfect song to use as her introduction on the reality show. Kacey wasn't particularly excited about *Nashville Star*, just as Miranda hadn't been, but she tried to make the best of it. "Kacey was aggressive," Anastasia Brown would later report in her book *Make Me a Star*. "In a good way."

She didn't do well on *Nashville Star*, which made sense in retrospect—like Miranda before her, Kacey wouldn't exactly relish the opportunity to be within the confines of a television-ready perspective. "She looked like she was disinterested," said Tracy, probably because she was. But instead of turning her away, that captivated Tracy further: it was a spark of someone who was never going to play by anyone's rules. That disinterest was intriguing—combined with her sheer talent, it unearthed a sense of mischief that was titillating to those around her. Tracy liked people, especially women, who seemed to have no interest in doing things in ways other than their own.

When things went south on *Nashville Star*, Kacey moved forward with her album anyway, and with the idea to move to Austin in the coming months. She held an album release party at Stanley's Famous Pit Bar-B-Que in Tyler, Texas (Kacey promised "loud music and great barbeque").

Mickey had tried out for *American Idol* season seven, billed as "Mycale," not Mickey, and with barely a few seconds of airtime. She made it to Hollywood before being cut when the group was narrowed down to twenty-four—the only time the audience at home got a peek at her was in a montage of contestants who had been let go. Mickey sat in a chair in shorts, a white lace top, and black heels in front of the judges. It was Randy Jackson who muttered the words that she wasn't moving on. All Mickey could say was a quiet "Okay." David Archuleta won that year, but his career never got much farther off the ground outside of worship music.

American Idol also had an opportunity to help reset country radio away from one singular blond and blue-eyed image, but, for the most part, it rolled out a successive line of women who, despite all being talented, fell exactly into that mold: Carrie, Kellie Pickler, Lauren Alaina. Blond, blond, and more blond. "When pop culture leverages 'blonde,' it is always as an unmarked racial identity. Blonde is code for white," wrote Dr. Tressie McMillan Cottom in an essay on country's most famous blond of all, Dolly Parton, called "The Dolly Moment."

Maren was flirting with reality show success, too—she also gave *American Idol* a shot in what she ended up describing as a "traumatic" audition that didn't at all mirror the reception she was growing regionally. Reality shows held a certain kind of promise for female artists who might not have a chance making it on Music Row from the ground up—it worked for Carrie Underwood, and it could provide a different path into the hard-to-crack industry atmosphere. Reality shows might edge an eyeroll from certain music consumers, but to small-town kids, they were a promise, a way to transcend class for a moment: maybe you couldn't afford yet to take that demo to Nashville, the way Taylor Swift had, but you could try out for *Idol*.

Maren felt burned by the rejection, but not enough to change direction. She hit the studio to work on her album *All That It Takes*.

"It was obvious that she was going to be a force to be reckoned with, and that she was going to be a star and win Grammys," said Taylor Tatsch, a fixture on the local Dallas music scene who started writing with Maren when she was only fourteen years old. He was quickly surprised by how she didn't seem to have much of a desire to showboat her voice in honky-tonks across Texas with cover versions of "Before He Cheats," but instead seemed focused on developing her unique sound. "She always had a really grounded relationship with songwriting," Taylor said. "We would play John Prine, Janis Joplin,

Patty Griffin tunes that were deep cuts, and that's in addition to the songs she wrote."

Patty Griffin, especially, had become a point of creative infatuation, especially her 1998 LP *Flaming Red*. Produced by Jay Joyce, who would become a go-to for Eric Church and eventually Miranda, it was a showcase of exquisite lyrical abilities and empathetic songwriting. Patty was never a country artist per se, but perhaps no one from outside the genre had been so peripheral and so central all at once, at least when it comes to this particular class of artists. For a certain kind of songwriter, Patty was, and is, everything. Kacey, Maren, Mickey, Miranda, the Chicks, Rissi, Taylor Swift. The Chicks had even covered several Patty songs, and "Truth No. 2" had been incredibly prophetic in its lyrics. *Flaming Red* included a song called "Christina" that became the gold standard to Maren. Eventually she would get a lyric from it tattooed on her back.

Patty's songs had become part of what shaped these women—she had been at Lilith Fair and seen the movement for equality in music reach the crests of waves and then slide back down again, touched the edges of country and retreated quickly when she realized that the bulk of what was making it to country radio was about beers and trucks, not the most basic human threads of life, like her songs. "Some of it sounds like a mess," she said. "Some sounds so misogynist. Like 'ok, just give it up, you beat that horse to death. But the women—the women are insisting. There's just something about women in music right now, the way they are supporting each other."

Patty would go on to be a consistent, influential force in Maren's life—and in Kacey's and Mickey's, too. Patty returned the admiration. "They are super talented," Patty said. "If I had anything to do with them and what they do, then I feel like, 'hey, I'm done.'"

The people sipping beers in the Dallas dancehalls didn't exactly know what was coming to them when Maren stepped out and started singing Beyoncé. But they liked it.

Maren was digging deep for songwriting and performing inspiration, from all across the spectrum: Beyoncé and Patty Griffin, Metric and Sheryl Crow. It was rubbing off on her friends, too, like fellow Texan performer Van Darien.

"She showed me that there are these really great writers that aren't necessarily in one genre that can influence your music," Van said, "and then you can pull it into that songwriter genre and make it more accessible. It's almost like baking a cake and taking different ingredients from different places and people. And then ultimately what you end up with is something that's uniquely you. And I watched her do that."

Trying to push past traditional country, or playing Beyoncé's "Halo" in a honky-tonk, wasn't exactly the model for Texas country success, but it fit Maren because she didn't. Maren had been making the rounds to the local Texas programmers with *All That It Takes*, trying to see it through to at least break some ground on the regional scene. "I remember her coming to the country station I worked at in Fort Worth and dropping off a CD," says former radio promoter Staci Kirpach. "I remember because I liked her name. Thought Maren Morris sounded slick. But it was going nowhere. The station wasn't at all interested."

Maren was getting more confident, though, even if others were not—and her parents kept up the pressure to stick with performing, even when she wanted to just stay home and try to be a normal teenager for a minute or two. Her sixteenth year came with a bit of teenager-appropriate validation: she bought her first car with money saved from gigs. "That was a really empowering thing to have for myself," Maren said. "All my other friends were either getting a free car from their parents, or a used one that their dad didn't want anymore. And I'm thankful for it now. After much therapy and songwriting sessions and seeing what I've accomplished, I don't think I would have the same work ethic if my parents hadn't rode me so hard about shows and paying the band and making the most of your time with the people, and treating your employees right. All of that was early coursework on what I do now."

She also wasn't thinking much about genre, or trying to conform to one particular type of lane. "When I'm writing a song, I don't think, 'Is this country or blues or rock?'" Maren told the *Fort Worth Weekly* in 2007. "I just write it, and then I sing it the way I think it's supposed to sound." *All That It Takes* had just hit the Texas scene, and had won Top Songwriter and Female Vocalist of the Year in the newspaper. "I always found her older than her years," said local reporter Preston Jones, who covered Maren intently in the region. That was the difference for him and so many others: Maren wasn't trying to capitalize on youth, or transform into a grown woman. She just exuded a lived-in maturity. "I was just blown away," he said. "I don't know how else to describe it."

The Chicks would infuse themselves into Maren more than she realized at the time. "Shut Up and Sing," that phrase lobbed at the Chicks ad nauseam, would eventually pop back into her mind when working on the song "Flavor" for her second album, *Girl*, in 2019. By then, she had already been testing the political waters heavily by speaking out in favor of gun control after numerous mass shootings, including one at the Route 91 country music festival in Las Vegas, and had experienced the trail of impact and swiftly assembling gate-keepers that come when anyone in the country industry dares to step outside their bounds.

Taylor Swift has openly spoken about how this message had been drilled into her head repeatedly and motivated every careful step she took as a young artist trying to play all the right games in Nashville, in the right ways. It was petrifying sometimes, turning creative, confident people into nervous wrecks when sitting in front of the press—the road map was just that clearly paved for anyone who dared to walk it.

"The number one thing they absolutely drill into you as a country artist, and you can ask any other country artist this, is 'Don't be like the Dixie Chicks!'" Taylor Swift told the *Guardian*. "I watched country music snuff that candle out. The most amazing group we had, just because they talked about politics. And they were getting death threats. They were made such an example that basically every country artist that came after that, every label tells you, 'Just do not get involved, no matter what.'" The Chicks would later sing with Taylor on her 2019 song, "Soon You'll Get Better," written in honor of Taylor's mother, who was fighting cancer, and Taylor would later emerge powerfully into her own political and activist voice once the constraints of country music were no longer placed forcefully upon her.

The "Not Ready to Make Nice" pathway notwithstanding, the absence of the Chicks in Music Row culture around 2007 did provide a different sort of gap that was just as profound—the lack of women to grab the hands of the new generation and lead them forward, especially since the men weren't going to reach a palm out to help. Many of the leading women of the nineties were being relegated to side roles behind their husbands: Trisha and Garth, Tim and Faith among them. Though the married-duo formula had always been a beloved mechanism for country, it worked well to diminish the role of women in leading roles, especially as country's men only gathered appeal and authority as they aged.

From the mainstream perspective, it had narrowed down the accepted path to two women: Carrie and Taylor. Shania had gone abroad. The Chicks had been taken care of. Radio had sufficiently chiseled its focus down so much to only let those two in at the top, with an occasional spice of Miranda, who didn't have a number one song until her third record with 2010's "The House That Built Me." And with Carrie and Taylor, at that point at least, no one had to worry about a boob flash or a political statement, while women like Pam Tillis, K. T. Oslin, Chely Wright, Mary Chapin Carpenter, and many others had been relegated to the footnotes of mainstream country. Once again, it became survival of the fittest by white, blond women only.

"They're both attractive, 25-year-old blondes with powerful voices," observed critic Geoffrey Himes in the *Nashville Scene* about Carrie and Miranda. Comparing and contrasting them, however, became the lazy crutch of not just the industry but the culture at large—you didn't need to let two of them in at the moment, and you certainly couldn't play them one after another on the radio. Meanwhile, legions of dudes with trucker hats were able to exist happily together, not battling for the top spot because they all were sure, in time, to be able to get their turn.

Blond women were interchangeable, but critics liked to be both above that and belaboring it. The Maren and Kacey paradox would continue the same—was Maren the new Kacey? Was Kacey the future Maren? Was Maren the past Kacey? And if there were barely two spots for women, how many spots would there be for Mickey, exactly?

The year 2008 got off to an auspicious start. If you held on to conservative values of what the role of a woman should be in the household, it was a year of discomfort: a Black candidate for president, Barack Obama, was shaking up the political landscape and the seeds of the Lilly Ledbetter Fair Pay Act, which gave new permissions for women at the federal level, were in motion—it would be one of the very first things President Obama would sign into law as soon as he took office. The woman's role in the household had obviously evolved past the point of constant, dutiful wife—but country music wasn't always so good at providing an environment that nurtured it. Sarah Palin, running for vice president alongside John McCain, had made sure to reinforce this model of a woman: a powerful one, a pit bull in lipstick, but still submissive to the man, still so intent on holding up conservative values. She would play Martina McBride's "Independence Day," at her rallies, mistakenly thinking it was a patriotic song.

Not everyone thought that new federal protections for women were even necessary or welcome. Maybe country music, in particular, wasn't so excited about the prospect of women gaining too much forceful ground, especially when pop music was swerving freer and queerer than ever. Country music's mainstream was decidedly not kissing girls, but pop was: the genre's biggest shake-up of the year,

Katy Perry's bi-curious "I Kissed a Girl," exploded in, of all places, Nashville. Just blocks from where country executives were lecturing their artists about keeping their politics tucked into their pockets, one station, 107.5 The River, helped the song take off.

Absolutely no one was going to let anything like that happen in country music, especially not in 2008, two years from Chely coming out, and five from Kacey even alluding to such a thing on "Follow Your Arrow." There would not be a major-label, mainstream country song explicitly about queer love or attraction, sung by a queer person themselves, until the Highwomen's "If She Ever Leaves Me" in 2019—though the singer Patrick Haggerty had started a revolution in his own right with what is regarded as the breakthrough gay country album, 1973's self-titled *Lavender Country*, it never, with tracks like "Cryin' These Cocksucking Tears," aspired for mainstream consumption.

The industry had also expelled LeAnn Rimes completely. In 2008, LeAnn filmed a movie with a married actor named Eddie Cibrian, and the two began an affair. Paparazzi caught the couple at a restaurant, and what ensued was a full-on scandal. It was on the cover of *Us Weekly*, and news outlets wrote rundowns detailing every gruesomely personal tidbit. She never quite recovered from it. After 2008 she barely had a country single break the top 30, with most failing to enter at all.

Country superstar Jason Aldean had an affair, too, also caught by the tabloids, in 2012. Like LeAnn's, it led to marriage. He's had eighteen number ones since then.

Chapter 7

ALL THEIR FAVORITE PEOPLE

How do you know a home when you find one, especially when you leave the one you are born into, the one sketched into your skin? How do you find the place you belong, the people who understand you, streets that feel familiar even if you didn't walk them when your feet were small? There's no real recipe, really. Country music is best at reminding you that home still matters, that it's okay to be from somewhere that has as many stop signs in a whole town as one small city corner. The Chicks even named their 2002 album after it: *Home*.

Kacey was trying to find her home, or at least a new home base, so she left Golden for Austin in 2008. It's where it made sense to go—Nashville was the obvious option for burgeoning songwriters, especially ones who had developed a newfound profile by appearing on *Nashville Star*, but Austin was where the Texas poets gravitated. It was the land of the Armadillo, the classic club that bred the Outlaw movement back in the days of a young Willie Nelson and now was a different sort of hub through music festivals Austin City Limits and South by Southwest that synthesized this artistry into cultural fuel.

Austin as a destination was quite different from Nashville, and Kacey's decision to try her hand there speaks to how deeply Texan success was embedded in the state's performers. It also spoke to how Kacey's designs were never really on massive superstardom but on a measured career simply built out of good melodies and great lyrics, and on gaining respect for the words on paper and the guitar in her hand. Willie Nelson had famously left Nashville for Austin in the early seventies after being completely disillusioned by the demands of the corporate country machine, letting his hair grow long and his creativity flourish back in his home state. And while Nashville was Music City, Austin was a music crowd: a listening audience, not an evaluating one. So instead of trying to make the big leap to Nashville, Kacey focused on a smaller market where she could feel more assured of genuine support for her work from both fans and peers, making herself less vulnerable to the whims of mainstream Music Row.

Kacey had gone back to Golden after *Nashville Star* and continued as normal at first. She appeared at a festival in Marshall, Texas, where she was described as having "Texas dancehall style" music, she played a fishing expo with Trace Adkins; she served as a vocalist for singer-songwriter Radney Foster at Gruene Hall, the oldest existing dancehall in Texas, where an attending reporter described her, uncomfortably, in the *Longview News-Journal* as "impossibly young, brunette gorgeous, demure and would make any daddy proud." In April 2008, she joined Blake Shelton at Miranda's Cause for the Paws benefit in Lindale—at that point, Miranda had already been well underway on her path to superstardom, which could have given Kacey even more reason to ponder moving to Nashville. But Miranda had done it all without relocating or compromising, so perhaps Kacey didn't need to, either.

Once in Austin, Kacey was determined to make things work, so she emailed a local label owner named Monte Robison, whose company, Triple Pop, managed a few artists around town. She invited him out to an Ethiopian restaurant, a place he'd never heard of despite being a longtime Austin resident (Kacey, not wanting to pick the spots usually beloved by Music Row, would later schedule press interviews at Ethiopian restaurants, Gojo on Nolensville Road in South Nashville being a particular favorite).

"I can tell you any number of stories of musicians that would give up, get a corporate job, and just make the music a hobby on the side. But I could tell from her that it was 110 percent that she is going to do music, and there's nothing else," Monte said. "I mean, that's it. I could just tell that that was her main and sole ambition or interest in life." Monte helped Kacey record a few covers that picked up a little steam online, like a dreamy version of OneRepublic's "Apologize."

Still, things weren't falling into place in Austin like they should have for Kacey. She wasn't finding a crack in any of it, short of her work with Monte and Triple Pop, and even that didn't feel exactly right. Money was tight, which Radney knew, so when his regular background singer left to take a job in Los Angeles, he asked Kacey if she might want to sit in on his sets, whenever they surfaced—not a lot of money, and nothing regular, but a semireliable three hundred bucks a pop.

"Well, that makes my whole month," she told him.

Radney and Kacey's friendship had been strong since she first opened for him as a fifteen-year-old, and he embodied a bit of that kind of Nashville success that appealed to her: respected as a songwriter but never cracking through the mold in a way that seemed to make him sacrifice his individuality. He liked writing songs with teeth and didn't have any desire to wrap them in pretty veneers—it's why the Chicks decided to cover his song "Godspeed" on *Home*. He became someone Kacey would come to, especially with matters of the artistic heart worth weighing.

"I'm still here in Austin, and no one is listening," she told Radney one night, growing increasingly frustrated. "I just can't find it." She felt guilty, though, about the idea of leaving Texas for Tennessee—she didn't want to betray her roots.

"Just because Austin ain't your town, it doesn't mean you have rejected your Texas heritage," he told her.

Texas is its own world and, in so many ways, that can be a boon for an artist: you can make a whole living there, never leaving state lines if you choose not to, playing to huge crowds and adoring fans, famous in San Antonio but anonymous in Seattle. Artists sometimes feel like they're leaving a corner of their souls behind or selling out if they decide to go to Nashville, the land of glitter boots and decorated dreams—the sentiment of those NUCK FASHVILLE shirts. Radney assured her that she'd be fine—he knew she'd be fine. He remembered how on the tour bus once, Kacey'd stuck her fingers in the chest of a bandmate to make a point, and saw instantly how headstrong and confident she could be, so committed to her own point of view. So one day, when Radney's bus was heading to Nashville, Kacey threw a bunch of boxes in the back and closed up her Texas life.

She moved into a house in East Nashville on Shelby Avenue, sight unseen, with a little money courtesy of her grandparents in her back pocket and two roommates, one of whom she found on Craigslist. An older woman they called Mama Sophia lived on the top floor and used to watch Kacey's dogs when she needed to go out of town for gigs. She was homeless once, and had a difficult life. Kacey paid attention, because she could synthesize suffering into art, and so Mama Sophia made it into a song: "Everybody's Got a Story," which the talented Chevel Shepherd eventually recorded.

Kacey shopped her demos to publishers during the day, picking her guitar at night, and hopping onto rounds when she could. It was a faster and more focused hustle than in Austin—becoming a songwriter, she thought, seemed at least like a more attainable goal than stardom through a Texas dancehall. For extra cash, she dressed up in costume for kids' birthday parties.

"I had to be Hannah Montana and sing one of her songs. They were pulling on my wig and saying 'You ain't the real Hannah Montana,'" Kacey told *American Songwriter.* "The next one was 'We need you to dress up in a French maid costume and deliver balloons to an industry birthday party at The Palm.' I'm glad I said no because it ended up being Blake Shelton's birthday party, and if I did that, I would have never lived it down."

* * *

That apartment on Shelby Avenue was important, but it was another house that mattered more.

It's full of gorgeous homes now, that strip of Villa Place, all renovated white-brick Airbnbs that have drawn pop star residents for temporary stays, up the street from a Spanish tapas wine bar and a boutique that sells cowboy boots for two thousand bucks a pop. But in 2008, it was home to a glorious shitshow of a place: Hotel Villa. Yellow brick, cheekily hideous Hotel Villa.

Hotel Villa wasn't a hotel. It certainly wasn't a villa, or conjuring anything romantic of the sort. Instead, it was a house near Music Row, where various casts of characters had lived, depending on the day. It was dirt cheap and dirty, and it was central for the group that would become a thriving creative class: a social center and a ragged heartbeat, driven by the bodies that gave it life. Hotel Villa had been the location for the very early incarnations of the Brothers Osborne, where T.J. and John Osborne would record vocals on a little Pro Tools rig, sitting on the edge of the bed. Albums and songs were born and made; friendships forged for life. Plus, if you needed some weed, you could probably find it there.

The Nashville in 2008 that Kacey arrived to was at a creative peak, driven by people who expressed their artistry and songwriting in ways both inside and outside of country music, and it was often far from the demands and requirements of Music Row—a thriving, collaborative crew. "No one was afraid to throw paint at the wall," said Madi Diaz, a musician who had come to Nashville with a fellow Berklee student named Kyle Ryan, who would eventually go on to become a member of Kacey's band and her musical director. "Just scribbling all over the outside of it." It wasn't just music, either: Madi and others were throwing art shows, scrappy events with food trucks, and anything that would be a sharp contrast to what was going on in the business end of things.

Madi wasn't a country artist, but none of that mattered much. The Villa world existed outside of Music Row but not intentionally so—it was a fertile place for artists like Courtney Jaye, who moved to Nashville after a record deal with Island had gone sour—whatever their vision had been, it wasn't exactly what she had in mind for the shape of her career, which was certainly not some manufactured vision of a pop star. She'd been coming to town on and off for writes, working with Kacey's future *Golden Hour* coproducer Ian Fitchuk in a band together and popping in for sessions mostly on the indie rock scene. Courtney had an album in her pocket already made—*The Exotic Sounds of Courtney Jaye*—which had been picked up by Universal for a singles deal. When they tried to push her toward country radio, Courtney backed away and put the LP out herself, and then made another one a few years later with Natalie Hemby's husband, Mike Wrucke.

Then there was Kate York, a master connecter on the scene and a masterful songwriter who seamlessly wafted between the indie rock world and the country mainstream. Kate moved from Los Angeles and had become a connective glue for the Villa crew. The Brothers Osborne—John and T.J.—were two siblings from coastal blue-collar Maryland who were on the cusp of their own label deal for their smart country-rock synthesis, driven by T.J.'s irresistible baritone twang and John's stellar guitar skills. There was Lucie Silvas, who had come from London as a pop star in her own right, now settling into her penchant for rootsiness and a soulful voice that could cut glass in rasp, belt, and tone. There was Elice Cuff, a publicist, there was Natalie Hemby and T.J. and John's sister Natalie Osborne, there was Kree Harrison, who captured the golden age of nineties country with a smooth Patty Loveless style and a quiet, skilled depth. They would welcome Mickey into the fold when she moved to Nashville, and eventually Maren, too.

Kree, in particular, had been in Nashville far longer than most of them, and though she would make her larger introduction to the country world via *American Idol* in 2013, she had been working her way through the Nashville system tirelessly and with a very specific vision for her own sound and priorities. Kree had lived more tragedy than most country songs—she lost her father in a plane crash off the coast of Spain in 2001, and eight years later her mother was killed in a car accident. She had been performing for most of her life, and had even become a favorite guest of Rosie O'Donnell back when she had a talk show and Kree was a young child, coming on and singing country covers in her uncanny twang.

She never fit the cookie cutters of what Music Row was offering at the time, and carried little interest to change her mold. Beyond her friend group she found herself more reflected in the older generations like Wynonna and Reba, and she stuck intently to her aesthetic, which did not include dying her hair—thick, black, and long, dusting mid-back, more Cher than Dolly—to a more bleached version of itself, or wearing sunnier clothes. She had been generally opposed to the idea of auditioning for the twelfth season of *American Idol*, but ended up caving to a bit of the peer pressure, and she came in as the runner-up behind Candice Glover, singing Patty Griffin on the finale.

"We definitely have a community," said Kree. "Not a 'you can't sit with us vibe,' but we stay close to each other. We hold on tight to each other because we have gone through so much shit together and grown together rather than apart, and it's a really beautiful thing. Success for us is having creative control over how we want to do it." Kree was a Texan, too, and familiar with the kind of world that someone like Kacey had come up in.

Outside of Hotel Villa jam sessions, much of the social life revolved around future *Golden Hour* coproducer Daniel Tashian's "12 at 12" showcase at Twelfth and Porter, where twelve up-and-coming acts would get a turn on the stage, and the dive bar Santa's Pub, where Kacey had worked before the money from songwriting and, eventually, the record deal was enough to keep her afloat ("beer is cheap, there's terrible karaoke," said Kacey once). And then songwriter rounds at places long gone—like Mad Donna's, which sat on a corner in East

Nashville across the street from Lipstick Lounge, the town's only lesbian bar—and some forever standing, like the Bluebird Café.

Another *Golden Hour* precursor created that year was *Stupid Love* by Mindy Smith, an artist who Maren and Kacey would both point to as being an influence on their writing and sound, right on par with Patty Griffin. Ian Fitchuk (with Daniel Tashian on guitar and vocals) had coproduced the seminal and important record from Mindy, who had moved to Nashville in the early 2000s after being raised in New York; she spoke, and still speaks, with the accent of a Long Islander with a penchant for the occasional Yiddish tidbit picked up anywhere but the South. After her mother passed away from cancer, she and her father lived in Knoxville for a stint, until she'd gathered up enough confidence from playing writers' rounds to make the transition to Music City.

Her songs were lyrically stunning but she didn't have the confidence to play her guitar at first—she would often bring it with her to rounds but never actually strum it. "I would just hold my guitar and sing a cappella," she said. It was at a Ladies' Night writers round in Knoxville at a place called Sassy Ann's that her friends gathered around and told her that next time she came she better be actually playing that damn guitar. Mindy picked it up every time, ever since.

Mindy headed to Nashville and embarked on the usual sort of journey, working odd jobs at a pawnshop, a Burlington Coat Factory, the flower store down the street—while playing writers rounds religiously. One of those included a lineup set up by Daniel for his 12 at 12, and their relationship blossomed from there. After covering Dolly Parton's "Jolene" for a compilation that garnered attention from Dolly herself, there was broader interest, and there were opportunities, but as Mindy toured the labels in town it was all the same: "We love you," they said, "but we just don't know what to do with you." Eventually she signed with Vanguard, but none of the Music Row players ended up coming to bat.

Working with Daniel, Kate York, who cowrote some songs, and

Ian Fitchuk as well as his coproducer, Justin Loucks, "was the most creative space I have ever been in," Mindy said. She had just finished treatment for anorexia, walking nearly straight from a performance on *Jay Leno* to a facility. She needed to pour her entire self into something creative, and *Stupid Love* is what came out. It became a permanent fixture in the collections of Kacey and Maren, especially. "She's an awesome songwriter," Kacey told *Esquire*. "*Stupid Love* . . . is folky, singer-songwriter music, but then she'll have a weird, electric moment, too. I can't stop listening to it."

Everything that happened among the Hotel Villa friends stayed at Hotel Villa. Almost everyone, from very early on, knew that T.J. Osborne was gay—he didn't hide it from them, but not one person in the group said a word anywhere before he was ready in 2021. Secrets and stories were all shared, but nothing left the house unless it was in a song meant for a wider audience.

When not at Daniel's 12 at 12, almost everyone found themselves drawn to the regular shows of KingBilly, a group that included John Osborne and Charlie Worsham, who was an ace musician and writer from Mississippi who had gone to Berklee College of Music in Boston on a scholarship after growing a reputation around his hometown as a virtuosic picker. Charlie eventually developed a name around town that would frame him as a young Vince Gill, and he caught the interest of Taylor Swift and Miranda Lambert even before he signed his record deal. Taylor "is the reason I even got my record deal," said Charlie, who also lived at Hotel Villa. "And Miranda would ask me onstage," he added, often spotting her in the wings as he played his opening set.

Charlie's tender, gorgeous creations would barely see the light of day on the airwaves—they were too emotional perhaps, too musical. Who knew, really, but he wanted to talk about songs, not strip clubs, with program directors, to his own detriment. After his 2013 debut album, *Rubberband*, failed to make much of a dent at radio, he regrouped and released an exquisite second album, 2017's *Beginning of Things*. It was positioned to be his breakthrough, and to some degree it was—in the media at least. But country radio completely ignored it, especially the stereo-perfect "Cut Your Groove." But in 2008, he was another struggling musician at Hotel Villa, looking for another story to tell and a song to sell, just like Kacey.

And Kacey, really, had just been looking for a little weed.

According to Elice Cuff, it was Natalie Hemby who suggested that Kacey meet her and Kree, knowing they might, at the very least, enjoy getting high together.

"You need to meet this girl Kacey who just moved here," Elice recalls that Natalie told the girls. "She doesn't have a lot of friends, but she likes to smoke weed."

"All right," said Elice. "Cool."

Kree had been living with singer-songwriter Ashley Monroe, who would eventually join Miranda in her trio the Pistol Annies, at an apartment on West End Avenue, and she arranged a gathering—almost everyone was broke enough to prefer cheap hangs at someone's house over drinks at the bar, especially when there wasn't a songwriter round to get to.

Kacey, as usual, was late. By the time she showed up, Kree and Elice were tired and high, but the first words out of Kacey's mouth gave each of them a bit of a second wind: *"Do you guys like to smoke weed?"* Soon, the three of them started hanging out every day they could, "like college sleepover time," said Elice. They called themselves the "Hasbeens," all living together in various combinations until Kacey moved into a house on Seventeenth Street in East Nashville, and Kree and Elice both met their significant others.

Every Monday night, Kacey would play a round with Brothers Osborne, Kree, and Carly Pearce at Hotel Indigo for "about ten people," said Carly, who, many years later, ended up signed to Taylor's ex-label Big Machine. It was clear to her, even then, that the talent she was seeing was on a different level of extraordinary. "You knew that people like that were a step above of what you saw every day," she said.

Even after they moved on from Villa into various more "adult" dwellings, they kept a group chat that still runs to this day for corny jokes, stories, and industry gripes. Over a decade of Grammy Awards and international tours, these friendships somehow never faded—in fact, they solidified. It wasn't so much about physical collaborations—formal writes together or cuts weren't the goal. Just friendship, and music. The people who gave life to Hotel Villa and who grew from its crumbling rooms to international fame came together because, in a town of artifice masquerading for truth, they chose their own truth instead of what was manufactured.

"What drove these people together?" wondered Elice. "I honestly think it's honesty. For this group, we can be ourselves and that's always been the thing. When you move to Nashville, no one knows each other. But when you find something like that, you don't want to let it go." Seven years later, Maren would find herself at John Osborne and Lucie Silvas's wedding—as John's "best man."

Back in Texas, Maren was seeing the response to *All That It Takes* grow. The *Fort Worth Star-Telegram* called her "one of North Texas' strongest songwriting talents." The title song was picking up steam on the Texas Radio charts, and live dates were rolling in: at South by Southwest, at a festival in France called Equiblues. She discovered an album, *Stupid Love*, that she would cherish. She dreamed and imagined where her home might be.

Miranda was thinking about home, too. She picked a song called "The House That Built Me," which had originally been written for her then boyfriend Blake Shelton, the next year. It was her first number one hit and a masterpiece of a performance, three albums into her career.

Chapter 8

BUTTERFLIES AND WILDFLOWERS

Before she remembered anything else, Beth Laird remembered the flowers. One of the only female song pluggers at music rights management organization BMI, Beth could picture nearly every detail from memory of Kacey's demo, the cover adorned in yellow sunflowers that made its way into her very busy, very infrequently rattled hands. Kacey had been circulating the six-song compilation around town, and it landed on Beth's desk in 2009, one of any number of CDs screaming for attention that floated by on a daily basis.

Beth grew up not far from Music Row in Winchester, Tennessee, interested in music and the business but not particularly sure how to make a dent in it—she wasn't motivated by any urge to be a performer, nor had she spent a childhood strumming away on a string instrument. One day wandering around at the Kroger in town nearing summer break from college, her mother ran into her old babysitter, a woman named Regina Stuve. Regina was one of the rare behind-the-scenes women working on Music Row at the time as head of publicity at Capitol Records, and she thought it would be worth urging more women to come try their hand in town.

"Why don't you let her move to Nashville and intern for me for free?" Regina suggested to Beth's mother, who would proceed to tell her daughter to move to Nashville for a few days a week, bunking up at an extended-stay hotel near Music Row. Eventually she made a permanent move, working at first for a biscuit company that manufactured goods for Pepperidge Farm, then to a receptionist job at BMG Music Publishing before finally landing the gig known as a "song plugger" at BMI, pitching songs to artists to record. She was the first-ever female rep at BMI and the only female rep there at the time—even then, it wasn't a particularly friendly profession for women, outside of the slightly more open fields of publicity or marketing. Nashville had seen a selection of women, specifically white women, break through in a few influential roles at times and do an excellent job of holding up the same machines that kept anyone but white men out of the highest-tier positions of power: to this day, the very top spots at the major country labels and publishers are all held by men.

Beth tried to operate the only way that felt appropriate: to "sit in" with the guys, to laugh at their jokes, to try to conduct herself like someone who could blend in or be unobtrusive in a room full of men. But it didn't work. "I hit a crossroads," she said. "I will never forget having a moment where I was like, 'I cannot try to be something that I am not.' I have to see being a woman as a strength and not a weakness, because the one thing they can't do is work with women and understand their perspectives. And once I changed my mindset, I feel like being a woman became an asset for me."

Another song plugger too married to whatever masculine version of a country music artist they were preprogrammed to gravitate to might have passed over Kacey, but not Beth. After a meeting in the office, she couldn't get Kacey out of her head. "I just kept thinking about Kacey after our first meeting," she remembered. "These songs were just so simple and great and her voice was so unique."

In 2009, Beth was underway with a showcase she had created called BMI Buzz at the Basement, where she would show off new acts she'd signed to try to get them in front of the most industry eyes at once—start early, end early was the idea, home in time to put the kids to bed. Most of the people who hung out there were much "cooler" by traditional (or stereotypical) standards than the country crowd, who would shuffle in wearing bootcut jeans to their sharp indigo ones from local denim shop Imogene + Willie.

But in those nights it could become magic, unlike most industry events in Nashville, which tended to land, and still do, somewhere between boardroom and beauty pageant, all smiles and handshakes and troughs of "Mexican" food in silver buffet servers and platters of meat or cheeses you have to hack at with a decorative cleaver. Social gatherings are part of the fiber of the town, and Music Row, per usual, focused on the "community" of it all: the same people in different jeans, the same talks in different rented-out bars, the same mostly white faces. You don't so much network as show up and prove to the people around you that you can remember their kids' names, where they live, what church they go to, what part of the Gulf Coast they went on vacation: it can be both an extreme strength and comfort in a cutthroat industry, and a handy tool to always limit who gets in the room or feels comfortable enough to stay.

Grimey's and the Basement had represented something different, a scene bubbling up from within Nashville that ran parallel, but separate entirely, to whatever was being pumped out of mainstream country. The Basement, run by Mike Grimes and his partner Dave Brown, had become a bit of an incubator for new talent, a tradition started when Mike kicked the East Nashville scene into gear with his venue called Slow Bar, a pioneering place for local music he opened in 2000. Kings of Leon played their first show ever there, and bands like My Morning Jacket and the Black Keys appeared there early in their career, before it closed in 2003. John Prine was known to regularly show up and take in the local talent over a few "handsome Johnny" cocktails of vodka and ginger ale.

Beth seemed to have a sense that melding those two worlds at her showcase, rather than posting up at some properly appointed watering hole, would give a different kind of cachet to the songwriters she was trying to put on display. Artists might actually want to come here—varied kinds of voices and perspectives with unique songs who were having trouble being heard, or were new altogether. Mike Grimes couldn't have cared less about what was going on in mainstream country from a profitability point of view, but he wasn't purposefully eschewing it, either—he was just as happy to have a burgeoning Music Row songwriter share the stage with a quiet folksinger, if the songs were any good.

"The Basement" isn't some kind of cool euphemism—it looks, and feels, like an actual basement, probably because it actually is one. Artists play on a small stage that's basically level with the ground, and guests have to walk right past it from most angles to reach the small bar in the corner, where the drinks are strong and generally hovering around decent. Over the years, it has hosted everyone from Metallica to Jason Isbell, and in 2020 its larger sister across the river, the Basement East, was ripped apart by a tornado that left the venue looking like someone had swung right through it with a monster-size wrecking ball. Mike and his partner quickly rebuilt, quietly providing the infrastructure of the good of Music City, the spaces where the real stuff seeps through when the building blocks of conformity separate or shift (though now the mural left intact after the storm is a common background for bachelorettes to stage an Instagram photo in matching pink cowboy hats, a clue to the newest battle for identity that Nashville began to undergo).

Which made it the perfect place for an artist like Kacey to debut. Ben Glover, an Irish artist and songwriter, shared the billing with Kacey that night, the usual sort of ramshackle lineup of baby bands and artists that probably had never met or seen one another before appearing on a lineup together. He'd moved a short time prior from a small village in Ireland and had plunged quickly into the local singer-songwriter scene; he was surprised at how crowded the Basement had been and how he'd looked around and seen the likes of influential publishing executive Jody Williams from BMI, who had hired Beth, and Keith Gattis, the songwriter known for his work with Dwight Yoakam, George Jones, and others, who would go on to write a song with Kacey after meeting that night.

They'd made a sweet enough little poster, purple and pink, with printed links to the MySpace pages of Ben, Kacey, and Eden's Edge, the other band performing that night. Rounds at places like the Basement were not only a way to meld the worlds of Nashville but also a nice reprieve from the standard culture at guitar pulls or rounds, where men often bullied their way into a better position, or the sound guys called them "sweetie," though that sort of misogynistic condescension toward female artists generally claimed no genre boundaries.

"I remember her being quiet and shy and reserved, but also thinking she had such self-assurance for someone who was really young," Ben Glover said. He didn't talk to Kacey much after his four-song set, but they spoke long enough that she would make plans to sing on a demo for a song he had written. "I just remember thinking after that this girl is really, really good."

Beth had the same reaction when she spun her copy of that sunflower-adorned demo CD, with songs like "My Own Road." There was something about her, enough to make Beth convince Luke Laird, a songwriter in town who happened to also be her husband, that he had to get his ass to the Basement that night for her showcase. "She came home one day, and she does this very rarely, but she told me about a new writer," Luke said. Luke didn't put up a fight—he listened to Beth, especially when she seemed this passionate about something. They made a plan to meet there after work.

Kacey sat on a stool on the dimly lit stage in a brown-and-white flannel, a guitar on her lap and a pick in her hand, her eyebrows raised and thin. Her phrasing, her delivery, her lyrical content: Luke, who had already had a few cuts for Carrie Underwood and Tim McGraw, thought it was fresh and different. He leaned against the wall in the back toward the bar, exchanging looks with Beth with each note that

Kacey sang. "I was just really blown away first and foremost by her writing," remembered Luke, who had come to Nashville from Pennsylvania for college, tour managing Brooks & Dunn until he got his first publishing deal. "I became a little bit of a fanboy." They talked that night over drinks, and agreed to write soon.

Early Luke and Kacey writing sessions were not much different from how they would evolve to be—just an instant connection. The first song they wrote together was called "Back on the Map," which ended up making the final cut for her first album, *Same Trailer Different Park*. Luke was the first component in the trio that would complete that record, and Shane McAnally was the second. If the group at Villa Place were her core for the heart, Luke and Shane were her core for the mind.

Kacey met Shane one night in East Nashville through a mutual friend named Ashley Arrison. She thought they might hit it off— that sort of Texas connection, with Shane hailing from the Dallas region. Shane went on to be one of the most powerful and prolific songwriters in Nashville and beyond, but he got his start at the same Opry house, Johnnie High's, as Maren and Kacey, but never crossed paths with them there (he's a "wee bit" older, as he might say). Shane had wanted to be an artist, but nothing had ever kicked into high-enough gear, and he, as an openly gay man in Nashville, came in as a sharp outlier. It was Reba McEntire, Lee Ann Womack, and LeAnn Rimes who first found the promise in Shane's songs and cut them for their records.

Ashley knew that Shane and Kacey would get along, but she didn't immediatley grasp just how profound the partnership would be. "There's this girl from Texas, and I think you guys are going to love each other," she told Shane.

She'd failed a few times to actually force them both into the same room, but one night, Ashley finally succeeded in getting them together in East Nashville, even though Shane was insistent that he wouldn't be writing that evening—he had done a "double" of writes earlier in the day, and he was tapped out, exhausted, and creatively drained. "I said, 'I cannot write tonight,'" Shane remembered. "It just will not happen. But we wrote two songs that night." Sometimes you just have to break out of the cycle of Music Row–sanctioned spaces and luke-warm coffee, to the places where lyrics don't have to happen under a ticking clock. They had a hard time staying apart after that.

"We couldn't be around each other enough," Shane said. "She was a combination of every female I love. Dolly Parton is one of the greatest. And my favorite singer of all time—and I will stand by this, because no one has affected me more—is Lee Ann Womack. And Kacey was just Dolly and Lee Ann Womack together. With a dash of Willie Nelson."

But there was one more unstoppable force to add to the equation—two, really. The songwriter Josh Osborne, and Brandy Clark.

Brandy grew up in Morton, Washington, an extremely small town about two hours from Seattle (and about two hours from where Brandi Carlile lived as a child)—it was country, a rural part of Washington that felt more like the South than anything else, flush with farmland and working-class people and small-town drama that made the daily soap operas seem tame—the perfect starting point for a brain that loved country music. Brandy's father died in a mill accident shortly before 9/11, the kind of compound grief that gets swallowed when the whole nation mourns for something else while you're still broken. Brandy was also a lesbian, and, at the time, Chely Wright had not yet come out of the closet. There was simply no model for someone like Brandy in Music City: plenty of reasons to stay away and be scared of what awaited her, but so many reasons coming up from her gut to go anyway.

She moved to Nashville in 1998 for Belmont University, a queer girl in a school full of anything but (or at least openly queer people). She'd gotten a job at a publisher right out of college, but her style—real stories of real people, the fuckups and the brokenhearted and the messy, messy ones—weren't exactly what was selling on Music Row. For over a decade, she toiled in writing rooms, crafting songs that only reached limited cuts, before she formed her most fertile writing trio with Kacey and Shane.

Radio had not been Brandy's primary point of contact—as a child, she saw her female icons sidestep the traditional modes and use film and television to reach a new fan base. It was Dolly Parton in *9 to 5*, Loretta Lynn as depicted in *Coal Miner's Daughter*, and whatever else she could catch on CMT or Great American Country. Aside from the occasional spin of Mary Chapin Carpenter, which she remembers relishing in the back seat of her parents' car, her idols came in through the television, or simply rifling through the record stacks to uncover Patty Loveless or Lee Ann Womack.

Brandy saw, and sees, the world differently than most do. The unsavory characters that most would ignore, or at least try to, became her point of fascination. It didn't hurt that, as a lesbian surrounded by a community that clings to every modicum of gossip like a rare unearthed jewel, she often felt as if she might fall too easily in the center of it if she wasn't careful.

At Belmont, she tried out for the yearly songwriter showcase, a tradition that has a history of helping to lay a road map for the genre's future stars: the first year, she landed on the bottom of the list. Second time, somewhere in the middle. The last year, she won it, graduating to a "baby deal" at a publisher where she still had to work odd jobs to make up for the only twelve thousand dollars in salary she was getting. Still, she was writing songs regularly and even scoring some cuts, though she, and her peers, kept running into the same roadblock: finding artists who would sing them.

"There just weren't enough women to pitch those songs to," Brandy remembered. When women wrote, the sensibilities, the subject matter, even the melodies often reflected their lived experience. At one point, Brandy nearly had a song cut by Kenny Chesney, which would have been a massive breakthrough, not to mention a financial boost—but he ended up skipping out on recording it because the melody was "too feminine."

Brandy's songs were too feminine for men to cut and, for herself, not feminine enough—she didn't care for dresses or the cookie-cutter versions of what a woman star was supposed to look like, and she was past thirty, the age she thought might no longer be acceptable to have a shot at a recording career (an assumption often mirrored by the industry itself). Country liked women in jeans and heels and dresses that glittered; Brandy liked slacks and boots, or a good pantsuit. Her hair, as dark as Loretta's (and her humor, too) and often hovering just past her shoulders, never seemed coerced into sprightly ringlets or "beach waves." She didn't fall into the only acceptable alternative to glamour, either, which was the scrappy redneck pastiche of a Gretchen Wilson, or Miranda on a casual day.

Brandy didn't think much about what everyone thought of her, but she knew she loved country music, and she felt like she fit because her words did. Soon she was writing for some of the best in town: Reba cut two of her songs, and eventually everyone from LeAnn Rimes to Toby Keith had her cuts on albums.

The year 2009 was a transitional one, prompting her to think about recording her own material, something that had never quite occurred to her in the whole push and pull life of a Nashville songwriter. She was, after all, a gay woman in a conservative industry, and in a format where there were, and still are, existing fears about mingling a gay artist on the airwaves under the same umbrella as a right-wing talk show host who chose to interpret the Bible as a vehicle of oppression rather than love.

Brandy's chemistry with Shane, in particular, hit fast and hard—a chemistry that would go on to breed Kacey's "Follow Your Arrow" and many more songs. They met in a kitchen at Brandy's publisher, lingering over the coffee machine and slim-pickings breakfast options, and wrote the next morning—they didn't come up with anything groundbreaking in that moment, but Shane called her shortly after. The session had been too heavy on his mind, too profound despite the lack of tangible output, and he had to see if Brandy was feeling the same. She was.

"I know nothing came out of today," he told her, "but I know we will write great things together." They were in a safe place, especially when they came out to each other, which they were nervous to do at first, both so conditioned by their experiences in Nashville. "And when we did," Shane remembered, "it was just like, oh my God, of course I was drawn to you."

They started getting together nearly every Monday, sometimes with a third person and sometimes just as a duo—and Kacey ended up being one of the writers Shane brought in, first to do some vocals on a demo, and then to participate in an actual writing session.

"Shane is a huge part of all of this for me," said Brandy. "Not only is he a genius collaborator, and such an encourager, but he is the missing piece for all of us. Josh Osborne always said we were all kind of like the misfit toys and Shane came along and knew how to play with us."

When Kacey started to get her footing in Nashville, Brandy and Shane were who she wanted to write and record with, alongside Luke, who would coproduce—this is what she told the label, not the other way around. Instead of the Nashville tradition of executives quietly (or not so quietly) suggesting who an artist might collaborate with, she was going to have it exactly as she wanted, or simply not do it at all. And it was Shane and Brandy, after all, who quietly helped create that blueprint.

Something about 2009 felt electric.

At Hotel Villa, music was spilling out: Kacey, Kree, Brothers Osborne, Charlie Worsham—a hotbed of creativity and energy. Taylor Swift released *Fearless* at the end of 2008 and was changing everything for Nashville—there was so much demand for Taylor and her songs that they would already be gold records by the time they were shipped to radio to play as singles. All country could do was ride the wave.

The year 2009 was also a year of another significant shift for the town, particularly thanks to a man named Jack White and some cans of yellow and black paint. White opened up his Third Man Records on an underdeveloped corridor between Lower Broadway and Music Row, though millions of metaphorical miles away from either. Jack's commitment to Nashville had already been developing steadily— from his production work with Loretta Lynn, to a decade later from that, when he would be the only one to stick his neck out for Margo Price, who somehow had gone unsigned with a brilliant finished album, *Midwest Farmer's Daughter*, that he let her release completely free of intervention.

Third Man changed the landscape, though, just as much as Jack changed Nashville. There was starting to be a very slight understanding that Nashville was more than just country music, but it was incremental at best. Jack White moved to Tennessee, as did the Black Keys, the blues-rock duo of Dan Auerbach and Patrick Carney. The press was picking up on it bit by bit, if not in depth.

"Nashville is more than country & western music," wrote the *St. Louis Post-Dispatch*. "Get over that 'Hee-Haw' hangover."

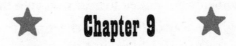

Chapter 9

IT'S NONE OF YOUR BUSINESS WHAT OTHER PEOPLE THINK ABOUT YOU

They were just so eager to find something wrong with Taylor Swift.

The year 2010 had begun with full-on Taylor Swift mania—at the Grammy Awards that January, she took home Album of the Year, not to mention a handful of others. But the night wasn't without incident: Taylor had shared the stage with Stevie Nicks for a medley, and had struggled to hit some of the notes—sound at those events could be notoriously fickle, and Taylor was understandably nervous about singing with an idol like Stevie. Coupled with her domination at the CMA Awards at the end of the year, discussion about whether or not she "deserved" any of it hit a feverpitch, especially as *Fearless* was approaching the status of most awarded country album of all time. Were her vocals always that troubled? Did she lip-synch? Did the rest of the genre, too? The country purists were eager to prove that she couldn't sing, and the pop purists, enamored with Lady Gaga, were just as eager to prove she was too vanilla to play in the big leagues. Music Row, still, was wondering if she was the barometer for the future, measuring every new woman that passed through the doors against her.

And despite the fact that there were so many girls turning up to see her concerts—women who wanted to hear women—that capital didn't seem to be enough to sway critics to her sheer power. At a concert in Miami, a reporter looked around at all the girls present and wrote that "it would have been nice if Taylor Swift spoke to all that girl power," as if the success itself didn't do that job: Garth never had to get onstage at arena shows and talk about "guy power." Taylor's talent and success somehow weren't enough, and neither were the opinions of millions of girls across the country. In a review of *Speak Now*, her next album that she wrote alone, the critic decided that the LP contained "nothing of any importance to anyone other than Swift," once again dismissing not only her songs but the intelligence of her entire fan base.

Despite it all, though, Taylor remained neutral in her early career: politically, culturally, smiling even when it would have been more appropriate to simply scream.

Chely Wright was sick of staying neutral. So in May 2010, after a decade of repressing her entire life, she decided to come out. Her book, *Like Me: Confessions of a Heartland Country Singer*, along with an intimate *People* interview, finally told her whole story.

"I knew I could force a conversation," Chely said, looking back. "I knew I could have every morning radio show, at least just for the day, having to reckon with saying LGBT or gay or lesbian on their morning drive without it being a joke. And many of them did make jokes on that day. But in my experience with country radio I had never heard anything mentioned about a gay person or a trans person or a person like me without it being a literal rim shot. I can't tell you how many times gay jokes were told and I sat through it and listened and I didn't speak up, and part of me died every time."

She received some cease and desist letters from churches, claiming it was "incompatible" with her Christianity. One afternoon over bagels in downtown New York, she met up with the bishop Gene Robinson, a pastor who had been one of the first to come out as gay and had become one of her mentors. It was crucial for Chely to incorporate her faith into her coming-out story and in the way she relayed it to her fans, who might just see not a lesbian woman but someone who was strong in their dedication to God and the troops. "I had amassed an entire collection of faith leaders. He said, 'I'm going to tell you something that will be helpful to you,'" Chely remembered. "As he smeared chive cream cheese on his bagel he said, 'Here is my advice. It's none of your business what other people think about you.'"

All Maren knew was that the walls were coming down around country music, led by Taylor and *Speak Now*. She'd even stepped out from them herself, spending 2010 with a local band called They Were Stars as the only woman in the quartet, playing the sort of indie rock that had found a home in the Dallas scene at the time. Maren was often the more calming, mature presence in the foursome despite being the youngest—but she was a veritable veteran at that point, anyway, and taking a turn into this sort of music wasn't exactly something that anyone on the scene would have predicted after getting acquainted with her as a pop country singer and phenom for most of her young life.

Her bandmate Mitch Lazorko was surprised to learn that this person he associated so strongly with pop country was also into scores of modern indie rock bands like the Cardigans, the Sundays, and Metric (her favorite), and she had been heavily swaying his own tastes. "Maren had always been one of those people you knew had the talent but didn't necessarily have the opportunity," he said. Maren would dress the rock-star part even if the audience was less than a handful—glittery stage clothes, a new angular and short chop to her hair. They played local venues like a club called Trees, which had hosted bands like Nirvana in their heyday. They sampled a world that was beyond the honky-tonks, beyond the lines drawn by regional country and Red

Dirt, "which began as a local songwriting scene centered in Stillwater, Okla., in the late 1970s," described Josh Crutchmer, author of the seminal book on the subject, *Red Dirt*. "The scene provided an early boost to the career of Garth Brooks before inspiring a roots movement that eventually merged with the larger Texas Music scene that Waylon and Willie made famous." For them, it felt like escapism.

"That music is still so good. It was such a moment," Maren said, recalling her time with the group. "It was so non-country, almost a rebellious phase against my parents. I was joining this pop rock band, had a crazy haircut, I'm going to play a MicroKorg. I think those were my rebellious years. I was nineteen and had just missed the high school window."

When They Were Stars fizzled, Mitch still stayed on playing bass for Maren, with Taylor Tatsch as a frequent producing and creative partner, and they did the local circuit together for the last years that she stayed in town. Her crowd was growing, but some days they'd be playing gigs to a couple of people max. One particular festival day was unusually cold, at least by Texas standards, and barely anyone showed up—just a few folks scattered in the parking lot. Maren kept her head high and played like she was in a packed club.

"It was disappointing to see," said Mitch. "But Maren had the talent and the drive, and there was part of her that seemed scared to take the next step. I was one of several voices that helped to encourage her: You've maxed out your potential here. You need to move on."

Maren was a little unsure of whether or not it was the right move to head to Nashville yet. It would mean leaving her parents behind, who had been her management and support vehicle, and had steered her right so far. But 2011's *Live Wire*, her newest album, was at least gaining critical respect and an understanding of her career and potential in ways that she had not quite seen before. Starting classes in Denton and the University of North Texas, she still balanced a course load with music. "Her weary, wary songs feel every bit as lived in as she likely intends them," the *Fort Worth Star-Telegram* wrote in May

2011. She kept hitting the roads in Texas, the idea of Nashville in her back pocket.

Though Kacey had made the move already, she was still connected to Texas through Josh Abbott—an artist who, with his band, has been one of the premier breakouts from the Texas Country scene, drawing ire from some and admiration from others in how he navigated somewhat into the Nashville market to achieve some modest commercial success.

Josh was a musician at heart but had gone to college, fostering a backup plan that was uncommon to most of his peers, even going on to graduate school at Texas Tech, where he met his bandmates. Music was, at first, a sort of hobby that was also nearly genetic programming, but the band got tight enough, and popular enough, that it seemed worth prioritizing. In the pre-Facebook days, Josh had often taken to MySpace to browse new artists or collaborators, and the fabled "top eight" feature would often serve as a hearty clue to the favorites of favorites.

"If you were in somebody's top eight friends, you were the real deal," Josh said, who was still in graduate school at the time, trying to balance his burgeoning band's success and finishing up his coursework to graduate. One day in a particular musical wormhole, Josh found himself on Miranda Lambert's MySpace page and started listening to songs from one of her Top Eight friends: a young artist named Kacey Musgraves. The profile photo was black-and-white—Kacey riding a horse, her body leaning on the neck with arms right around it, long dark hair falling over the animal's mane and blending in. She looked young, but it could easily be a photo from any year in her career.

Josh was sucked in, listening to a few of the originals but especially a cover of Neil Young's "Heart of Gold" that she played harmonica on. "I just loved the shit out of her voice," he said.

Soon after, he called up his manager. "I think I found a girl you need to sign," Josh said. "Her name is Kacey Musgraves."

"Dude, did she put you up to this?" the manager asked. Turns out,

Kacey had been working the front desk at his management company, and he realized that he'd probably spoken to her hundreds of times by now.

In 2010 Josh was working on a song called "Oh, Tonight," for his album *She's Like Texas*, and his fiddle player, Preston Wait, thought it might be good to add in a duet. "I knew Musgraves was the voice," he said, calling her "Musgraves" as he always did. "It didn't matter that she wasn't a name. It was just, let's just grab the person who makes the most sense." Josh had always been a sucker for an ace duet partner, especially when the vocals came from a woman—and he didn't care if that person was known or not. Beyond Kacey, he would go on to record with Carly Pearce and then later with Catie Offerman, all before their profiles changed and grew considerably.

Josh hadn't planned for the song to become a single, but the band started to play it live in concert, and it began to be requested at radio stations around Texas—mainstream stations, growing up from inside San Antonio and then out from there. They hired a radio promoter, and "Oh, Tonight" started to blow up, at least by modest non–Music Row standards.

"I genuinely think that happened because of Kacey," Josh said. "Before they knew her, they knew it."

In February 2011, someone had the idea to play a set at Freddie's Place in Austin, a dog- and kid-friendly spot near South Congress for southern comfort food. Kacey and Josh set up at a table in the middle of the outdoor restaurant, surrounded by families having lunch. Kacey's thick bangs swept her eyebrows and Josh, in a flannel and reading glasses, looked like he could have been a patron who just happened to burst out in song. "We both looked like an ad for Cavender's and I was wearing my fricking glasses," Josh said.

When it comes to Texas, bands could exist massively within the sphere of the Lone Star State but rarely venture outside the border for larger stardom—sometimes by absolute choice and others by circumstance. It's a universe in and of itself. But the Josh Abbott Band was starting to gain a bit of traction, as was a sort of renewed global interest in all things country and western, across Europe in particular. Tents were erected outside Paris to house faux rodeos where chic clothes were traded for overalls and drawn-on freckles, and preparations were in the beginning stages for the very first C2C, Country to Country, the UK's massive festival for the genre. Though it may seem like country music and Europe weren't exactly a synchronous match, there's less daylight between rural communities in Scotland or England and those in America than one would think—issues of class and caste in small-town living cross every border.

Josh had scrounged up some interest for a European tour, so he recruited Kacey to come along overseas. There were stops in France, and then there was a small festival in Savoniero, Italy, a hilly town about an hour and a half outside Bologna. It was truly an all-hands kind of effort: the local women spent days beforehand preparing the pasta, and there was a huge citywide potluck where men in white aprons and TV mustaches presided over the Italian plancha, simmering and sizzling meats.

The stage was assembled on the middle of the town tennis court, which left little room for any sort of proper greenroom and changing area, so Josh and Kacey were left to hole up in a converted bathroom near the site to prep before going onstage—nothing glamorous, but the smell of the grills and wafting scents from the buffet probably usurped any American fruit tray, and the room had decent acoustics.

Kacey started strumming a few songs that she'd been working on back in Nashville with her new team of trusted cowriters. One was "Mama's Broken Heart," which was being considered for a cut by Miranda. For most songwriters, that's the dream—get your song recorded by a major star, hopefully a number one thereafter, and the world breaks open. But Kacey wasn't so sure. "What young songwriter is about to land their first major cut with a major artist, and is hesitant because she wanted to keep it for herself? All along I think she knew what kind of artist she wanted to be and the kinds of stories she wanted to tell," Josh said.

And then she played another. It was called "Merry Go 'Round," a frank depiction of real life in a small town, where places and people are imperfect and it can feel more like a trap than a comfort. It was painful, but honest, and a stark contrast to a song like Jason Aldean's "My Kinda Party," where only life and love happen by the tailgate, never desperation or desolation.

Josh blinked hard. He was going to have to play after that. He'd never written a song that good, he thought. He still doesn't think he has.

When Kacey returned from Europe, she released big news into the world: she would be signing with the label Lost Highway and had a cut on the new Martina McBride album. She was still working as a karaoke singing waitress at Santa's Pub, a dive bar by dictionary definitions and a second home for left-of-center musicians, but something else entirely to the Nashville community; a place made up of a trailer converted into a bar and not much else, thick with so much smoke that a musician might walk away from a gig with a newfound rasp.

How she ended up at Lost Highway had a lot to do with a woman named Stephanie Wright. Stephanie had heard Kacey's name around town and popped in to see a show at the Basement and set up a meeting, cold-calling her and inviting her out to lunch at the Copper Kettle Café, an old-school kind of place where folks took low-key meetings far enough away from Music Row but close enough that if someone spotted you, it was clear you weren't trying to have a clandestine affair. They had a long meal and talked about everything over the course of two hours—music, plans, how Kacey's ultimate measure of success at the time was to afford a place where she could live by herself without a crazy landlord, and to be able to buy her grandmother a set of red kitchen cabinets that she had her eye on.

"There was this overwhelming feeling, like she's just got this magnetism about her that I really couldn't even explain," Stephanie said. "I felt all these butterflies that were happening and I thought, *My God, I don't even know how to describe this because she's just the most enamoring person.* She had all the things an artist can hope to get—sometimes you can't describe it on paper, but it's just there."

It took over a year and a half to convince everybody at the label to move forward with actually signing her, and, by that time, there was already a considerable buzz—buzz that gave Kacey some leverage. "Lost Highway was more abstract and to the left," Stephanie says. "There was a prestige that came with it."

Lost Highway, which shuttered in 2012 before being absorbed by UMG Nashville, was the perfect home for Kacey—like Mindy Smith years prior at Vanguard, it enabled her to be who she was over what worked best commercially. Formed in 2000, it had come to prominence by releasing the soundtrack to *O Brother, Where Art Thou?* and set a mold for a roots-music release that didn't necessarily need the love of the mainstream country airwaves (though the single "I Am a Man of Constant Sorrow" was a massive cultural phenomenon, very few country program directors felt the need to actually play it). Luke Lewis, who founded the label, had created a special model that stuck out in the homogenized system—despite having worked with Shania in the past, he became an expert at sourcing artists who carried heaps of talent but didn't need or want the support of radio.

Stephanie's path to Nashville wasn't traditional by any means, either. Born in Utah, she married young and came to town to visit her cousins, Kristyn, Kelsi, and Kassidy Osborn, otherwise known as the country trio SHeDaisy, and was lured into making the move not long after. A mother to a young son, Stephanie couldn't afford to take the fifteen thousand dollars a year that most assistant music industry jobs paid, so she worked administrative tasks at an air-conditioning manufacturer in town. One day, looking through the paper, she found a listing for a job at Capitol Records and applied—her non-music credentials were actually what helped to seal the deal. Kacey was her first big signing.

"It was just such a pure sound. It reminded me of when I would listen to Karen Carpenter with my dad. Every song was her, every time," Stephanie said. "The ability she had to be this conversationalist within the songs she was writing. They all sounded fresh." The signing became official in August 2011. "I've waited a long time for this next step, and I couldn't be more ecstatic to share a label home with so many artists I've looked up to all my life," Kacey said at the time.

Kacey was assigned to a label publicist, Fount Lynch, a Tennessee native who started off his career as an intern at Universal in 2001. Like Miranda, who had walked straight into that room back at Sony, Kacey set the ground rules from the start, and the team could only follow.

It was working for Miranda anyway: her 2011 album *Four the Record* eventually sold a million copies, and included a song written by a beloved but then somewhat under-the-radar singer named Brandi Carlile—as well as Kacey's "Mama's Broken Heart."

"She couldn't be shaped or molded or manufactured in any way," Fount said. "She would never fit the mold, and I don't know anyone had the balls to challenge it. Kacey is a brilliant artist. Why in the hell would we ever want to stop that? Why would we ever want to get in the way of Kacey Musgraves?"

Out in Los Angeles, Mickey had still been working two jobs to make rent. Every day that she had shifts, she would smuggle her blind dog into the restaurant and tuck him beneath the hostess stand—it's not like he would know where he was, she thought, and at least she'd be able to keep an eye on him. Days at the restaurant were long and commutes on the interstate were longer—an interstate in a city that she didn't even really want to be in but felt she had to. But unlike many service workers in Los Angeles, this wasn't a side road to a dream career in film and television—Mickey wanted something else, somewhere else, but she had gotten mostly used to keeping it to herself.

It's not that California didn't have a connection to country music—of course it did. The Bakersfield sound, and the class of musicians that included Merle Haggard and Gram Parsons, defined and influenced an entire generation. For Mickey, Los Angeles represented a way to try to convince herself that there was something else out there. But it was no longer working.

One afternoon off work, she went for lunch with her friend Jessica Bendinger, a screenwriter who had written movies like cheerleader-empowerment film *Bring It On*. Mickey and Jessica had become close through *American Idol*'s Randy Jackson, who made the introduction shortly after Mickey left the show.

Mickey had been singing demos for a project that Jessica was working on, and it had provided a nice way for her to reconnect with her country tone—a tone that Jessica had noticed and embraced. That afternoon over lunch, though, Mickey started to cry. She felt directionless.

"Mickey, you sing incredibly. What kind of music do you want to sing?"

"I want to sing country music," Mickey replied.

"Then do it," Jessica deadpanned.

The next day, Mickey was wandering around a local mall when she ran into DJ D-Wrek, whom she had met previously and who had worked with Nick Cannon on his show *Wild 'n Out*. L.A. being L.A., there were a million malls she could have gone to, and a million people she could have run into, but this particular shopping expedition she decided to explore one she had never been to before, to find her mother a birthday present. D-Wrek spotted her roaming, stopped to chat, and the topic of country music came up—Mickey had just been fired from her job, and, fresh from the conversation with Jessica, she was sick of trying to stifle where she envisioned herself being. She was considering moving back to Texas, since she was out of ideas and soon would be out of money, too.

"This is so crazy," he said, "but I know a producer who had produced Glen Campbell, and he is looking for an African American female country singer, if that even exists."

"Well, I'm your girl," Mickey said.

That man, Julian Raymond, wasn't a country producer exclusively—he had worked with acts like the Insane Clown Posse and Cheap Trick, as well as Glen Campbell. But he had been attending a golf fundraiser for his child's school in Los Angeles when he struck up a conversation with an older white man about the genre, and the man, a grandparent of one of the students, had a question.

"You know what? I'm really into country music," the man said to Julian. "Some of the stuff is really amazing, but there is one thing that is missing, and that's African American female country artists, because they just don't exist. And I don't understand why."

Julian couldn't get the thought out of his mind while trying, to no avail, to focus on his golf swing. One day, he called up D-Wrek, with whom he'd been working on sessions. Did he know any Black women country singers, he wanted to know? Julian understood that the problem wasn't that they didn't exist but that they weren't getting the same level of interest and support that white, mostly blond, women did. D-Wrek didn't know any at the moment, but he got right back to Julian as soon as he ran into Mickey.

"She was the real deal," Julian said. "From-Texas kind of real. Her vocal style reminded me a little bit of Dolly Parton, a younger version back in the day, and I thought she just had an incredible range."

Julian couldn't let talent like that sit, so he introduced her to managers Gary Borman and Steve Moir, who had long track records of working with artists like Faith Hill, and knew how to grow an act from infancy. This could be easy, Gary thought—she was talented, could sing beyond belief, looked the part. They all took Mickey to Nashville and New York to court Warner Music, Capitol, and other labels during CMA Fest in 2011. The response, to his surprise, was pretty instantaneous.

It was quickly clear that Warner wasn't going to be a fit, though. "They started testing me, playing country songs that they didn't think I would know," Mickey told the *New York Times*. "And I was like, 'Oh, that's Joe Nichols.' And they were like, 'Oh, well, you know country music.' I was like, 'Yeah, I *actually* do.' Country music is a way of life. It's not just about whether you know a song. I grew up in the country, on gravel roads. But because I was Black, I wasn't enough."

It was Capitol that offered her a deal. "I'm sitting here in front of this massively successful [label head] Mike Dungan seeing all these plaques," said Mickey. "I'm singing my country song and I sang a cover of Patty Loveless 'Blame It on Your Heart,' and I went to the Riverfront Stage after that meeting and he offered me a deal that day. Through all the chaos, the twists and turns and roundabout ways, country music still found me, and I still found country music. And that was the easy part."

Yes—that was the easy part. And that's where the easy stuff ended, too.

If the mainstream was so restrictive and competitive to women, and that door was only cracked, it was closed for Black women. Sure, Frankie Staton and others came through on occasion, but they weren't allowed to walk through—they had to sneak in behind everyone else, or through the gap on the bottom and were never allowed to blossom by the gatekeepers or achieve the success they deserved. Julian thought that Mickey could make a difference, though—both in voice, which could battle with Carrie Underwood for those highest and biggest of notes, and in a genre that seemed not only stuck in the past but fully willing to ignore any of its transgressions, historical or current, in favor of the status quo. And now Mickey had a record deal, a future in Nashville. And somehow, soon after the deal was signed, a date to go sing for President Obama. Without even a formal song to her name, she had been invited by the Obama administration to come sing as part of

PBS's regular special from the White House, her first real performance as a signed artist.

They had not even planned on inviting Mickey initially—the ask had gone out to another artist on the label. But having Mickey there to sing country music to the first Black president, and to reclaim the tradition from what it represented in the Bush era, seemed designed by something far beyond simple coincidence.

Arriving in Washington, Mickey barely ate a thing. She had a little wine at night to help her sleep, but even that didn't really work. The group was tasked to come for several days, and Mickey would call her parents crying—she wasn't sure if she could do it, wasn't sure if her voice would hold up to the immense pressure, the immense weight. She had gone from working at a restaurant in Los Angeles to dropping everything to pursue country music in Nashville, living out of suitcases, and was suddenly supposed to sing for the first Black president of the United States?

Once she got on that stage, to sing Patsy Cline, everything changed. President Obama stared up from his seat, directly aligned with the mic on the White House stage, flanked by Dr. Jill Biden to one side and Michelle Obama to the other, listening to a classic country song. Famous for his yearly playlists, President Obama had always made sure to keep as inclusive as possible when it came to the sort of music he welcomed inside his walls—his administration, contrary to what would come after under Trump, was a revolving door of creativity and artistic presence. In the company of Lauren Alaina, the Band Perry, Dierks Bentley, Alison Krauss, Kris Kristofferson, Lyle Lovett, Darius Rucker, and James Taylor, Mickey delivered a polished version of Patsy Cline's "Crazy" that met the past and the future in the most perfect place.

For Mickey, appearing at the White House and singing for a president was the pinnacle of a career—a moment that could, and should, usher in a new era. She took it as seriously as anyone could, if not more, honing every syllable in that song and deliberately choosing something that even casual listeners of the genre might recognize. But it wasn't the jumping-off point she thought it would be: in country music, you have to have a record label willing to immediately release and push a single to country radio, ready to dump endless dollars of promotional budget your way. And that promotional budget wasn't going to Mickey.

"I thought it would be a massive thing," Mickey said, looking back. "I thought I would immediately sell out an arena tour. I was quickly shown that it was not happening. Too many white men making decisions for me."

Too many white men making decisions for everyone, really. But Leslie Fram was going to try something different.

In 2011, Leslie was living in New York, working for a hybrid rock station called WRXP and doing the morning show with Matt Pinfield, a bald sort-of iconoclast who had been known, in his heyday, or at least the heyday of music videos, for hosting *120 Minutes* on MTV. They spent their days treating the lineup like a "local" station, and when your local is New York City at the height of the indie rock boom, things are going to get a little wild and weird. "Mainstream country," Leslie said, "just wasn't part of my world." Her world was Passion Pit and Vampire Weekend, the cool shit that played venues like Bowery Ballroom and that made the covers of the good music magazines, or the ones you wanted to show up at your Fashion Week party in a leather jacket with a lit cigarette. The kind of music that you were supposed to resent if you liked country music, and made for the kind of fans who assumed that country music was the domain of hicks and rednecks only, and that hicks and rednecks were pejoratives to begin with.

Clothed most of the time in black and with an obsession for folk art and working out, Leslie didn't fit into the usual blueprint of a Nashville executive. Nor did she really have much of a working knowledge of the genre to begin with—she had barely been more than a casual fan despite being born in Georgia and spending a long and storied run in Atlanta, focused on the rock scene there. But she was about to take an opportunity that would change that permanently.

Leslie's old friend Skip Bishop had been in town for a Miranda show, and had brought Leslie along. She fell in love with Miranda and brought her on the show with Matt Pinfield in the morning (unlike country radio, they had the fluidity to be able to host a country act one minute and a Brooklyn indie pop band the next). She knew about classic country, but not a lot about modern mainstream, and the biggest impression she'd had so far was interviewing Johnny Cash in the studio, who had made a rare crossover into "cool" with his Rick Rubin–produced album.

Leslie had also gone to see a Keith Urban show, and as rock was starting to veer away from guitars, country music filled the void. The Fenders and Telecasters that Leslie knew had been slowly and surely replaced by computerized synth sounds. "This is where all the guitars went," Leslie remembered thinking. "They went to country." Jack White had already been colliding those two worlds in Nashville at Third Man, but would also help put country on Leslie's radar when she went to see Wanda Jackson, the rockabilly legend, play Music Hall of Williamsburg—Jack had produced the album, and like his work with Loretta Lynn, it shook everyone's understanding of just exactly where these women of country existed on the radar of pop culture, especially older women.

The year 2011, like every year since the Telecommunications Act was passed in 1996 and consolidation tightened the market more and more, was a bad year to be a radio station—and like so many others, WRXP was sold and reinvented as news talk, leaving Leslie without a gig. CMT was looking for a new senior vice president of strategy, so then president Brian Philips invited Leslie to Nashville for the weekend a few months later.

"Why don't you look outside of radio?" Brian said.

She stayed the weekend, hopping around to local spots, getting to know the restaurants and clubs, and at the end Brian offered her the job to come and take over the music programming at CMT. She said yes without even thinking about it—her life in New York had reached a logical end, and Nashville was invigorating, intriguing, and certainly more relaxed.

This could be a cool opportunity for me to really shake things up, she thought. *Go from rock to country and radio to television. Next thing I know, we're moving to Nashville.*

It took Leslie a few months of getting a grip on the Nashville landscape to understand that she was dealing with a much different perspective than in pop. She spent a year trying to capture how the format works: going to a lot of shows, putting her head down, sometimes hitting a different songwriting round every night. It took a bit of training to reprogram herself from Manhattan to Nashville, but her new town was thriving in ways that New York City had limited long ago—music was everywhere, artists could still find cheap apartments within a reasonable drive of any venue, and studios could be found on Music Row but also in the backyards of East Nashvillians like the one that belonged to Eric Masse, who would go on to eventually coproduce Miranda's *The Weight of These Wings* there.

Leslie realized, though, that the landscape of country radio was completely different from what she had been used to—that the atmosphere was closed rather than open, and so narrowly focused that there was almost zero room to play. CMT wasn't beholden to radio, but country music was an ecosystem where every part was nurtured by the other, and necessary to grow. Mainstream stars were still made on the airwaves, whichever way you looked at it.

"The first year, I didn't really recognize any problem because we were playing Sara Evans and Martina," Leslie said. "But then we started to say, What's going on here? There's a shift." Jason Aldean's "Dirt Road Anthem" and Jake Owen's "Barefoot Blue Jean Night" were dominating the airwaves in 2011, the beginning of a trend favoring the party and the tailgate. She asked Brian if she could start a franchise to support female artists and he was on board—they called it Next Women of Country. After all, she knew a great song when she heard one. "The format is in danger of becoming all about baseball caps and partying," she remembered thinking.

What alarmed Leslie more than simple airplay was how limiting it was to women who wanted to pursue a mainstream career in country music. Without support on radio, there wasn't the infrastructure building around them to allow the kind of profile that opens up enough doors. "Unless they have a song on the radio, they aren't going to get on a Luke Bryan tour," Leslie said.

There was too much good and groundbreaking music in 2011 to not do anything about it, anyway, especially from women. Nikki Lane's debut, *Walk of Shame,* was one of the best independent country introductions in recent years, gritty and unique. The Band Perry, led by Kimberly Perry alongside her brothers, dominated on the heels of their self-titled debut, co-writing nearly all their songs and grounding them in mandolin and banjo (eventually the trio fled the genre for a score of reasons, including being asked to compromise their sound to chase trends). And Miranda Lambert was good for not one but two exemplary records. *Four the Record* was a sonic breakthrough, the work of a superstar and true songwriter in a rare embodiment of both. But first, there were the Pistol Annies, a trio she launched with friends and songwriters Ashley Monroe and Angaleena Presley, that shook the country world with their fiery, naughty, and country as hell first album, *Hell on Heels.* It made it even harder to define or pigeonhole Miranda, or even predict where she would zig or zag next.

"Hopefully, groups like Pistol Annies are breaking down the doors for artists like me who are really honest," Angaleena, a brilliant artist in her own right, as was Ashley, told the *Daily Oklahoman.* "And talk about things that need to be talked about."

Chapter 10 ★

CAN'T REMEMBER SHIT

Did that just happen?

It was around noon on a strangely humid February day in downtown Nashville—not the kind of hour when you want to be onstage, as the southern sun hits the Ryman Auditorium's stained-glass windows, if you had your choice—and Kacey was set to make her debut at the storied venue, a place where so much of country music history has been born and blossomed. Her grandma and grandpa had driven in from Texas, extra puffs of hair spray and pomade applied, just for this: the annual Universal Records "Team UMG" lunchtime event during Country Radio Seminar, known as CRS, where artists new and old sing their songs to woo a crowd of radio programmers, hoping they'll feel motivated enough to add their singles into rotation. It's not exactly glamorous, crawling from bed to the makeup chair to the stage before it's even happy hour, but this pageantry was and is, as most things in Nashville are, accepted tradition. And a coveted ticket, too: this is where the stars, like Eric Church, Keith Urban, and Carrie Underwood, can be found, making it the perfect early-afternoon chance for humblebrag social media posts that send outsiders drooling, sniffing that juicy steak of celebrity smoking on the fire.

Up in the stiff wooden pews the radio programmers, record executives, and DJs ate their boxed lunches as lanyards dangled around their necks—the performers had to play to the sound of crunched chips and sandwich chewing, hoping a particularly potent verse doesn't get lost in the rustle of a cookie being unwrapped. Not ideal, but it's better than having to dog-and-pony in the crowded, sticky bars they'll take to later, enduring unwanted advances from men who feel entitled to ogle their legs, steal a hug, or smell their hair, drunk on power and gratis tequila (there's hardly a faster way to a radio guy's heart, and playlist, than through a bunch of freebies, after all). This is how CRS went, anyway, with the lines between professionalism and the party blurred into an amorphous smudge of a week—to the point where the entire event had become known to attendees as "Can't Remember Shit."

For now, though, in the daylight hours, it was still supposed to be about the music, the business. The *format*. Kacey, new enough to town that her name was still unknown to many in the audience (unless they'd paid the attention they should have to the songwriters on Miranda's "Mama's Broken Heart"), smoothed her dress down, grabbed her guitar, and made her way out to middle stage, where she glanced at the crowd—mostly men, mostly still lunching and ready to talk over a young woman with a guitar if they had to—and introduced her song at the Ryman for the first time. It was "Merry Go 'Round," that potent, scorching indictment of small-town life, myths, and complacency, and she had insisted that this was exactly the way she wanted to introduce herself to country radio, even if it wasn't a breezy anthem or polite ballad. "This song is inspired by growing up in a small town in the South," Kacey said, setting up the audience for what they were sure would be some kind of classic country lament for the bygone days at the tailgate, those idealized Friday night lights and holy Sunday mornings. Or maybe it would be a nostalgic nod to teenage love by the single stoplight, a diary entry set to simple chords, the way Taylor Swift had done it. It would be, they imagined, something well within the parameters that Music Row had neatly established for success.

They were wrong. She started strumming, her voice hitting crisply against the Ryman's wood interior as she stood solemnly in a black dress and white heels, a streak of blond hair bisecting her dark bangs. Bandleader Misa Arriaga flanked her to one side and Emily Nelson, a cello player who came up through the Vanderbilt Blair School of Music, on the other. They peered at each other on occasion to keep the time, but mostly Kacey stared up to that top pew, looking both forward and into her past.

The room fell silent from the first note. There were no cookies opened, no sandwich bites taken, the fingerpicking on her guitar resounding in perfect echo, the way it can only when the people in the audience are frozen still and shocked into full attention, without an accidentally buzzing phone or whispered conversation. She received a standing ovation, rows and rows of crinkled chinos and checkered shirts visible above the railings. The only other artist to get the crowd on their feet that day was fellow Texan George Strait, for whom the lack of due respect would be akin to blasphemy. "Merry Go 'Round" wasn't a drinking song, a party anthem, an ode to a boy long lost. It was a mirror to themselves, their friends, to the life they could have had or the one they left behind. It stung—no one had rubbed alcohol on a wound like that in years, especially not here, at Can't Remember Shit.

Kacey walked offstage shaken. "Did that just happen?" she asked Stephanie Wright, who was waiting in the wings, watching the crowd as best she could from behind the drawn curtains.

"Yes, ma'am," Stephanie replied. Luke and Shane both breathed sighs of relief—Luke, in particular, had been sweating the whole thing out harder than usual, even worse than Kacey herself. He was always the worrier, absorbing any of the stress that others might be able to shake off better, and these were tender, special songs they'd all written together not long ago. "She didn't even seem nervous," he said. "But I was nervous. I knew it was a lot of people's first time to hear her. It was huge." Shane, as soon as the room stood up when she hit the chorus, couldn't help but cry.

CRS at the time had already been a strange, even troubled place for women like Kacey to make themselves heard, and a risky one, involving more than just the temperamental taste of a program director. Sometimes, it was a dangerous place, where women found themselves in hotel rooms and dirty bars with DJs who had had too much to drink, or too little respect for the women around them. There were panels and constructive events, for certain, but then day turned to night, or events turned from public spaces to private hotel suites, where men with power to throw around became bolder and more aggressive. Sometimes, no matter how uproarious the standing ovation, or how brilliant the performance, nothing was going to sway the artist into radio rotation other than some backroom deals that had already been made, weeks before the event even began.

But opening up 2012 with a CRS debut like that was a promising start for someone like Kacey, and with a song she had fought so hard over to serve as her debut—the buzz about it was palpable, as program directors messaged their partners back home about what they'd just seen, and label executives bemoaned what they'd lost out on by not being the ones lucky enough to sign her. Kacey, mostly, was a little shocked. "She was taken aback," Stephanie recalled. "It was pretty magical to see her get up there. That room was just overcome."

There were plenty of women at CRS that year who thought they might break through, too. One of them, Katie Armiger, was also having a banner CRS week, with a showcase at Nashville club 12th and Porter, where she was able to hobnob with journalists and industry folks and start the arduous process of drilling her name into their heads long enough to enter into the territory of "familiar." Katie had moved recently from Sugar Land, Texas, and she was on the brink of landing her own promising career, with a sweet but biting vocal style. She would eventually end up in a sexual harassment lawsuit with the very label that had signed her, alleging that they encouraged her to make herself appear more available and enticing to radio programmers. She went back to school years later, and the label, Cold River, dissolved, as did her dreams of being a country music artist. Though Katie gave up pursuing music full time, she became a Time's Up–supported victim who ended up taking ownership of her masters and devoted her studies to feminist research and social justice.

But this day, Katie did the dutiful rounds. She smiled and shook hands in an outfit that she felt was conservative enough for people to take her seriously, but tight enough to appease the men at her label who wanted her to look a little sexier, leave a little bit up to the creative imagination. She was grateful for the chance, at least—other women, like Rissi, had never even gotten the support to have an official CRS-sanctioned event, even at the height of "Country Girl."

But Kacey had fought like hell to make her introduction from that stage with "Merry Go 'Round," even though she'd been told time after time that maybe it would be best if she were to release something happy, something less critical, something a little . . . easier to take. Like Miranda when she first walked into that meeting with the label bosses at Sony, Kacey wasn't going to waver. "I found myself being told that I really shouldn't write about certain things—weed, homosexuality. . . . I was told that a debut female had to release something upbeat. . . . I really fought for my first single," Kacey said at *Variety*'s Power of Women event, "saying, 'I am willing to go down in flames for this song you are saying just isn't going to work.' And I was met with this word-for-word response, from a grown man who runs a company: 'Well, sometimes in this business you have to do things you are not proud of.' And I said, 'That's where me and you are very different.' I was appalled.'"

Country music, and especially Music Row's money machines, loved to praise small-town life and the people who make it vibrant, and, to a large degree, that's a foundational part of the genre: the music, quite literally, of the country. But somewhere along the way, the meaning got lost—instead of asking questions, it became candy-coating. There could be no mistakes in that sort of life, no wrong opinions or wrong turns, only the right amount of tailgates, trucks, tan lines, football games on Friday nights. The men were all singing about these things from the comfort of Nashville mansions and Gulf Coast beach houses, but none of this seemed to matter to fans who found them to represent that space they had always felt lost in—and a space they felt was increasingly being swallowed in a culture that was drifting away from the conservatism they knew and toward a much more socially progressive atmosphere than they'd been raised in.

"Merry Go 'Round" wasn't interested in painting a rosy picture of the kinds of places Kacey grew up in, though, as much as she loved them and understood them. There are no heroes in the song, only humans, the kind of stuff that the teacher John DeFoore always knew Kacey had in her. A song like that would win as many fans as it would alienate. You had to be willing to be a little self-critical, and that wasn't on the agenda: self-critique doesn't make for a fun party.

"It's sort of the musical version of [the movie] *American Beauty*," said her then publicist Fount Lynch. "These are hard things to accept, especially when it's nine a.m. on a Monday and you are driving your kids to school and the song comes on. And at the time, things were just very, very safe on country radio."

How do you compete, anyway, with the guilty pleasure ease of Florida Georgia Line's "Cruise"? Or the movie theater adaptation of small-town life as Jason Aldean tended to depict it in songs like "Take a Little Ride," where the genre's leading men praised dirt roads and truck rides? It's not easy, if you want to play with the boys on country radio. And Kacey tried. She did. She had the conversations and played her songs for regional radio stations; she packed her bags and made the necessary stops along the way. Country music was supposed to be about the truth, but somewhere that started to fissure. Jason Aldean's version wasn't the whole story, but it went down easy. Kacey had the truth, but maybe no one wanted to hear it. Maybe we would stop wanting the truth: an Instagram filter on our country music.

"Coming from a small, conservative Texas town, I've grown up with this. We're all guilty of having something that keeps us distracted—no matter the vice," Kacey said to *American Songwriter.* "Our comfort zones make us settle and I think there's hope in knowing that everyone has felt this way."

A few weeks after CRS, Kacey found herself back at the Basement, where she would properly announce that she was going to be opening for Lady Antebellum (now controversially known as Lady A, a name they adopted in the wake of the Black Lives Matter movement that had also been used for decades by the blues singer Anita White). The small venue was packed so tightly this time that people were trying to watch from up the ramp across the stage past the bathroom to the front door, standing up on tiptoes to get a glance of her in a pink skirt and her blond-striped bangs. It felt like a convergence: the usual crowd who makes the rounds at kiss-ass number one parties, but also the kids who you'd see at small clubs on a Tuesday night. Kacey played "Merry Go 'Round" and other songs she had been working on for the upcoming album at a writing retreat in Texas, but she also played one about smoking weed with John Prine that some chuckled at uncomfortably: "I ain't one to knock religion," she sang, going exactly where you're not supposed to, "though it's always knocking me."

The dates with Lady A took her abroad, opening shows in Europe in the shadow of massive tours like Taylor's and Carrie's, where she'd be left to make sure the merch table was running smoothly and she had enough gear to get herself stage-ready before the show each night (John Mayer had even handpicked her as an opener based on the strength of her CRS show, the video of which went somewhat viral, before having to cancel due to problems with his throat). "Merry Go 'Round" hadn't been released as an official single to country radio yet, but it had been circulating online enough to pick up steam. One particular night in Ireland, Kacey had stumbled upon a group of fans gathered outside the arena: to their surprise, she approached them and asked if they might be able to help her find a curling iron. At one point Kacey ducked aside to check her Twitter in between stops, and saw that Katy Perry had been raving about "Merry Go 'Round" online. One of the fans tagging along for the hunt remembers Kacey freaking out: approval from someone beyond the country genre signaled to Kacey that she was doing something right, and that maybe her world could crack open the way she had imagined.

By September, journalist Jody Rosen was calling Kacey the future of country music in *Slate*, and even infamous gossip blogger/cultural phenom Perez Hilton had signed on. Though Perez would grow to be a divisive figure, for good reason (especially due to outing multiple queer celebrities without their consent), he was an odd but influential advocate for women in country music. That October he recruited Kacey to play his "One Night in . . . New York City" show at the Highline Ballroom, an annual benefit for the VH1 Save the Music Foundation. Perez, like many gay men before him, had been drawn to the women of country music for their bold and open-arm qualities. "I grew up in the nineties, where it was Shania and the Dixie Chicks," he said. "And others like them and, of course, Dolly Parton. They really welcomed non-country music listeners into their worlds of country, because their sound transcended the genre and was accepted by other radio formats."

That Kacey was headlining a show for a queer pop culture blogger at the same time "Merry Go 'Round" went to country radio spoke directly to the degree to which she felt comfortable bucking tradition, even a little intentionally, sometimes. "At soon as I heard 'Merry Go 'Round,' I felt like it was unlike anything I had heard before, and continues to be that way because it felt dangerous," Perez said. "And it *was* dangerous."

Seeing Kacey get signed and start touring gave Maren hope, but she also wasn't quite sure anymore that she even wanted to pursue a career as an artist. The dusty bars, the drifting faces, and that life of being a soundtrack to other people's drinking habits was wearing on her—or maybe it was the insular world of Arlington that had put her in a box since before junior prom. But she was still doing it anyway, still racking up the accolades in Texas as if she'd been around for three times as many decades (*Fort Worth Weekly* joked that "Maren Morris won the Female Vocalist category for, like, the 20th year in a row"). Her album, *Live Wire*, was "a mature effort from a singer who's practically grown up on record." But it was still an independent release, and she had bigger hopes, her producer and collaborator Taylor Tatsch remembered: hopes that it would catch the ear of some label somewhere or radio outside of Texas. Somehow, neither seemed to happen.

The delta for women on radio was growing stranger and stranger, though—there was mass superstardom like Taylor Swift, reality-born stardom like Carrie (who, by this point, had proven that her talent transcended any gatekeeping filter of *American Idol*), and then little in between, short of the legacy acts paid some sort of sideways respect on behalf of being in the public eye for so long, like Reba. Not the degree of respect they deserved, but respect that made people feel a little bit better about ignoring the work of women overall. Miranda, as usual, was the lone mainstream female rebel, but it wasn't even a straight-ahead road for her, especially when it came to radio. The gossip about her love life and relationship with Blake Shelton drowned out so much else far too often. "I did tell Miranda, we need to get people talking about your music again and not your life," Natalie Hemby remembered.

On the Texas scene, it was even more limited. You had to be either full-on country or something entirely separate from the genre— especially for women, who always ended up in teeny-tiny print on festival rosters or smashed into "Girls Rock Nights." "Bars were always patting themselves on the back for it," said Taylor Tatsch. "Like, 'oh, we're doing an all women night!' But that's not what they needed. They needed to be opening for the big Texas headliners. But by the time Maren was twenty-two, and still working that Texas scene, everyone still thought of her as being, you know, fourteen. So she was spinning her wheels, as a mature woman writing mature songs and not getting the love I think she deserved from the Texas music scene."

She was also intent on pushing what exactly she could do in the frame of—and outside of—country music. For *Live Wire*, she made a conscious decision not to incorporate steel guitar or too much twangy instrumentation, experimenting instead with piano-based songs. Taylor could see that she really wanted it to stand out and stand alone.

"I must have been nineteen when I realized I had been touring Texas for almost a decade," Maren said, "and I needed a new challenge."

Not thinking much of it, Maren and the band headed to New York in June 2012 to compete in the New Music Seminar. An eighties-era institution, it had faded out and shuttered in the nineties after festivals like South by Southwest turned the endeavor into a full-on business, where it became less about spotting unsigned acts and more about labels building their marketing plans for artists already on the rise and looking for a good party to drop a lot of swag. But the founders resurrected New Music for a few years due to the almost unmanageable amount of good talent that, in the age of the internet, was able to find an audience, changing the meaning of what an independent career in music could look like to begin with.

Maren and Taylor flew up to New York from Texas, staying at a hotel downtown and staging practice at a house in Brooklyn referred to as "The 1984," a place where a bunch of ex–Dallas area musicians crashed or cohabited, including ones who both of them had gigged or crossed paths with over the years, like Nolan Thies and Cooper Heffley. The 1984 house was prime artistic mayhem—at least eight or ten musicians living in the same Williamsburg apartment, somehow cramming their bodies and day-to-day belongings in with an ungodly amount of recording equipment, crappy, cheap instruments, or whatever you could bang on or squeeze a sound from. Books propped up computers and monitors, mics wrapped up with packing tape. It was chaotic, but it also felt perfect.

Maren had gotten to the Artist on the Verge Finals at New Music, to her surprise, and any free moment would be dedicated to rehearsing and tightening up their set. Taylor practiced on a broken-down drum kit, barely giving any thought to the potential weight of the moment—his wife was pregnant, and they were enjoying being in the city together before they'd become parents soon. Maren, in a Hawaiian-print tube dress, tinkered and tuned her guitar. "Should we be nervous about this?" she asked Taylor. He didn't know how to answer: there were hundreds of bands and they had no real expectations—Maren was already on the fence about making the move to Nashville anyway, and this was another chance to play a show and sample another city, another way of life. Maybe she'd move here instead, transfer schools, get a bartending gig? Or should she hang it all up for a little while, go back to college in Texas, study history or writing?

They caught a few odd shows around the city after rehearsal, some Chinese food and cheap drinks, and the next day headed to a since-shuttered venue called Santos Party House. The vibe was crowded and hot, with plenty of people exhausted from the previous day's activities. Local DJ Jonathan Clarke from the station Q104.3 introduced Maren—she was in a white skirt, black tank top, and angular crop to her hair swinging by her face, the antithesis of what anyone had come to generally expect when they thought about women in country music and their long blond hair extensions.

Maren was the only country or roots-leaning artist in the bunch—other finalists were rapper Black Cobain, duo Ninjasonik, and indie rock band the Dig—out of one hundred contenders. The room was full of, as Maren put it, "movers and shakers," including even some Nashville executives. Maren put on a pleather skirt and brought out her acoustic, playing songs off *Live Wire* with a bit of extra fire—and, to her utter surprise, ended up winning the whole thing. "I was the only country artist and everyone else was really artsy or hip-hop, and I thought there was no chance in hell that I am going to walk away with anything from this other than a key chain," Maren remembered. There was no big party for the band after, no late-night drinking at the bar. But something felt as though it had finally shifted.

After some additional reassurance from her friends and parental encouragement, Maren spent the last few months of the year settling things up in Texas, playing gigs, and searching out cheap houses on Craigslist to rent in Nashville. Her last official performance as a Texan was a night at the Grease Monkey, swapping sets with her friend Van Darien as she'd done so many nights before. She sat on the rickety wooden stool one last time, tuned her guitar, and then, by the first week of January 2013, she was gone.

It was an anniversary, and it was also a first of hopefully many nights back at the famed Ryman Auditorium. Mickey had moved to Nashville herself just about a year before, and she was looking back on those months with a sense of wistful nervousness: there were the huge steps forward, like signing her deal with Capitol Records, and there were the huge steps back, which usually came with the utterance of words about her skin color or the way she wore her hair or her gender, or knowing glances in boardrooms when they discussed the marketing plans around her music.

The year 2013 was kicking off as custom: with CRS, and it was set to be an important one for Mickey. The Ryman felt no different, really, than it did the year prior, gathered for the same Universal Records showcase, with mostly the same radio programmers in the same "Nashville-ready" outfits, which meant jeans with a little bit of extra flair and a windbreaker for the rain. But this year, it wasn't just Kacey who was the talk of the Ryman Auditorium, playing "Follow Your Arrow" to yet another stunned crowd—it was Mickey. Mickey was already getting the usual feedback awarded to any Black artist trying to make a space for themselves in the genre regardless of how they actually came across sonically—too R&B for country, too country for R&B. But Mickey had champions at Capitol, vice president Cindy

Mabe and Lori Christian, who worked public relations for the label (handling her press coverage).

Even with an executive like Cindy on her side, Mickey still had to play by the rules—to keep the decorum up, to smile and shrug; and Cindy, beholden to the bottom line, had to do the same. The "lessons" of the past echoed in Mickey's head: the Chicks. Rissi. Stand still, look pretty. Shut up and sing. They were only lessons, however, if you erred on the side of total compliance.

"Seeing the Dixie Chicks canceled really affected me," Mickey said. "That was a little more terrifying to me than anything else. Shut your mouth, don't have any kind of opinion or anything remotely unaligned with the country music industry or you will be canceled. And I feared that. That fear is very much in the community today."

It wasn't easy for Rissi to watch Mickey taking these steps and to start to grow even a small platform—she had never gotten the support to be able to play an official showcase, never gotten the industry backing that at least seemed, from the outside, to be surrounding Mickey ("seemed" proving to be the operative word). But it was thrilling at the same time, to watch a legacy that she had helped start ease just a bit farther through Mickey's voice. "I'm gonna be completely transparent," Rissi said. "My feelings were hurt. And I took it very personally. It wasn't *her*. I wasn't ever upset with her, or angry with her or anything. But seeing her and seeing the fact that it appeared she was welcome—that was hard."

Mickey didn't exactly feel welcome, but she sure tried to look like it, especially backstage, where she and her upright bass player were the only Black people in the entire room, and everyone tried not to notice, or maybe they didn't even see the problem to begin with. That was nothing new anyway, the lone person of color in a space full of white on white. Mickey's top was white, her skirt light gray, appearing white when the cameras snapped. Maybe she could soak it up, blend in, not have them see her for anything but her voice and her songs.

It said a lot, though, about the space between the two women (and

the space allowed to them) that Kacey had been able to run success-
fully, so far, with her commitment to her own compass, while Mickey
shivered at the thought. "I'm kind of a big believer in people doing
whatever the hell they want to do, since I feel like society is probably going to have an opinion either way," Kacey had said before she
introduced "Follow Your Arrow." If Mickey had said that, as a Black
woman entering into this nearly exclusively white space, she would
have been shunned.

Mickey had been rehearsing hard in the days prior, though, running through takes of her planned single "Better Than You Left Me"
over and over, pacing the apartment to get her notes right and puff-
ing a little white Vicks inhaler to keep her nasal passages clear. She'd
never even entered the Ryman before, let alone had a chance to walk
out onto its stage as a performer.

"I had no idea what CRS even was," she remembered. "I thought
I was just doing writer's round, but I didn't know it was a possible
career-changing moment."

She felt like she was floating out, her skirt dusting the Ryman floor,
the unbroken circle of country music, when her name was called. The
Ryman treated her with the same response they did when Kacey took
the stage the previous year—a standing ovation. "She's a superstar in
the making!" wrote the website Sounds Like Nashville. Twitter lit
up with praise. A debut CRS song, a standing ovation, but eventual
crickets when it came to airplay, when the label finally decided to push
the single two years later—this would be a pattern that Mickey would
come to know again and again. For then, it felt like victory.

Mickey walked offstage and shot a look at one of her label reps. She
blinked and smiled.

"Did that just happen?"

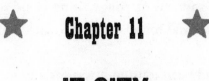

Chapter 11

IT CITY

Young women come to Nashville with a dream and a guitar from all across the country and beyond: Missouri by way of Pennsylvania, like Rissi Palmer. Those cornfields of Iowa, like Hailey Whitters, who packed her parents' van the summer before college and headed down I-64, her whole family squished in tight and probably breaking seat belt laws across state lines, stopping for fast food and milkshakes and gas station restrooms. From Canada where the young artist Tenille Townes came from, all forty hours from Alberta in a converted RV she used to kick her career off, parking in supermarket lots and doing makeshift showers in the bathroom sinks.

Maren barreled down that highway with her mother on January 4, 2013, more familiar with those long stretches of Texas roads and Nashville's nonsensical, winding interstates than most. She'd done the journey plenty of times, even slept on Kacey's couch when she would come for writing trips, but never with the permanence of that day, her hair freshly shorn, her U-Haul packed with belongings that felt both trivial and all-important, like her guitar and songwriting notebooks. It was all a perilous but intriguing backdrop to arrive in, renting an apartment for $350 a month on the east side of town and ready to seek out a publishing deal, because things were dried up in Texas: like Kacey and numerous other artists before her, that world had only been able to feed her to a certain point, and not even a move to Austin, like Kacey had tried, would prove to solve that ache. She was both revved up and tired—tired of the artist life, willing to put that path on hold to focus on songwriting alone, and ready to jump headfirst into writes and rounds around town, a handful of demos in her back pocket.

"I realized I had been touring Texas for almost a decade," Maren said, "and I needed a new challenge. I was still a kid, flying from the nest. It was one of the best decisions I have ever made."

Those previous trips to town and late nights in East Nashville had set her up well with a group of friends ready to hold her up—a whole team of them, far beyond just Kacey and the folks she knew from the touring circuit or back in Texas. The whole Villa crew, really, became her crew, too: John and T.J. Osborne, Kate York and Natalie Osborne, Lucie Silvas, Kree Harrison, Natalie Hemby, Daniel Tashian, and many more. She became familiar with the insides of their writing rooms or cramped apartments where they could carve out a corner to create, until those storied doors on Music Row started to open up, which happened much faster than she could have imagined.

Where this particular collection of artists fell was both in and out of Music Row. On the surface, it would seem as though Nashville had two country camps: the East Nashville indie underground and the mainstream, major-label lot. That had never been exactly true, though it was the easiest way for folks, especially outside of town, to understand everything under a neat umbrella. But with these artists something different was emerging. It was becoming a thriving group that respected and enjoyed both the traditions and the subversions, the songwriting community and the space in between: they often went on to describe it as a "modern-day Chelsea Hotel," where they would hop from home to home writing and strumming their guitars, camping out on back porches to smoke weed and make the best of pre–record deal life with empty pockets and overdue electricity bills. On holidays, they'd often assemble together for "friendsgiving" or other occasions where they were too poor to go back home to Texas or Maryland or wherever they had come from, eating buffet style, rolling joints, writing songs until bellies were too full. They'd since moved on from Villa—Brothers Osborne signed to EMI Nashville and Charlie Worsham to Warner Music Nashville—but were as tight as ever.

For Kacey, that community was everything—a group that she could come to after the just-bubbling trappings of real and true fame were starting to explode, where she could wipe her stage makeup off and roll a joint. "She's still that girl from Texas who loves to sit and get high with her friends and be unique and funny and quirky," said Fount. "And have really unique and funny things to say that could be off-putting to others, but her friend group, they get it. Man, the sheer level of talent and artistry in that one room all together, it was stupid." Mickey had hit it off with the group, too, especially with John Osborne, whom she counted as a close confidant and ally. "John stands up for what's right," she'd later tell *Billboard*. "I've seen him go to bat for me in times where I felt so small and alone. And he would give me encouragement that nobody else did. He saw me when nobody else did."

When Maren arrived from Texas she settled in easily but quietly, laying back most of the time as an observer, and Kate York hadn't even quite figured out just how good she was up until one night at Santa's Pub when Maren took the mic to do a karaoke cover of Beyoncé's "Halo." That had been her signature move back in Dallas, her way to level the crowd and set the stakes from the ground running—Beyoncé was also from Texas, and it was Maren's subtle nod to her understanding that the musicality of her home state wasn't limited in any way, shape, or form to just country or western music. When she did it that night, to her unsuspecting new friends, they were flabbergasted.

"I just started laughing out loud because it was so good," said Kate. "It was just so crazy." Maren didn't always take out her guitar or start singing when they were hanging out, but from that moment Kate knew that it absolutely wasn't for lack of talent, and started talking Maren up to anyone who would listen.

"It's just a family of encouragement, lifting each other up," Kate said. "It never felt competitive." Even as they got more and more famous, the glue stuck (years later, in pandemic times, Kate would quarantine at John and Lucie's house, hanging in a bubble with Kacey, the singer-songwriter Fancy Hagood, and T.J.), and they all maintained group texts and hangs and as many chances to see each other away from the red carpets and spotlights as they could. "No one really gives two shits about if you are doing well or not," Maren said. "Everyone is just more concerned with, How's your heart? How's your family?"

Kacey, meanwhile, was taking off in 2013. Not as far as she should have—"Merry Go 'Round" should have been an easy number one song, and it ultimately only made it to ten on Billboard's Country Airplay. But it was climbing steadily and surely, doing well enough to foster a fan base that existed beyond just mainstream country or niche Americana.

Kree, Maren, Kacey, and especially the musicians they played with also managed to toe a collective line to what was happening over in East Nashville, which was gaining more and more attention for its new class of country-adjacent and independent Americana musicians— Caitlin Rose, Jason Isbell, Amanda Shires, Joshua Hedley, Margo Price, Sturgill Simpson, and Elizabeth Cook, who was a favorite of David Letterman as well as an omnipresent guest at the Grand Ole Opry without ever being invited into membership. And Holly Williams, granddaughter of the great Hank Williams Sr., whose album *The Highway* was a lyrical breakthrough and proved that legacy had made it to her pen, not just her blood. Like the movie *Heartworn Highways*, which followed the likes of Townes Van Zandt and Guy Clark, this was shaping up as a new generation of left-of-center musicians who managed to thrive completely independently from Music Row.

At the center of it all was undeniably Jason Isbell, who was starting to lead the town into a new reality when his LP *Southeastern* was released. As much as Nashville in 2013 was about mainstream truck songs, or as it was about Kacey, it was also about Jason: the album landed like a bullet in the hearts of anyone with one. Jason was married to Amanda Shires, who would become Maren's bandmate in the Highwomen, and he had written the album sober after a long battle to get clean of alcohol addiction. Its success—and Jason's future success—had stunned everyone not for the quality (most knew that his songwriting was exemplary, as evidenced by his work with his former band, Drive-By Truckers) but for how it was able to be a financial and chart success without the help of a major label. *Southeastern* was distributed on Thirty Tigers, an independent company that held the top office of the same building as the Basement, and it shook the entire system to its core—Thirty Tigers founder David Macias described it as a "lightning bolt." Though Jason wasn't, and isn't, country music proper, the album was everything Music City was supposed to be—just a bunch of timeless songs. His next three albums would all hit number one on the folk, rock, and country charts, and win him four Grammys.

Southeastern was good—stunning, in fact. It was good and it was independent and it was successful, things that were the antithesis of regularly scheduled programming over on Music Row.

It also introduced a new producer into the cultural mix: Dave Cobb. Dave was not new by any means—he had started out with Shooter Jennings in 2005, but his work with Jason was shaping him to be one of the most coveted in town, and he had also been working on an album with Sturgill Simpson at his home studio. The album, *Metamodern Sounds in Country Music*, would change the landscape when it came out the following year and would position Sturgill as one of the most elastic, creative musicians around. His next album, *A Sailor's Guide to Earth*, would take home a Grammy for Country Album of the Year before he would make a rock album, then a bluegrass one, shape-shifting like a Kentucky David Bowie.

Maren's first gig as a permanent Nashville resident was in a slot at the Basement, opening for an up-and-coming Sturgill: owner Mike Grimes had recruited her to the gig on the strength of another performance he'd seen a few weeks earlier. Maren opening for Sturgill epitomized exactly where the city was, spiraling out in a hundred creative directions at once. Both artists were interested in the roots and legacy of the genre and places from which they were born, but not at all interested in feeling like they had to make art just to exist in a specific genre box.

Sturgill had booked a monthly residency at the Basement, for a five-buck cover charge, and the buzz around town was growing exponentially with every show. One afternoon, Mike was running errands when he realized that he had forgotten to book an opening act for that evening. Mike was so old hat to the Nashville scene that he wasn't worried that he wouldn't be able to find someone to snag the coveted slot, but he did have to act fast.

He thought back to a woman, Maren Morris, who had played a New Faces night a month or two back, before her official move to town, at the recommendation of Kate York. "I was just scrambling the day of," Mike remembered, "and I thought, well, Maren Morris just played here and she's great. So I called her and said, 'hey, can you do thirty minutes opening for this guy Sturgill Simpson?' She said yes and so Sturgill Simpson had Maren Morris as his opening act, for an audience of about thirty people."

Maren hadn't heard of Sturgill yet, but she liked his name—alliteration, just like hers—and that the set was just short enough to cover the minimal material she had worked up. "I was like, that's perfect," Maren said. "Because that's literally all I have. I just remember he was wearing Chuck Taylors. And he had his band and he started singing and it was like, *holy shit*. Who was this? It was very Waylon. It just felt like I was listening to an old radio but very unique, and he was super nice."

John Strohm, now the president of beloved roots label Rounder but then Sturgill's lawyer, had been trying to get him playing in front of as many Nashville eyes as possible—the album, after all, was truly that good. Maren, opening the show, was just alone with her guitar, singing the songs she had been writing and workshopping since she had been coming back and forth to town. The next major time Sturgill and Maren would reunite would be at the Grammy Awards in 2017, less than five years later.

The gig drew the usual sort of crowd: some of the people there were enraptured, and some of the people there were completely ignorant to exactly what was going on right in front of them. As is Nashville custom, going to the show is more often than not saying you've gone to the show, past tense, rather than absorbing every moment—you could tick off a box on social media that you'd been there. There's great talent onstage any night during the week in Nashville, but this was something else. "Half the audience was outside on the patio," John Strohm remembered. "I thought, 'What the fuck is wrong with these people? Don't they hear what's on the stage?'"

John had worked with the Civil Wars, the duo of Joy Williams and John Paul White, who would go on to win Grammys and escalate Americana into pop consciousness with their album *Barton Hollow*, and seen firsthand the reluctance that Nashville can have when someone receives fast success without going through the traditional ranks of country radio. He had been somewhat hoping that Sturgill could be a person who could reset the country pendulum—with the exception of Eric Church and Miranda, mostly, the mainstream area had become monotone. He had studied the past, and thought that it was time for a reset—one that would come a few years later, to some degree, with the arrival of the brilliant Chris Stapleton's debut solo album and his explosion on the mainstream scene. Sturgill's career would end up evolving in a much different direction, having scared the shit out of Music Row and been rejected by the mainstream despite the fetishization of "outlaws."

The next few months saw everything happening fast for Maren—especially her publishing deal. Laura Wright, who worked at a publisher in town called Big Yellow Dog, had flagged her thanks to a recommendation from Jody Williams at BMI, who heard of her after she won the New Music Seminar in New York City and gave Laura a call. "That next night, I went to Whiskey Jam, and ran into Kacey Musgraves, someone I believe in so much. And she said, 'My gosh, Laura, you have to meet my friend Maren who just moved here from Texas.' I said, 'Is there a sign on my face that says I am supposed to meet Maren Morris?' It was a match made in heaven."

"Come by the office tomorrow," Laura told Maren. "I'd love to connect with you."

Maren was already being pursued by other publishers, but Laura jumped first and hard. She went to her boss, Carla Wallace, and made the case. Carla, too, was sold, and they made her deal with Big Yellow Dog official.

Laura started to work fast, booking cowrites with Luke Laird and Natalie Hemby and Shane McAnally. "This girl just moved to town. I don't have a clue what she's like in the room, but I know there's something there," Laura said. "Every time they would get in the room they would be calling me, being like, 'Laura, holy shit, I love her, please put more dates down.'"

One day Laura passed a CD to the songwriter Ryan Hurd and asked him to listen and tell her what he thought. He popped it in while riding in his truck and immediately called Laura. "Put as many days as you can down with her," he said. They got together for a writing session, and then another. That professional relationship blossomed into a friendship, and then a romance—they would tell each other "I love you" over drinks, a moment Ryan would eventually turn into a song called "Love in a Bar." He proposed by the lake in his native Michigan, and Maren and Ryan would marry in 2018, Maren wearing a short white dress modeled after the one her mother wore in the eighties.

Maren was still unsure if she wanted to go the artist route, though, but those around her were intent on convincing her—she was having trouble getting other songwriters to consider cutting what she came up with, because they were just so uniquely in her own lane and voice, or at least that's what they told her when they didn't want to say so overtly that there wasn't really a space for female artists, especially one with such a sharp point of view.

"I remember thinking, some of these songs are hers. Just who else would sing that?" Laura said. "I said, 'If you want to make an EP, do anything, let's just try. She's a really, really, really strong songwriter, and if you can be that first, then you have the voice and the artist.' It was a really pivotal moment because I really believed in someone for the first time."

Word was getting out to other artists as well, even beyond the country music community, in part from friends like Kate York making sure to advocate for her. "Kate sent me some of her demos and at the time she was just trying to be a writer," says Courtney Jaye. "I heard the demo and I was like, 'No no, you need to be an artist!' Hearing her first in demo form and seeing her play live—it's a no-brainer." Courtney, Maren, and Kate enjoyed their share of partying together, goofing off late in local dive bars and hitting up Mule Mondays at a place in East Nashville, where you could get drunk for cheap.

On other nights, she'd head to 3 Crow Bar with fellow songwriters Abe Stoklasa, Kate York, and Chris Gelbuda. At the time, 3 Crow was the center of the East Nashville bar scene (it took over the space of the former Slow Bar), the Cheers of the Five Points area. The air was always thick from cigarette smoke and the smell of fresh burgers on the grill, which were uncharacteristically good for a local dive. It was far enough from the Music Row writing rooms to be a safe respite, and not have to feel like you might dangerously run into someone when you were only trying to disconnect and talk shit over a grapefruit vodka and soda or Bushwacker, the signature drink that was something white, slushy, and far too boozy for reasonable human consumption. "Maren was as real as it gets, as a person and a writer," Abe said. "No bullshit. Just oozes talent and experience. She never tried to chase anybody else's sound. She knew what she wanted to do."

She would also take her cuts and holds (when an artist calls dibs on your song in case they want to "cut" it, or record it for their album) very seriously, according to Abe. A hold doesn't always mean that appearing on a record is a sure thing—sometimes, a writer can have their songs on hold for so long that they eventually disappear into purgatory, or the trends move on without them. "I remember her getting very emotional when she thought she had lost what would be her first cut with Tim McGraw on the *Sundown Heaven Town* record," said Abe about the song Tim did eventually record, "which happened to be my first cut too (different songs, same record). She wasn't angry or ungrateful but she was tearing up in the office one day. It was her baby. Most writers shake it off and move on or carry a chip on their shoulder. She just was really disappointed and let it out and then moved on. I think that says something about how deeply she cares about her compositions as opposed to a lot that go for quantity over quality. I hadn't ever seen anybody be so emotionally struck by something like that."

Like that moment, everything felt both in and out of reach. The scene was more vibrant than ever, and Kacey and Miranda were reaching critical success and new fan bases, but the bro-party revolution was also getting too loud to drown out—it danced around in writing rooms like a pesky gnat you couldn't catch, buzzing in the ear, a ticket to bigger meals and bigger stardom. Florida Georgia Line's "Cruise" had already become a near-global smash, and the pressure was on.

The town was changing, too. In January 2013, Kim Severson of the *New York Times* had dropped a bomb: Nashville was the "it" city, transforming into a place people wanted to come to en masse. Add the emergence of the TV show *Nashville* to the mix and suddenly a full-on tourist boom was underway: starring Connie Britton as an aging country star, the show launched in 2012 to enormous fanfare and put beloved local venues like the 5 Spot on the map. Guestrooms in East Nashville had never been fuller; parking lots shifted from vacant gravel to paved asphalt or, worse, foundations for future high-rises. The seeds of Nashville's next phase beyond just hipster tourism—bachelorette mania—were starting to sprout. Bachelorettes seemed to fall straight into the roles that here-for the-party country songs were ascribing to women: chugging beers in short shorts, climbing into the passenger seat of a truck (or a pedal tavern). And the eternal country bacchanal was the perfect soundtrack to their pursuits. Soon it developed into a symbiotic relationship, where the tourists needed music for the party, and the music needed the tourists.

Country music was reaching new heights in terms of global popularity, but even in the days of Garth and Shania the city itself had never proven very desirable to coastal folks. Here was the new Nashville: an "it" city where gentrification was turning historically Black neighborhoods into homes for white Brooklynites looking for a weekend out of town, where they could rent an Airbnb and eat hot chicken, a playground for the party to belt "Cruise," a place full of thriving creativity but crushing exclusion. East Nashville had been reshaping and pushing out its longtime residents since a 1998 tornado brought in a sweep of revitalization and rebuilding, and affordable local grocery stores were being shuttered in favor of artisan cocktail bars.

Nashville itself had been a mixed blessing—it was blowing up the demand for the city to enormous proportions, but it was also providing a platform for writers like Kate York to pitch their songs. Kate, writing with Sarah Buxton, was churning them out by the day, spending nights at karaoke with the actress Hayden Panettiere, who played a lead on the show. The actors were becoming part of the fiber of the town in their own ways, while writers were balancing being critical of a show that commodified their town to a new degree without biting the hand that fed them. Maren and Kacey both had several cuts on the show, an opportunity that seemed to conspicuously elude Mickey.

Despite stellar albums that fell across the year from the Pistol Annies, Natalie Maines, Sheryl Crow, and Kacey, the fog of the testosterone party was getting too hard to shake. By August, critic Jody Rosen had coined the phrase that defined the phenomenon of the Lukes and Jasons of the world in *Vulture*: "bro country." It was a smart moniker for a train that had well left the station—a type of country music that by definition could allow the radio programmers to laugh and play into a trend that kept advertiser dollars rolling in. For as helpful as it was to have a name to put on the thing, it also primed Nashville as a recurring target for beloved hick jokes and made it easier to dismiss the music as low art. Not everyone loved it. "When Jody coined 'bro country' I was kind of mad," said Lauren Tingle, who was working at the industry trade *Country Aircheck* at the time. "I was like, damnit. You gave it a name, and now we have to live with that."

Jody Rosen was a little annoyed, too. He didn't mean for it to take on such a pejorative connotation. "It was really a descriptor," he told the *Guardian*. "I was simply trying to characterize the music and place it in a broader social and musical context. It feels weird to me that bro country these days is used really as a cudgel. It's sort of by definition an insult if you call something bro country. It means you're saying it's crap."

There were terrible, no-good bro-country tunes. But some were fun, joyful even, sugary candies not ever meant to be the whole meal— "Cruise" was, and is, the definition of easy, party-friendly listening, a part of the genre that had always been important. It was just never supposed to be all that there was.

"What is it about 'Cruise' and its Nelly-featuring remix that so epitomizes the bro-country ethos?" Brittney McKenna asked in *Rolling Stone*. "For starters, the lyrics cover all the bro bases: driving in jacked-up trucks with the windows rolled down; nameless, faceless, long-legged ladies in bikini tops; back roads and farm towns; and plenty of alcohol. Then there's the melody, which is infectious enough to have even the staunchest of country purists humming along, if reluctantly. 'Cruise' is the song that launched a thousand ships with lift-kits to country radio. Better to hop onboard and sing along than get caught in its frothy wake."

The press was as fascinated by bro country as radio was, but the difference lay in artists like Kacey—critical due was plentiful, but airplay wasn't. Suddenly the dichotomy between "quality" and bank-ability had never been stronger. *Entertainment Weekly* called it a "civil war," even tracing the whole thing out in a timeline that charted from when Blake Shelton called lovers of traditional country "old farts" and "jackasses," to Jason Aldean's atrocious song "1994," to "Cruise" reigning as the longest-running country number one in history. Even Tom Petty chimed in, calling modern country "bad rock with a fid-dle." Kacey (along with the likes of Sturgill Simpson and Jason Isbell) was presented as the foil to all this—not only did she have to carry the weight of the music, but she had to carry the weight of somehow saving country from this direction, a beloved story line for more pop-oriented press.

It was all far too simplistic—on one hand, "Cruise" was emblem-atic to some of a corner of country music that epitomized heading in the wrong direction away from "three chords and the truth," and their visions of country music being exactly what the book says, banjos and steel guitar. And its success got Music Row absolutely beside itself with greed—if this sound worked this well, what could come next? How many other people could they manufacture to sing about trucks and cruising? On the other hand, it symbolized a further opening of the genre in ways that appealed to artists like Brittney Spencer, who came from Baltimore to Nashville in search of a songwriting career, and who saw it as the genre making space for different points of view—and, she hoped, as a Black woman, different races. If Flor-ida Georgia Line was duetting with the rapper Nelly on a remix of "Cruise," maybe that meant there would be room for an actual Black country artist like her?

Brittney had been busking downtown and working odd jobs while attending Middle Tennessee State University, and she would often hear covers of "Cruise" alongside tracks from the Pistol Annies. The difference was that one of those artists would get played on country radio, and the other would barely merit consideration.

In a separate interview with journalist Grady Smith, who composed the *EW* timeline, Luke Bryan mulled over the situation. Rarely were men asked to be accountable—rarely were they asked anything of substance, leaving the women or, on occasion, the rare artist of color, to account for all the injustices and imbalances in the world while the men in trucker hats just rallied for tighter jeans and liquor sponsorships. You'd hear them welcoming you to Nashville when you arrive at the airport as you fetch your bags on the carousel over the PA system; they get to headline arenas and promote beer lines and answer questions about their new puppy, or how the baby is doing, or how they liked working with that new producer this go-round. They don't have to go to bat for anything, because they are given the space to live high up in the clouds.

Grady Smith attempted, at least, to see what Luke had to say.

"A lot of times girls, you know—it's just a tough time for girls to pull off those early days and radio tours, too," Bryan continued. "And I don't want anybody calling me saying, 'Why are you saying girls aren't tough enough?' But I've thought about it a lot and why it happens, but at the end of the day, I can't put my finger on it."

But did Luke Bryan have to endure comments about his legs—or much worse—while trying to promote a song? And if he didn't, would he not be "tough" enough? It was shocking that so many were unable to see that these expectations to buddy up with radio programmers or be able to absorb the "toughness" of the road were maybe more indicative of a larger problem. Maybe he could put his finger on it, maybe everybody could. Maybe no one wanted to. Why spoil the fun?

At CMT, Leslie Fram was devising her own way to help move the needle, though, and CMT's Next Women of Country initiative was meant to offer some counterprogramming to this idea that only men could lead. Leslie had been pushing internally and, to her surprise, got CMT on board fairly easily—after all, women had been the cornerstone of the video boom in the nineties, so betting on them now seemed like a reasonable practice.

They announced the first Next Women of Country class in early

January, which included Ashley Monroe, Holly Williams, Jana Kramer, Kacey, Brandy Clark, Lauren Alaina, Sarah Darling, Rose Falcon, Rachel Farley, and Kelleigh Bannen. There were no Black women until the next year, with Mickey—there were no other Black women signed to labels, after all, to even invite. These "classes" would be replicated over the years, and come to include the likes of Carly Pearce, Kelsea Ballerini, Maren, and 2021's roster, which finally broke through the white girl barrier with a diverse, and also spectacularly talented, group of women including Brittney Spencer, alongside Chapel Hart, Reyna Roberts, and Tiera as well as the openly lesbian Harper Grae. It would be the first time the program boasted multiple Black women in one year.

Even with new spaces like Next Women of Country emerging, women, and especially Black women, just couldn't seem to pass the authenticity test in mainstream country. Kacey always had developed a certain kind of country-quirk aesthetic, glittery cowgirl things that would work for the rodeo or the drag show. It rejected the traditional molds for country "authenticity" that only cemented themselves further for a new generation as Americana became an even bigger and more powerful force (and solid option). Country boys, "real country boys," were the authentic ones who had a right to sing about real things and didn't like anything but jeans and a good belt buckle and boots just as good for stepping onstage as on horse shit. Artists like Michael Ray would spell this out explicitly on songs like "Real Men Love Jesus," where "real men" were religious, watched football, and loved cars, beer, and women (just women, only women).

By default, a woman's path to "authenticity" went two ways: Gretchen Wilson, scruffy and wild like the "outlaw" boys, or Patsy Cline, captive to traditions. Kacey was inherently interested in the entire visual package as part of her art form, which existed in neither of these categories. "I think the fact that they drape themselves in rainbows and butterflies rather than plaid and beanies is the real difference. If it doesn't look 'serious' it can't be serious," said Staci Kirpach.

Once again, it was also very clear that this definition of "authenticity" was only specific to one skin color. It was a no-win game: if you were Black, and you followed the rules of how a man, or even a woman, was supposed to present themselves—in other words, looking "authentic"—you were accused of trying to be someone you weren't. If you leaned in any other direction, you weren't authentic enough: *You should pursue a career in R&B*. It had already caged Rissi to the point that she wasn't even attempting to make country music for a broad audience anymore, and it had stuck Mickey in an impossible corner.

Mickey would often walk by the R&B programmers at radio station visits even faster than she ought to—she was purposely trying to evade any impression that she was interested in playing to that market, since she had to try so hard to prove at every step of the way that she was country. She had to overcorrect so far that she was losing sight of who she even was.

Chapter 12

WHERE MY GAYS AT?

The bells were ringing loud in New York City on the morning that Kacey hopped into a car uptown from the Gramercy Hotel to film her first appearance on national television—metaphoric bells for certain, but actual, thunderous ones, too: it was March of 2013, just as Pope Francis, aka the new pope, was officially being installed at the Vatican. In a city that loves the sinner as much as the saint, or at least makes it possible for both to share an apartment, this whole week felt unusually holy, and with good reason—on the subways and in the streets, people remembered to wear their rosaries, dangled lightly and proudly around necks next to tight spring coats and hanging out of skinny denim pockets, clicking against subway poles as the trains swayed.

Kacey had rolled into the city for the usual stream of prerelease press, which had become a Nashville rite of passage—that all-important time to engage the New York media and try to break past the country walls alone. It's always an awkward shuffle: How country is too much country? How much can you tone it down before alienating your fans back home? Some artists pack and repack their bags before settling on a look or approach; others throw in nothing but cowboy boots and belts, defiant as always.

It was a ludicrously busy day at the *Today* show, as it always was, but producers were scrambling to cover what was transpiring across the ocean in real time—with the benefit of an increased captive audience, and one more religiously observant and conservative than normal. This was not the kind of day to look the other way and let a curse or unwelcomed body part pop out as they cut from Times Square to St. Peter's Square, lest they alarm anyone at home clutching their Bibles, or their pearls, tightly. This was not a day to make a fan or the FCC upset over an errant curse word or boob slip. It was a day for recipes and family-friendly products and puppies, the kind of content that makes morning shows a safe and risk-free sort of space. Under normal circumstances, it would be a pretty good day for wholesome, Music Row–bred country.

It also happened to be the same day that Kacey was booked for this all-important breakthrough moment to get her face in living rooms across America, and the same day that *Same Trailer Different Park* was released to the world: Kacey Musgraves, the girl from Golden, and the new pope, a matchup that absolutely no one would have expected (or, perhaps, recommended). The night before, Kacey and the team had stayed up and had drinks at the posh hotel downtown, just talking about politics, love, and weed, and they'd all gone to bed only a little bit tipsy, ready for an early morning in the makeup chair. Kacey, by no surprise, was going to play "Merry Go 'Round" and not some bubbly offering to appease a general (half-listening) audience—the song was gaining critical steam and moderate airplay anyway, but, more than anything, she felt like it was the best possible introduction that she could make to a national audience, dumping it all on the table out of the gate. Fount Lynch had been in tow, and he was preparing himself for the eventual conversation that would unravel: he was a good, God-fearing boy himself and he, too, understood the significance of the day. He said his prayers literally and figuratively that morning, remembering that it was ten years almost to the day of the Chicks' famous anti-Bush "gaffe," and he knew as well as anyone how little it took to deeply unsettle country's conservative base.

It was a celebratory morning—for Kacey, not just the pope, since

the album was officially out in the world, the day she had been waiting for since arriving in Nashville. Shane and Luke, in sweatpants
and jeans, had run over to the local Walmart first thing to grab a
copy, where it sat on the rack smack next to Luke Bryan's newest. It
had even shot to number one on iTunes. Friends from Nashville and
beyond were sending selfies of them holding the record or snaps of the
charts.

One of the producers grabbed Fount, lanky and quietly dressed,
outside the greenroom as soon as they arrived in the chaotic halls of the
morning show. He could tell from their facial expressions that this was
not going to be good news. "At the end of the song, you know where
she says, 'Mary doesn't give a *damn* anymore,'" the producer started to
explain. "Well, we're covering the Vatican and the pope this morning,
going back and forth to Rome, so maybe it would, you know, be a good
idea not to say that word 'damn' at the end of the song?"

Fount nodded—that usual reserved publicist nod, the polite "fuck
you," stoic and gracious (known, in the South, more specifically as
"bless your heart"). Sure, he said. He would see what he could do, no
problem, he'll talk to Kacey. He smiled because he knew, in practical-
ity, he could do absolutely nothing.

The walk back to Kacey felt like a mile, and, after taking a breath
in the hallway, he already knew the answer. He had to do his label
duties and present the producer's case to his artist, but to tell Kacey
to change her song would be like telling Lady Gaga to curb her
New York accent—and besides, she wasn't going to do it anyway. In
fact, the sheer idea of Fount telling her to change her song would
make her even more fired up to sing it exactly as it had been written.
Fount sat down next to Kacey, crouching in his tight work slacks.
He rubbed his palms together while he figured the best way to get
the words out.

"Would you think about changing the lyrics?" he asked tepidly. She
was in her stage clothes, a pair of candy-red pants, a denim shirt, and
high black heels, fixing her own makeup.

"Those are the lyrics," Kacey said plainly. "This is what it sounds like. I'm really uncomfortable changing it."

Fount shrugged and rested his case there. He didn't see any value in pushing Kacey to think any differently, because why bother? This is what was working, anyway. He paced the halls outside the green-room, wondering what might happen. He didn't expect much, other than maybe a race in the *Today* show control room to do whatever they could when she hit that word, cutting to commercial or silencing the mic. They were focusing on that word "damn," but "Merry Go 'Round" contained far more assaults on blind faith and organized religion than that alone. The truth was in there, hidden behind pretty and solemn chords.

When it was time to go live, and with her pink rhinestone–encrusted banjo in tow, Kacey walked into the studio and plugged in. The live cameras counted down, and they were rolling. "A lot of new artists would have buckled under that," Fount said. "But not Kacey."

"You're known for being blunt and speaking your mind," *Today* anchor Jason Kennedy, who was hosting the segment, said to Kacey once they started rolling. She smiled. That was true enough, though surely it was supposed to be, for an effective artist?

Kacey cued up the band and started strumming, the studio lights gleaming off the pink rhinestones. It went off smoothly, perfectly, so relaxed that it looked like she'd been doing live television for years, save for the treacherous heels. And when she got to that last line, she sang it just as it was. She said "damn" loud and clear, with no hesitation at all.

No one heard it at home, though. The mic cut out, her mouth moving with no words to be heard. It didn't matter. She wasn't going to change a thing, and everyone else would simply have to bend and twist in her way.

"Where my gays at?" Kacey shouted from the stage at the Bowery Ballroom, where the only chance her mic would go out would be if an overexcited fan accidentally dumped a few beers on the control board. It was the encore for her show that kicked off her "Same Trailer Different Tour" run in September. Opening things up in Manhattan, with Brandy Clark in tow, made sense: it's where she first garnered the interest of Perez Hilton, and where she firmly established that she had no plans to cater to The Way Things Are Always Done in Nashville, anyway. Kacey had already been speaking freely to media about where exactly she felt she stood in the Music Row landscape, which appealed to East Coasters who loved the sound of banjo and steel guitar but didn't quite love the idea that who they are—liberal, gay, trans, anything non-Christian white—wasn't part of the accepted model of what the genre likes to present. If it wasn't enough of a signal, Perez was watching from the balcony, intermittently taping segments on his phone.

Brandy opening the show was a double down on this reassurance: this is a country concert, but you're safe here. She was still trying to find a niche where she could speak freely about her identity without having to be tokenized by it, a balance that is infinitely hard to achieve in a place where an understanding of sexuality is that it's supposed to be repressed or perhaps turned into some sort of commodity. Like Kacey and Maren, she was sometimes unsure if her destiny was as an artist or just behind-the-scenes songwriter, but her voice had propelled her above and beyond any reasonable doubt, and her debut album due that October, *12 Stories*, was so unconscionably good that it seemed as though there was no denying her potential onstage. For Kacey, she had become an invaluable partner and a key to opening up the genre to the queer experience in an authentic way, moving it from the fringes and into the mainstream.

That opening gig had not even been a sure thing for Brandy—it was a one-off, and she hopped on the bus with Kacey from Nashville, which broke down along the way, grabbing a hotel room in Chinatown. It felt like a moment to Brandy, just something brewing strong. "I was just blown away by the New York audience," Brandy said, who watched Kacey's set after her own from the balcony, surrounded by the local press. "I thought, man, this is gonna be huge."

Chely Wright had also found solace in New York. While her personal sense of freedom had never been better, her place in the Nashville country community was all but gone. She had moved to the city with her wife and had two sons, and was living a parallel existence away from the Music Row ecosystem. It had hurt too much to stay, even though a coalition had been forming in her wake with voices like Brandy's.

This was in the early stages of what Hunter Kelly, who launched a show called *Proud Radio* on Apple Music in 2020 dedicated to songs from LGBTQIA+ artists in the genre, once jokingly called the "Nashville Gay Mafia," which included Kacey's manager, Jason Owen, Shane McAnally, and other artists, writers, executives, and managers in town who were finding strength in numbers together. Though there was a small contingent of openly gay people on Music Row, and a much bigger number who were not able to comfortably live their lives publicly, these men found potency, and some safety, in weathering the often oppressive environment as a team. Hunter was just one who gravitated toward the women of country music: Kacey, but more specifically the "divas" like Reba and the Judds, because they represented a way to subvert the masculinity that the rest of the genre was most interested in peddling. And "authenticity" in country music so often served as a near antonym for queerness (thinking back to that Michael Ray song and his "real men"), something that Dr. Nadine Hubbs explores in her book *Rednecks, Queers, and Country Music*.

"Women are our mouthpieces," Hunter said. "Not in that we are telling them what to say, but that they are what we, the gay people in town, want to see. If we don't have diversity of voices, it doesn't really feel like a place for us gay men. And for us to even have a chance to have gay artists on the radio." Hunter shared an office space with Jason at the time, working at ABC Radio as a reporter and host, so he had the opportunity to see how Kacey moved around in her career through his eyes in real neighborly fashion. "She just didn't bend over backwards," Hunter said. "She called stuff out, and that was new."

It helped to have someone like Jason Owen in her corner, who had been an instrumental part of Shania Twain's career as well. Jason knew how to navigate outside the walls of country music if he needed to, and how to make the world conform to the talent, not the other way around. "Jason gave her the space to develop, and not feel the pressure," Hunter said. He was also supportive rather than discouraging, when she told him how she wanted to embrace and not shun some progressive ideals. Kacey had even made it part of her press plan—though she and Fount were picky about her media interviews, being inclusive of queer press was an easy yes. They turned down classic Nashville outlets, like *Country Weekly*, press opportunities that any musician in the genre would be programmed to do out of the gate, on instinct, and booked up publications like *Out*. Not only was she giving space to those corners of the world, she was chasing it herself—no one in the mainstream had done that before, short of Dolly Parton.

"I'm not really into giving my favorite recipes or my favorite Mother's Day memory," Kacey told Fount at the time. "I really want everything I do to be about my songwriting and music, I don't want to do anything that ventures away from it." When Fount went on to work with Maren a few years later, the same pattern emerged: it had to be about the music first. Fount's response to both? "Yes, ma'am. We should keep it about the music, because you are different."

Kacey's first roommate out of high school had been gay, and though Golden was a small town, her parents never raised her to think of anyone as more or less deserving of love or the right to it. She saw the pain it caused when her friend had to hide that part of himself, like so many young kids growing up in America had gotten used to, sometimes dangerously so. "That really opened me up to a different opinion," Kacey told *American Songwriter*. "It bothers me that because of religion this subject is taboo. People are driven by the same emotions, to love and want to be loved. The younger generation needs to know that it's okay."

That all kicked "Follow Your Arrow" into high gear, the anthem she wrote with Shane and Brandy, and the anthem she was going to close the show with that night. "I'm not gonna say it's not from some personal experience," Kacey said to *Pride Source* about the song, written at a retreat in Texas with lots of tequila and plenty of weed, "but we were writing it and with the 'kiss lots of boys' part I said, 'I wish, because of the nature of the song, we could just say "or kiss lots of girls,"' and Shane was like, 'Why can't we?'"

Writing a song about a gay embrace just felt natural. And needed. "It never happens and I'm sick of it. It's ridiculous," Kacey had said about the lack of queer representation in country music—in lyrics, artists, or otherwise. "Whether or not you agree with gay marriage or the fact that people don't choose to be gay, we share the same emotions, needs, and wants. I just think that everyone should be included in that. It's definitely time."

It had always been women in country music who were the most visible allies, after all, with the exception of Little Big Town's "Girl Crush" (whose bandmembers were half men) and Garth Brooks, whose song, "We Shall Be Free," cowritten with Stephanie Davis after the 1992 Los Angeles riots, sang about all Americans being free to love anyone they choose—as with the Chicks, the song received a substantial airplay ban, proving that not even the genre's biggest star was immune to censorship when speaking out against extreme conservative ideals. LeAnn Rimes, too, had worked vigorously on LGBTQIA+ rights, to the point she'd go on to be honored by multiple gay rights organizations (a point that didn't gain her any friends in conservative Nashville, already eager to find ways to expunge her from the community). "Is not a political thing for me," LeAnn said, "but much more about humanity and feeling like we should be able to love who we want to love. I was always told not to have an opinion about anything because if people don't like it, they won't buy your album."

Chely Wright signing photos and greeting fans at Fan Fair in 1996. *(Photo by Debra Liebig)*

Mickey Guyton posing with her grandmother, Mary Roddy, who helped spark her love for country music. *(Photo courtesy of Mickey Guyton)*

LeAnn Rimes, one of the biggest inspirations for this generation of female country artists and one of the genre's all-time talents, belting a song. *(Photo courtesy of LeAnn Rimes)*

Miranda Lambert performing in 2009 at the Stagecoach festival. Her success on her own terms was a huge influence for women like Maren Morris, Kacey Musgraves, and Mickey Guyton. *(Photo by Whitney Pastorek)*

Patty Griffin playing a music festival. Kacey, Maren, Mickey, Miranda, the Chicks, Taylor Swift, and Rissi Palmer were all inspired by her songs or covered them. *(Photo by Whitney Pastorek)*

Maren rehearsing in Brooklyn for the 2012 New Music Seminar, where she won the Artist on the Verge contest. Taylor Tatsch, Maren's early bandmate and collaborator, took the photo. *(Photo by Taylor Tatsch)*

Mindy Smith performing. Her album *Stupid Love* was a seminal influence on many women in both Americana and country. *(CC BY 2.0/Janet Dancer)*

Kacey, Carly Pearce, Elice Cuff, and Kree Harrison posing in the Hotel Villa days. *(Photo courtesy of Elice Cuff)*

(Above) Natalie Osborne, Kree, and Elice with Kacey on tour as she opened stadiums for Kenny Chesney. *(Photo courtesy of Elice Cuff)*

(Right) Kacey giving a thumbs-up to her publicist, Fount Lynch, before taping a TV appearance at Austin City Limits. *(Photo by Fount Lynch)*

Mickey opening up for Brad Paisley at the Xfinity Theatre in Hartford, Connecticut. *(Photo by Sean St. Jean for The Country Scene)*

Leslie Fram and Brandy Clark celebrating Brandy's album *12 Stories*. *(Photo courtesy of Leslie Fram)*

Ian Fitchuk, Abe Stoklasa, and Maren at a bar in East Nashville, talking about songwriting. *(Photo courtesy of Abe Stoklasa)*

Margo Price, playing Nashville club 3rd and Lindsley in 2016. Her debut album, *Midwest Farmer's Daughter*, had come out that March, but country radio ignored it despite massive critical acclaim. *(Photo by Jordan O'Donnell)*

The Chicks performing "Goodbye Earl" on tour in 2016, in front of a graphic of Donald Trump with devil horns. Years after their country music expulsion for speaking out about the Iraq war, they were still refusing to shut up and sing. *(Photo by Meghan Stabler)*

Mickey performing at CMA Fest in Nashville in 2016. Despite a glowing reception to her set, country radio still didn't respond to her singles. *(Photo by Lorie Liebig)*

Kacey, Shane McAnally, and Brandy Clark after their pivotal, historic moment: winning Song of the Year at the CMA Awards for "Follow Your Arrow." *(CC BY-ND ABC/Image Group LA)*

Kacey and the author's son, Stone, at a performance promoting *A Very Kacey Christmas* at Grimey's. The record shop, now located in East Nashville, is a center of the town's creative community. *(Photo courtesy of the author)*

ʳoud Radio's Hunter Kelly and acey after a media roundtable scussing her Grammy-winning bum *Golden Hour. (Photo ʲurtesy of Hunter Kelly)*

(Above) Maren popping in to sing "Greener Pastures" with Brothers Osborne at the Ryman Auditorium. (Photo by Jordan O'Donnell)

(Right) Tracy Gershon and Brandi Carlile (in white) embracing, celebrating the success of Brandi's album By the Way, I Forgive You. (Photo courtesy of Tracy Gershon)

Brandi Carlile and producer Dave Cobb at the piano in RCA Studio A during the recording sessions for the Highwomen's debut record. (Photo by Alysse Gafkjen)

Yola, Maren, and Sheryl Crow work out arrangements for a High-women song while Jason Isbell takes a supporting role on acoustic guitar. *(Photo by Alysse Gafkjen)*

Tanya Tucker embraces Loretta Lynn at Loretta's birthday celebration at Bridgestone Arena. *(Photo by Alysse Gafkjen)*

The Pistol Annies (Ashley Monroe, Miranda Lambert, and Angaleena Presley) pose with the Highwomen backstage at Loretta's birthday concert. *(Photo by Alysse Gafkjen)*

Mickey poses with two of her most valuable collaborators, Karen Kosowski and Victoria Banks. *(Photo courtesy of Karen Kosowski)*

Executive Producer of Newport Folk Festival, Jay Sweet, and Brandi embrace at the end of the festival weekend. Jay had charged Brandi with a mission to bring more women to the stage. *(Photo by Nina Westervelt)*

Maren, Yola, Amanda Shires, Brandi Carlile, and Natalie Hemby onstage for the Highwomen's debut at Newport Folk Festival. *(Photo by Catherine Powell)*

Our Native Daughters (Rhiannon Giddens, Leyla McCalla, Allison Russell, and Amythyst Kiah) showing off their jean jackets at Newport Folk, where they gave a transformative performance. *(Photo by Nina Westervelt)*

Amanda, Jason Isbell, and their daughter, Mercy, who helped inspire Amanda to create the Highwomen, onstage at Newport Folk Festival. *(Photo by Catherine Powell)*

The author's daughter, Dylan, in front of a Highwomen mural at Grimey's. *(Photo courtesy of the author)*

(Below) LeAnn Rimes performing at the Ryman in 2019. *(Photo courtesy of LeAnn Rimes)*

Margo Price backstage at a benefit for the March 2020 Nashville tornado. It was one of the very last shows in the city before everything shut down due to the COVID-19 pandemic. *(Photo by Catherine Powell)*

Rissi Palmer recording her Apple Radio show, *Color Me Country*, which helped spur a movement to rethink and rewrite the past, present, and future of country music. *(Photo by Bryan Stypmann)*

Chaka Khan leads Allison Russell, Adia Victoria, Yola, Amythyst Kiah, and many more at Newport Folk 2021, where Allison curated a stage called Once and Future Sounds: Roots and Revolution. *(Photo by Sachyn Mital)*

Reyna Roberts, one of country's newest stars and part of a new generation of artists who finally are seeing themselves in country music, at the piano. *(Photo by Alyssa Donyae)*

Brittney Spencer opening up for Jason Isbell in 2021. Brittney's career exploded when she released a cover of the Highwomen's "Crowded Table" on Twitter during the early days of the pandemic. *(Photo by Catherine Powell)*

Mickey Guyton opening for Jason Isbell at the Ryman, full circle after debuting her song "What Are You Gonna Tell Her" in the same spot during CRS in February 2020. *(Photo by Catherine Powell)*

Miranda had become a subtle breed of ally with "All Kinds of Kinds" on 2011's *Four the Record*, inspired by seeing the struggles her own brother, who is gay, had gone through. Dolly Parton surely, and Carrie Underwood would eventually tiptoe around it herself, dangerous waters for someone so beloved by the genre's Christian conservatives. Maren followed an equally passionate path, and eventually Mickey would be instrumental in underscoring how deep the connection between Black and queer artists in country radio truly was: no one can be free, after all, until everyone is free. But there would be absolutely no question on what side of the fence Kacey was on. She knew that this wasn't just a matter of gaining fans but helping to make people feel that finally country music was a place where they could see a little bit of themselves. It was, as Chely always said, about saving lives.

Kelly McCartney, Apple Radio host as well as a longtime journalist and activist for a more diverse and real-world reflective roots music base, felt a shift with what Kacey was bringing to the table. "I think it was important," she said. "Because I think allies and accomplices and coconspirators are absolutely vital. She had to stick a foot in the door as a straight white woman and say it's cool: love is love."

Over the next year, the tide started to change: Chely's Kickstarter, to make her comeback album, raised over $250,000, breaking records. Ty Herndon, who had some successful hits in the nineties but never fully realized his career after some difficult personal hurdles, came out to *People* in 2014, followed hours later by Billy Gilman.

Though some, like Hunter, had found that bit of recognition in the divas, there had not yet been such a strong, and young, country force willing to put it on the line for them from within the mainstream. And there, in New York City at Bowery Ballroom, was a living and breathing one right onstage, and one as casually subversive—and straight—as this one. There wasn't much flair, just Kacey in black jeans, an olive-gray tank top, and sneakers—around her wrist, a bracelet of silver spikes. Her stage set had been taken up a notch since the last run as an opening act, with giant HEY YEAH letters (plucked from the lyrics of "Follow Your Arrow") hanging above her head. There was tequila poured, glasses raised. New York City is always a place of freedom but on that night, it felt more free than usual. It felt like the world was opening up to some in a way that hadn't been afforded yet, doors swinging open that they thought had always been cemented shut.

She played "Rainbow," the song that would later become *Golden Hour*'s breakout anthem for the broken-down, though the guitar would be replaced by piano, it carried the same solemn weight it would later develop in Sheryl Crow's home studio. Kacey had written the song with Natalie Hemby and Shane, and she wasn't afraid to try it out on the road. "I was going through just some weird stuff at home," Natalie said. "And we were just all having a hard time, and so we wrote 'Rainbow.'" Kacey shelved the song for several albums until it appeared on *Golden Hour*—the timing just hadn't been right, but it filled that room with a sliver of love and hope. Even in the gentle, unknown moments, the audience stayed captive, resisting the urge to duck outside the venue walls for a cigarette or gasp of air.

"Follow Your Arrow" came at the end, in the encore, and though the song had not been released as a single yet, the audience was already fully engaged and singing along. Somehow this woman from a small town in Texas had managed to create an environment for jaded New Yorkers; those New Yorkers who were sometimes programmed so strongly to hate everything that country music stands for and taught that it was only pop or hip-hop or rock where they could find something to relate to. But here it was, in simple clothing, with a steel guitar.

Chris Payne, a journalist in New York who worked for *Billboard* at the time, attended the show with a friend—he remembers trying to push his way through the crowd to get to the middle of the venue floor, where he might be able to get a good view. "We were just so tightly packed," he said. "People seemed to really want to get close to the stage. You could read the room that people were really psyched to see a country artist getting popular while singing songs about tearing down binaries of attraction, like how it's not a big deal to do drugs. I think a lot of people like me and other New Yorkers had gotten a lot of stereotypes about popular country over the years, and how culturally conservative the country music industry was."

The city in 2013 was already running more counter than ever to what was brewing from the likes of Florida Georgia Line and bro country—references to drugs, girls kissing girls or boys kissing boys or any element of a normal, inclusive life that country music might have viewed as "counterculture" was just a part of any given night. So when Kacey arrived, blending all of these worlds, "they were ready to cheer her on," Chris Payne said. "It's the first new country album I can remember listening to. *Same Trailer* changed me. A progressive voice in mainstream country was missing."

They were clearly ready at the Bowery Ballroom, which had sold out with ticket scalpers down the block. This wasn't supposed to be what they had been conditioned to expect of country, all redneck stereotypes and an image of post-9/11 conservatism that stuck deeply in the hearts and minds of New Yorkers who still can't look at a plane in the sky without heart palpitations. It was a genre that seemed to take as little pains to understand them as they took to understand it.

In January of 2013, New York had also crossed an important milestone in its country-ness: the launch of Nash 94.7, the city's first exclusively country station in seventeen years, since 1996. The lack of a local station had been a frustration for many, and a point of division: Would New York audiences embrace the genre beyond occasional kitsch? The subject had come up many times before to varying degrees of success and influence, especially after the CMA hosted their awards show in town. It even spurred entire examinations in trade publications like *Billboard* Radio Monitor: "Ain't no dang country radio station in New York City," Ken Tucker wrote in 2004. "I can't believe there is still not a full-signal station in New York," the radio consultant Ed Salamon told the magazine. "What a huge missed opportunity." The station would ultimately go off-air in 2021.

It was—telling New Yorkers that there wasn't an appetite for country music reinforced the thinking that city folks shouldn't actually like that redneck shit, because it was just that: redneck shit. But New Yorkers don't just grow out of the concrete, they come from everywhere, dirt, corn, and all, and the rest of them had just become obsessed enough with the show *Nashville* to finally play along. The growing love for Kacey was proof that there were scores of dormant country fans dotted among the masses, who spun Reba in secret on their morning commute, who perked up at an errant lick of telecaster among the usual soundtracks. Their cowboy hats were metaphorical, but they were still on their heads like hidden halos.

Kacey, surely, was different, and that was showing in the increasing amount of New York (and Los Angeles)–based press that was starting to flow in, and a massive *New York Times* magazine piece had landed the week of the *Today* show appearance. This wasn't the sort of stuff that always made its way to the heartland, but the piece, accompanied by photos that found Kacey in a gemstone-blue high-fashion Proenza Schouler dress styled by renowned magazine go-to Kathryn Typaldos, one of the most coveted stylists in the business, was sure to raise the antennae of the not easily persuaded blue state population.

Journalist Carlo Rotella had followed Kacey on the road and down to Nashville for a stint for the *Times* magazine piece. At the time, Kacey was thinking about what the next single would be, and was absolutely stuck on "Follow Your Arrow." It wasn't the one that was "testing" the best (that was "Blowin' Smoke"), but her gut hadn't failed her before. These kinds of sweeping stories in publications like the *New York Times* were never easy to come by, but the interest in Kacey felt authentic, and new. "If you had a 615 area code you had a strike against you," Fount said. Cracking through that credibility wall of "coastal" media didn't come without work, and there were very few artists who passed the mold—Miranda just barely, and Eric Church among them. But it was an uphill battle, even for a publicist skilled in navigating those waters closely. It was different for Kacey, because she was different.

"You're already uncool coming from Nashville, so you had to prove why you were cool," said Fount. "At that time, Nashville was just starting to become a hot city—not 'hot' yet, but at the forefront of that. But if you are a critic in New York, you've already made up your mind about what you thought about country music. We really had to break down those walls with Kacey, and we did that, and I think that opened the doors to a lot of other artists, male and female. I think once we started saying, 'Hey, you may not like mainstream country music, but you're gonna love Kacey Musgraves,' and we delivered on that promise, then we had their attention. They would trust us from that point on." Gaining that trust from someone like Carlo Rotella was the doorstop they were looking for, and would eventually open up a new world to artists like Margo Price and Sturgill Simpson to capitalize on that truth.

"She wanted it to be 'Follow Your Arrow' and they didn't," Carlo remembered of a conversation with Kacey about what single might come next. "There's often a way in which an artist might just appeal to the person writing the profile and say, 'Oh you know, I love this song, I am really passionate about the idea in the song,' and she did all that. But she also said, 'Look, I think it's actually a better strategy to offend everybody you're going to offend right away, and get it over with, and then announce to all those other people who might be interested that you're out there and that you're different.' The way she was able to see it not just as a matter of passion, or politics, but also as just more of a sophisticated move to play the long game and do the controversial thing first." It worked, clearly. The reception to the album proved to be bigger than anyone predicted, and she didn't ask permission once.

Ashley Monroe wasn't asking permission, either. A few months before she'd join back with Miranda and Angaleena Presley for their second Pistol Annies record, she made a solo offering of her own.

Like a Rose came out the same month as *Same Trailer Different Park*, and despite few similarities other than genre and gender, the media went to great pains to categorize them together at any possible chance. Many reviews found them packaged as a twosome, but short of subject matter that looked deeply into the motivations of small-town life, this was often unfair and inaccurate. Ashley suffered for it in the early press—"we've already covered Kacey Musgraves," they'd say, pitting woman against woman in the eternal battle we've all come to know well. A *Spin* interview that was supposed to be about Ashley—and awarded her album a 9 out of 10 rating—ended being equally about Kacey (they both sing about sin and cigarettes!). Produced by Vince Gill, *Like a Rose* was country as country could be, twangy and rich and full of vibrant tales, that voice that had stopped Jack White in his tracks, so much so that he made note of her name pulled over on the side of the highway after hearing her on the (independent) radio station.

"I actually pulled over, because I was going into a shop but I was like, 'I gotta wait and hear what this girl's name is, because I really love her voice,'" White had said. "And they finally said Ashley Monroe, so I tried to remember that."

In some spaces, Ashley's album was reviewed as even more breakthrough than Kacey's: Ashley sang of "Weed Instead of Roses" and sultry moments stolen. There was a mature sensuality to it, and the *Washington Post* said it was "the first great album of the year." And not just great country album, great *album*. "Time to scrub that 'I like all kinds of music, except country' line off your OkCupid profile," critic Chris Richards wrote. Not only that: "it's the first in a cascade of discs from female country singers plotting to dominate annual best-of lists eight months down the road." He was right about that: add Brandy's *12 Stories* to the mix, and the quality work of country music was almost exclusively dedicated to women. These songs created "essential tension that helps define the genre."

What these albums all were rooted in was tradition while investing in a new future—*12 Stories* for Brandy was bringing back to life a dream that she had long let go of. She'd later see the same path emerge when she tried to push singles to country radio—despite a Best New Artist Grammy nomination in 2015 and many other accolades, the airwaves didn't budge. "You can keep knocking on this door that's not opening," said Brandy. "Or you can just walk through others that are." By the time she got to 2020's *Your Life Is a Record*, she stopped trying to play in country radio's waters altogether, marketing the album more toward Americana. Country radio could, after all, make space for allies on occasion, but not quite enough room for queer people themselves.

The uniter of all these albums, Miranda told the *Boot*, was "Truth. Kacey writes about trailer parks, we write about trailer parks. Ashley sings about weed and roses. It's like, just lay it out and maybe people will like it. And people do. They feel like it's not a fantasy world."

Like a Rose and *Same Trailer Different Park* did group together sensibly in one way, though, as albums from artists who had clearly departed on paths independent of the classic Music Row machinery while never trying to fully subvert it—they shipped songs to country radio, they followed the framework when it suited them. Like Ashley, Kacey played by plenty of the time-honored traditions when she found they fit: she made her Opry debut in a pair of white cowboy boots and a lace dress, hit the road with Little Big Town (whose singer, Karen Fairchild, had been a fierce leader for women within Nashville), Kip Moore, and Lady A while also launching that same tour that began in New York. And the sales were great, better than anyone could have hoped for.

The headlines meant well. They did. "Kacey Musgraves, Pistol Annies Prove Country Girls Rule 2013" was how the *Boot* put it. But these were not just women's albums, they were the best albums. The hyper-categorizing was creating problems of its own.

To the shock of no one, this was translating poorly to the radio programmers. Kacey had been making the radio rounds, and it hadn't been going well—she wasn't keen on the usual instructions to smile nice and let the program directors ogle you in favor of putting a single into rotation. One particularly bad interaction came with a visit to New Country 93.1, and the host, who goes by "Broadway," would not stop making comments about her legs (her thighs, to be specific). He kept talking about them even as Kacey looked visibly uncomfortable, asking to touch them, even taking to Twitter to complain, with a "frowny face," that Kacey had called him "creepy." She was being kind: he doubled down on social media later with photos and specifics, including an analysis of the "Tennessee-shaped birthmark" on her thigh. He received no penalty or even a flag for his actions; this was just part of how things were done and how men were expected to talk and interact with any young woman who came through their doors under the guise of "keeping it fun." Miranda had felt this, too, while starting out, who, despite needing the boost at radio, never had any interest in being an object to be admired, unless it was the songs themselves getting the admiration. Rissi remembers going to a station and having programmers crack jokes about the size of her breasts, while Chely "had one radio guy leave a message on my phone about the state of his erect penis." Katie Armiger remembered being asked when she was going to be "legal" while touring radio stations under the age of eighteen.

A few months later Kacey would appear on *The Bobby Bones Show*, and the two were not a match for gregarious morning programming like he'd hoped. Notoriously arrogant, Bobby held immense power in the world of country radio and beyond, well before he became a household name through his role on *American Idol* as a "mentor." A stop at the *Bones* show is a must for total and complete stardom, one that even legacy-level artists endure with a forced smile. He was, and is, not someone whom anyone hopeful of a future in radio would want to piss off, but that did not hold Kacey back from talking about how his interaction had led her to develop a reputation: According to Kacey, Bobby had edited the conversation to play into the mythos that had been building about Kacey, she would say, which was that she was "cold" and unapproachable by making it seem that her answers to his questions were short and dismissive—something that DJs would later claim was part of the reason they failed to "connect" with her music.

Since when does connectivity have anything to do with radio success? Everything, when it comes to country. "Kacey is not going to be Miss Bubbly but she is very authentic and real," said CMT's Leslie Fram, reflecting on the Bobby Bones incident. "That's when I knew she was just going to be Kacey Musgraves, take it or leave it."

Radio tour was never a thing that Kacey expected to like—everyone hears the warnings—but the freedom of DJs like "Broadway" to fully unleash at will on female artists who came through their doors is a timeworn foundation of the country music industry and was continuing to grow rampant and unchecked. Maybe they felt they had permission: 2013 was dominated by those songs from men, dominated by the party, and by male singers who were up for absolutely anything on their station visits. And if you could go hang out at a strip club with a famous male country star, why couldn't you make crude comments about Kacey Musgraves's legs? Country music could somehow simultaneously be the genre fearful about saying the word "damn" on the radio but support a culture where making a comment about a woman's body wasn't just part of the program, it was encouraged.

"The artist is supposed to do a lot for country radio, well above any other format," said Leslie. "It's just what is expected. I understand it's great to build relationships, but that's just not how it is in any other formats. Artists are programmed to thank country radio. You are expected to do a lot of free radio shows. I came from a format where people did do free shows, but the difference is we played the music, not buried it."

Miranda always told a story about the first time she went on radio tour, and she and her reps had to take a local program director out to dinner. He ordered a five-hundred-dollar bottle of wine, a bill she would have to foot out of her advance, and all she could do was sit there and smile. This business of payola lite had been going on for ages, and for the women trying to be heard, it made things often impossible. It might not have been actual dollars used to bribe for radio spins—the technical and legal definition of payola, which has been outlawed since 1960—but favors and backstage passes and free shows and even Super Bowl tickets sometimes held an even stronger currency, as they carried an exclusivity and cachet that money couldn't buy but fame sure could touch. There were the nights out at strip clubs, and the unwanted glances—or more—that sometimes came along. "She really did not cater to sucking up to radio people," says Luke Laird. "There were times where I was like, 'Come on, Kacey.'"

And though it had not been made public yet, it was Taylor Swift who would eventually help draw a greater awareness to just how sinister and empowered some of these radio programmers could be. It was June 2013, and Taylor was making a usual stop for meet and greets backstage on her *Red* world tour—one of the most painful parts of the process, if you ask most artists, especially female ones. Radio programmers often love to come to shows and stock up on the free snacks and booze, padding around with a VIP pass and an ego pumped with gratis bourbon. If you dropped down from space, you'd think the DJs were the celebrities and not the actual artist performing, based on the level of royal treatment that they were accustomed to getting, drunk on access to fame.

Taylor was doing her usual photo line backstage at a show in Denver, posing with DJs and program directors one by one, smiling dutifully. She had always been notoriously gracious, not only agreeing to photos but sending handwritten thank-you notes and gifts to her supporters in country radio—she knew how tenuous that relationship and line could be, and how easily it could crumble if you broke order.

When David Mueller, a DJ for Denver's KYGO at the time, had his turn, he didn't just cozy next to Taylor or put his arm around her in the usual, but already borderline, custom. Instead he, according to

Taylor's testimony, grabbed her "bare ass." There's a photo to back it up, and Mueller's hand appears to be in the exact suspicious place that she had claimed it.

Taylor told her security team what happened, and Mueller would soon be fired. But he wasn't done with her, suing her for defamation two years later—she sued back for $1. Taylor finished up the Red Tour, but it was her last foray for years in the world of country music. She was done. In 2017 after the story became public, *Time* magazine would name the "Silence Breakers" as Person of the Year, with Taylor among them. "I figured that if he would be brazen enough to assault me under these risky circumstances," she told the magazine, "imagine what he might do to a vulnerable, young artist if given the chance."

Taylor's story was one of many stories owned by women who didn't have the ability to make their experiences public. Women in front of whom men had exposed themselves at CRS, or asked for them to sit on their lap, kiss their cheek, flirt. "It's accepted behavior, so it's protected behavior," one major-label female artist said. "I wish I could be like, 'Hey, everybody that touched my ass during a radio tour, I am calling you out.'" A former female label executive described it to *Rolling Stone* as a "culture of acceptance. I've seen it happen a million times, and everyone else in the room has to play along because they don't want to offend the artist or the radio station. You know that's affecting the lack of artists that are female [on the radio]. If they can't make radio gatekeepers happy, they don't get a spin. It's a direct correlation."

"I don't want to be at the mercy of country radio," Kacey told the *Guardian* in August 2013. With stories like that, who could blame her?

By November 2013, Kacey was up for several CMA Awards, and she had prepared a very non-CMA type of performance: she would play "Follow Your Arrow" in a bright yellow dress, in front of a display of neon arrows pointing left, right, and back again. The censors ended up muting some of the words about rolling a joint, though they did manage to leave in mentions of crack, inexplicably. "I think it's super awesome that country music has been so supportive of [my] message," Kacey said backstage after winning Best New Artist, a sign that while radio might not have approved, she had the respect, at least, of the voting body. "I mean the fans, too. I think people are just really ready for a message that's just encouraging of all kinds."

Ty Herndon sure was, and remembers sitting in the audience and watching her play the song onstage, and being moved nearly to tears—this would have been a time for Kacey, trying to make a good impression at her first industry awards, to play it nice and safe. Kacey, instead, decided to go with "Follow Your Arrow," and leaned straight into it.

Ty, whose last number one hit was "It Must Be Love" in 1998, was still closeted and had come to the event with his (still secret) boyfriend, Matt—though he was thinking about finally telling his truth in public, which he would in 2014, about a year after this performance. He remembered looking up at Kacey and having a hard time believing what he was seeing, shuffling in his seat like a popcorn kernel dancing closely to the pan and ready to explode. This was country music, singing of weed and gay love and free sex, and in a track cowritten with a gay man, Shane, and a lesbian, Brandy? Could it be? That wasn't Ty's world, the world that sent him into addiction and immeasurable pain trying to hide his truth. For these three minutes, from the spikes of Kacey's heels to the tip of her guitar, it was something different.

"The stage was lit up like a Pride festival," he said. "I thought, 'Wow, welcome to 2013.' I was just like, 'Holy cow.' I was so proud of her and I was also like, 'My God, look at those shoes! Because I am a cowboy, but I also appreciate beauty. And bravery."

It signaled something even more profound, though. Something far more life-changing than that.

"I turned to Matt and said, 'I'm going to be okay.'"

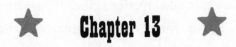

Chapter 13

FAITH IN THE HEARTLAND

It was just another write really—"a done by one," as they call them—when Maren sat down with Maggie Chapman and Dan Layus, member of the band Augustana, who had moved to Nashville just short of the new year. A little bit Sheryl Crow, a little bit Dolly Parton, it was called "Loose Change," and they demoed it in the first few weeks of 2014. Dan, like Maren, was pretty fresh to town and was trying to find a way and a place to make his point of view fit in among the Music Row culture. "I was a pop-rock guy trying to fit in," he said, adding with a laugh: "Then you realize you are completely out of your league."

Dan was part of a contingent of musical folks who moved to Nashville in the early 2010s in search of cheaper rent, more land, and a break from the pressures of L.A. or New York—but folks who existed outside the usual country realm. Playing in Augustana, a band known for their 2005 hit "Boston," Dan hadn't exactly set himself up for a path in country music songwriting, but like Chicks cowriter Dan Wilson before him, and other pop-rock band members turned Music Row hot commodities, he saw Nashville as a place where he could hone his chops while being surrounded at all times by creative people without some of the traditional traps. He lived in the suburb of Franklin, Tennessee, with his wife and four kids, but he still talked faster and with more gusto than anyone else in town, like he was still trying to get his order in at an L.A. bar.

Maren was an early writing matchup, but Dan was instantly stunned by the concepts and creative agility that surrounded her—she was at once proficient in the bones of country construction and open as can be to genre experimentation and play, tradition and futurism all in one voice. And it was easy—so easy, the way the lyrics just rolled out onto the page and her voice dipped through, effortless and calm but full of fury.

"She was just an unstoppable force," Dan said, "just that energy. Something in that time and place was really fresh." A year or so later Dan would find Augustana opening for One Direction at the O2 Arena in London, and he ran into an executive from Sony who had just signed a few acts he was excited about—one of them ended up being Maren Morris. "To roll into a room where people were looking for a song that had a different dimension, and be able to have one of my first sessions be 'Loose Change,' it was amazing. And then have that be born to the public so many years later," he said.

Maren posted "Loose Change" to her ReverbNation page once they had a solid demo, and though it became a song that helped get her some early recognition, it didn't even end up making her first record. Dan didn't think much of it until 2019, when he heard that the Highwomen had cut it for their debut record, *The Highwomen*. Producer Dave Cobb had found it when they were sifting through some demos to see if any of Maren's early work might make a good candidate, and he loved it right off the bat. When Amanda, Natalie, and Brandi sang harmony on it, and the melody sped up, it became a pithy kiss-off, with Maren's voice approaching Dolly Parton textures, her country warble emerging stronger than ever, those vowels swinging toward twang.

"Every once in a while there are artists and writers that come along that are just going to take you on the ride as long as you don't get in the way, which is hard sometimes," Dan said. "Like for your own pride or your own ego. It's like you want to throw your perspective in but sometimes if there is someone who is going to take you to promised land as a writer, that is the place you want to be no matter how you get there. And she is just one of those people."

Maren had rung in the New Year with friends, and opened up to a 2014 full of writing and touring—from "Loose Change" to the songs that would become *Hero*, working with a producer and writer named Mike Busbee (known to everyone as "busbee"), who had been growing a reputation for working with more pop-oriented stars like Pink and Katy Perry. They had been set up through their publishers to write, but ended up at Lucie Silvas's house at the same jam session, known as a guitar pull—busbee was immediately struck by Maren's voice. They went out to breakfast shortly after, and it was clear that he saw something in her that didn't involve tweaking or shaping her into anything she was not.

"Sometimes, with certain artists in those early days, there's a bit of a thing in there, and you're helping develop it," he said to *Hits Daily Double* 2016. "That wasn't the case with Maren at all. From my perspective, it was like going, 'Hey, do you see that big red dot on your forehead?' It was that clear. For me, it was already there."

Busbee understood Maren, and he got her voice, but he could also push her to go places that she didn't think she was comfortable going vocally. It was an instant creative match, and Maren started going to his house out in Los Angeles to record and write at a little outpost in his backyard that he'd built specifically for both.

She had gotten her first cut with "Last Turn Home," for Tim McGraw (per tradition in town, she went to Target to pick up a shrink-wrapped CD copy with Ryan Hurd, who cowrote it), and spent the remainder of 2014 working with every writer she could, including busbee, laying the bones for what would eventually become the album.

The summer of 2014 was by no means quiet for Kacey, but things had settled into a somewhat predictable pattern on the road with Kenny Chesney, until the award nominations started to roll in. She had taken Elice Cuff on the road, and they would spend their days on the bus laughing, getting stoned, or thinking about where they might get stoned next. Everything sped up when the Grammys were announced: Kacey was up for Best New Artist and for Best Country Song for "Merry Go 'Round," as well as Best Country Album and Best Country Song as a writer of "Mama's Broken Heart."

All eyes were on Kacey as she headed to Los Angeles in January for the big awards. The past year had positioned her, after the CMA Awards in November, as a bit of a black sheep favorite. Country music had a habit of eschewing certain records on radio only to have those same records go on to be rewarded with Grammy recognition—look no further than the Chicks—and this was poised to be no exception.

Luke Laird remembers being spectacularly nervous in the audience, and Kacey was, too—vindication from the world outside country always meant something different. And though it wasn't customary, Kacey wanted Shane and Luke to come up to the stage with her if she went to accept an award, which she did, for Best Country Album. "I remember her saying, because a lot of times the producers don't go up onstage for that," Luke said. "But she told me, 'Hey, if I win, I really want you guys to come up there,' which I thought was really cool. And I just remember them announcing that and us running up to the stage, and just standing there, and I couldn't hear anything she was saying. All I remember is being up there and seeing Jay-Z and Beyoncé in the front row."

That wasn't the only award she took that night. Best Country Song for "Merry Go 'Round" was given during the pre-broadcast, and Cyndi Lauper, who read the winners, botched their names as she opened the envelope: "Kacey McGrath" and "Shane Mick-Nally," though she got Josh Osborne right. Shane turned to Josh and asked, "Well, did we win?" And Josh said with a smile, "Well, I did!"

For Luke, it was an instant lesson. "It can still be success without the radio success," he said. "And it can be a longer and harder road, but in the end, it will be a lot more satisfying. And I think that she probably influenced and inspired a lot of new artists that come into this town and think, 'Hey, you know, Kacey Musgraves can do it. And I can do it, too."

That Grammy opened up her world to new collaborations—with Katy Perry, who had already been a fan and sent those tweets that got the world's attention. Kacey had gone to L.A. the year before with Kate York to watch Kree make her big performance on *American Idol*, and took a stopover to write with Katy while she was in town—Kate laughed in hindsight at the casualness of Kacey going from supporting her friend one moment to writing with one of the biggest pop stars the next. They would take the relationship and collaborations beyond just that writing session, when Katy ended up inviting Kacey along for a tour and a *CMT Crossroads* special with Leslie Fram at the helm.

Something about Katy Perry and Kacey meeting for a *CMT Crossroads* felt wild and perfect all at once—"Follow Your Arrow" had been written with Katy in mind, but she passed on it, thinking it was much better suited for Kacey to keep for herself. The tour and pairing between the two felt unconventional even to those close to her, but Kacey knew how to trust her instincts.

"I remember thinking how mismatched that was, but then when we went to see the show how beautifully what Kacey and Katy were doing at the time blended so well together. And I was like, 'Oh my gosh, she can totally play with the big boys,'" said Stephanie Wright.

Katy Perry's background could have actually led her to Nashville—she was raised a devout Christian with little but gospel music around the house. For some in Music Row, the dichotomy between the "Jesus" tattoo on Katy's wrist and the subject matter was more proof that women could be unpredictable, scary things, ready to pivot in any possible direction at a moment's notice. Growing up in Texas, it wasn't an upbringing that was outside of the familiar for Kacey, where religion becomes a battlefield, and morality, or the appearance of it, is more important than anything.

"We left those worlds, but we kept our compasses," Katy told *Bill-*

board for a dual cover story on both artists, written right around the time of their *CMT Crossroads* show. "I think [Kacey] straddles the line like I straddle the line of appropriateness and still maintaining a sexuality that is healthy and exciting. And it's not all about that. It's about sending inspiring and empowering messages and being a think-for-yourself type of woman."

The authenticity crowd had their feelings about this. It couldn't be her decision, it must have been the label's, forcing her against her will to join forces with a pop star in hopes of some bigger success outside country music. The idea was that women needed to stay fiercely loyal to the genre no matter what, but, at the same time, they needed to keep plugging away when that same genre was repeatedly signaling that there's no place for them in it. For Kacey, it was just playing with the rules the way she always had. But the "traditionalists" weren't too keen on where she was heading. They were confused, in fact.

By November 2015, when Chris Stapleton emerged on the CMA stage with Justin Timberlake and began to build a similar partnership, the reaction was the exact opposite—good on Justin for dipping into his Tennessee roots, and good on Chris Stapleton for seeing a window into bigger mainstream appeal. It was referred to by many critics to be one of the biggest moments in modern country music history.

"I can't imagine doing a *Crossroads* with somebody like a Katy Perry," says CMT's Leslie Fram, who had organized the event for the network. "What I saw in Kacey was total confidence in how she wanted her songs to work. A producer can be in there but the two artists are working it out on their own. I got to see Katy listening to and respecting what Kacey had to say. It was really magical to watch these rehearsals." Leslie flew out to L.A. for the show and noticed that while Kacey had brought a few friends, Katy rolled in in true pop star style: late, massive team and entourage. "That's another huge difference between those worlds," Leslie says, but Kacey, entourage or not, seemed to be able to waft through them both. She had even managed to get the attention of legends like George Strait and Willie Nelson and other pop stars like Harry Styles, who tweeted: *"it's impossible to listen to @kaceymusgraves too much. Don't tell anyone."*

Though the Grammy Awards were the first cherry, the real change came, somehow, with the ACMs and then the CMAs, the most profound of all. Though many country artists find a sort of validation from getting critical acclaim outside the bounds of the genre, Kacey had that from the very beginning. She was more interested in investing in the future than the weight of any personal accolade, and that had to come with the help of the country music community.

First up was the ACM Awards, when she took Album of the Year. "Coming offstage, it was one of the first times I had seen her overwhelmed," said Fount. "She had been happy before, but it was just this overwhelming joy and relief: *they finally get it.* It was almost like this comfort and this peaceful joy that she now had tapped into because the world and the industry had received the album the way she hoped they would. Winning Album of the Year unlocked a different part of her. She was in a moment of just pure joy and it was so cool. Let's soak this in, because moments like this don't always come. God, she was happy."

To add to the joy, Kacey had run into George Strait, who won Entertainer of the Year, in the pressroom—Kacey poked her head in quickly to say, "George, I love you." When George realized it was Kacey, he stopped his interview and said, "I love you, too." "It was Texas," Fount said, "and Texas."

When CMA day finally rolled around, it was the usual sort of spectacle—a tent erected all around the Bridgestone Arena in Nashville to house the massive red carpet, with press lined up trying to steal time from bands coming down the line.

The night had been going well, mostly in accordance with usual CMA standards: goofy jokes, a stage full of mostly white people and a mostly white audience. When Kacey's category, Song of the Year, came up, the room quieted: in Nashville, Song of the Year held the biggest weight of all, and Kacey won, with her name pronounced correctly this time. It's a songwriter award in a land of songwriters—an idea that Vince Gill reaffirmed to Kacey when he grabbed her later and said, "You just won the biggest award you can ever win. I know, I've won them all and this one means the most to me."

The category included Eric Church and Miranda Lambert, and while Kacey was certainly the favorite for "Follow Your Arrow," nothing was predictable, especially when you were the kind of artist who clearly refused to play by the standards and rules of the Music Row ecosystem.

"Do you guys realize what this means for country music?" Kacey said when she made it to the stage to accept the award. She was flanked by Shane and Brandy, and had wanted to make sure they would join her, too, because the most historic part of all was that this was the first time two openly gay people had stood on the CMA stage to collect an award. "I think I can speak for all of us when I say that this award means so much because our genre was built on simple, good songs about real life. And that's what this was," Kacey said. "And it was because of the fans that connected with it who spread it and took it farther than I ever could."

"It was just a huge moment in the pressroom," said Hunter Kelly. "It was the beginning of my work in *Proud Radio*; everything led to that moment. It moved everything forward." If a song about smoking weed and loving who you love could be embraced to this degree by the biggest institution and voting body in the industry, what else was possible? Could actual queer people be the artists up front, and not just allies?

That night Kacey also performed a duet with Loretta Lynn, which provided a crucial point to more conservative fans—this woman might be singing about embracing all walks of life, and the queen of country, Loretta herself, was backing her right up. They sang, of all things, Loretta's "You're Lookin' at Country," her 1971 hit, in complementary rhinestones: country could look like this. Like her.

"When we won, it was shocking," said Shane. "Shocking. Talk about jaw-drop. There have been many times in my life where I thought we would win, but that was not one of them. For Brandy and I standing there thinking, 'Look what just happened' and really believing it could happen for us. Kacey made so much of that possible. She opened more doors than people will ever realize."

He remembers looking out and seeing Keith Urban in the crowd, smiling. "He was just so happy," Shane said, choked up with tears. "He just looked so proud. They were so genuinely happy for us."

The next morning, Brandy Clark got a telegram, of all things, from Faith Hill and Tim McGraw. "It said, 'Congratulations on a historic night in country music,'" Brandy remembered, emotional at the sheer thought of it all. And it was a historic night. Though everyone went back to work as if nothing had changed, there had been a rip in the seam of the Music Row establishment, a ripple of that old "crisis of credibility" coming back to haunt Nashville once again. It wouldn't change things overnight, but it would start to loosen the reins on the types of songs that could be written, the types of voices that could make it through and rise to the point of recognition. Well, everywhere except radio. And for as many people that found solace or hope in its message, it sent panic to some others.

Brandi Carlile was watching, nodding along, getting excited that the genre she loved and left might be breaking a little. "I was like, 'Good.' The queers are influencing and platforming themselves through mouthpieces from people that are palatable and acceptable, and making leeway," said Brandi. "And then soon, we'll be able to say something like that, kiss lots of girls, if that's what you're into, and then we won't be shut out permanently. It's that coming in on someone else's arm, but then staying put when you're in there. And I saw it immediately and saw what they had done and went, Fuck yeah, thank you, Kacey. But well done, Shane and Brandy."

And with that win, suddenly conservative radio was interested—but not in a good way. The song wasn't getting much traction to begin with, even banned in some places, but once those particular talk hosts began to get ahold of it, a similar cycle emerged—a coalition that didn't care about Kacey either way began to care very much. During a Right Wing Watch broadcast, a pastor named Kevin Swanson said that Kacey and "Follow Your Arrow" were "promoting homosexuality." "Let me say this, if she had sang [sic] that thing in a country bar in the 1920s or 1880s in Denver, Colorado, somebody would've called for a rope," he said. "So she's got to promote homosexuality and she's got to promote the abandonment of the traditional church in the same song. That's critical for the dismantling of the Christian faith in the heartland."

The dismantling of faith in the heartland.

Could that be part of these fears? What did Pastor Swanson think about Shania Twain—was she dismantling faith, too? Would Brandy Clark? Not to mention Mickey. Maren would, too, when her clothes were too tight or too short for their liking, her opinions too big. Is that what made years like 2014, when music from men was tame and focused on the girl or the party, so fearful of anything that might be pushing us out of institutionalized norms? "I don't want to knock religion, but it's always knocking me," Kacey sang in a still unreleased song called "John Prine," about smoking a doobie with the songwriting legend.

The world was changing, after all. Not just country—America was only a year away from making marriage equality a right, and it had already passed preliminary rulings in 2013 that took couples all over the country one step closer to being able to experience and share the exact same rights to love and be loved as their straight friends and neighbors. As vice president at the time, Joe Biden was taking an active lead that summer in mobilizing a "global front," according to the Associated Press, on antigay violence and discrimination. "I don't care what your culture is," he told a gathering. "Inhumanity is inhumanity. Prejudice is prejudice is prejudice."

Though he was speaking internationally, many took that mention of "culture" as an attack. The feeling of having a threatened faith and sanctity was nothing new to country music, and the chiding of its biggest stars served as a convenient vector with which to project. Women like the Chicks and LeAnn Rimes had let the genre down, they thought, while men were more efficient at peddling their God-fearing nature. LeAnn committed adultery (pay no attention here to the fact that Jason Aldean did the same and suffered no real consequence). Women like Kacey in country music often had to come with a bit of a caveat—Loretta was still waiting for her man to come home, even if she might pop the dude in the face if he fished for some loving she wasn't in the mood for. Chely Wright had come out only four years earlier—just four. Conservatism was having to come to terms with a world where religion couldn't be used as the same repressive tool it had always been, when same-sex marriage received full and undying support from the American federal government. And country music was its last, most potent hold on popular culture.

"'Follow Your Arrow' is hands down people's favorite off the record," said Kacey to the *Guardian*. "It's the one they instantly recognize or freak out about. Whether or not they like country music, they seem to really like and relate to that song. But even with all of that, and country radio always looking for its next hit, they are still scared of it. Most radio program directors that I talk to say, 'That's my favorite, I wish we could play it.' I'm like, 'Well then, fucking play it!' I just hate that people are scared of it. But I don't want to be begging. . . . It's gonna have its own life regardless, so I don't really want to ask their permission."

When Josh Abbott heard it, a few years after their work together on "Oh, Tonight," he wasn't surprised—it was the Kacey he'd always known. "It goes back to her empathy, and her really just putting a song out there that says, 'I don't care if this goes against traditional sense or what works at mainstream radio," said Josh. "Just, this is the song I want to put out as a young artist to represent who I am and my brand and who I'm about. And she didn't care if it was number one, or top 10. But she wanted stations to play it. Because she wanted the LGBT community to hear it."

"I think it's time," Kacey told the Associated Press, "that a new normal was created."

Mickey was working on songs that could change the culture, too. She had been writing constantly, and the newest one she had come up with was called "A Woman's World." She had written it with Liz Rose and Cory Crowder, and it was edgier than anything that ended up on *Unbreakable*, the EP that she put out at the beginning of the year. Mickey had been working to get in writing rooms ever since she got to Nashville, and the four songs that went into that short collection were expertly sung, if not her truest stories possible.

"Woman's World," though, was different—country as hell, straight out of the nineties female powerhouses. *"They say this town is run by men, well close your eyes you better look again,"* Mickey sang in a punchy, perfect quiver, somewhere between Patty Loveless and Trisha Yearwood, with her unique signatures all over it—Texas twang mixed with pop star prowess.

The label, Mickey remembered, was lukewarm on it. She couldn't understand it. It seemed to check all the boxes.

"This is why I felt like I was horrible," Mickey said. "I couldn't wrap my brain around it."

★ **Chapter 14** ★

YOU SAY TOMATO, I SAY FUCK YOU

In May 2014, Maren tweeted a photo with the caption: "these ladies. Changing the scene." It was her, Lucie Silvas, Kate York, Natalie Hemby, Kacey Musgraves, and Kree Harrison. And there was no doubt about it, they absolutely were—every single one was carving her own unique path through the wilds of Nashville, kicking the door open and leaving it there for one another, from Kacey's monumental night at the CMAs to Maren's inroads as a songwriter.

Kree was taking her time after coming in as runner-up on *Idol*—everyone had told her that the right thing to do would be to immediately release a record, but she needed a moment to regroup herself. Maybe that wasn't the right business move, but she had to do things on her own terms. She had been through enough loss and disappointment that the wall she put around her creative heart was unscalable without ropes, and she kept in there in part to make sure that no one would soil her sense of individual drive, either.

Maren had spent the bulk of the year writing and demoing songs feverishly, and doing the usual songwriter rounds—including one particular round at the Sutler Saloon, where Maren and Kacey played the Wreckers' "Leave the Pieces" with Michelle Branch.

Another was a round at a place in the Gulch area of town with Lilly Hiatt, daughter of John, who is now known as a wildly creative songwriter on the indie/Americana side of the spectrum. It was still possible to see artists from divergent worlds on the same kind of stage (and a pattern that Maren would embrace with the Highwomen, in her partnership with Amanda, Natalie, and Brandi). Lilly remembered being "blown away" by her. The venue, Two Old Hippies, which ended up closing during the pandemic, was one of those singular Nashville places—you could buy a guitar for five grand or a paisley patchwork item suited for the office secret Santa party, not to mention stumble upon a round of future Grammy nominees.

"I told her that her voice sounded like rich chocolate," Lilly said. "Rounds like that are why I have never taken a stance on what qualifies the scene. It's just a songwriter's town."

For all this creative renaissance—the awards, the recognition, the everything—nothing was moving the needle at country radio. It was another dismal year on the charts for anyone except white men, because not only were men dominating what was being played, the subject matter itself had devolved into its own subcategory: women weren't getting spun on country radio, but songs with "girl" in the title, sung by white men, seemed to have no real problem. Almost everyone in the industry recognized that number one songs were rarely some sort of magic, an organic feat that just happened because of eager fans. Number one songs were most often built with promo dollars and budgets: backroom trading and deals between stations and labels helped to boost hits.

The only way to get a country song on the radio as a girl was to be a girl in a country song.

Maddie & Tae, a duo of Madison Marlow and Taylor Dye, had gotten fed up enough that they decided to sing about it: "Girl in a Country Song" was written out of their pure distaste with the predictable cycle of dudes singing about cute blond girls in short shorts, which they were able to harness and reclaim—country music doesn't have a lot of meta-moments while still adoring being self-referential, but this was a duo taking to task the culture of the very songs that country radio banks on, going to number one.

It was a whole odd equation to deconstruct—they were on a label, Big Machine, owned by Scott Borchetta, the place that had first signed Taylor Swift, and were white blond girls criticizing the very idea of fetishizing themselves. They took "Girl in a Country Song" and turned it into a moment for commentary for country music while in the machine and breaking the machine at the same time.

"Thanks for saying what we all want," Maren tweeted.

The song would go to number one, but it would nearly become more famous than the band itself. Maddie & Tae would struggle after that, never reclaiming the kind of success that came along with "Girl in a Country Song," shifting around to different labels, though always being quite good.

And what happened next turned the discussions into downright fury: *Tomato-gate.* "If you want to make ratings in country radio, take females out," Keith Hill told *Country Aircheck*. Keith had previously spoken about the topic that spring at CRS, in a panel called "Unlocking the Secrets to Country Music Scheduling"—secrets that included, as the anonymous advocacy group WOMAN Nashville uncovered in their report called Breaking the Bowl, treating women as something you should not only use sparingly but program your software to do for you, something that occurred as far back as 2011, if not earlier. WOMAN, created "by women who felt compelled to stop being complicit in an industry known for bad practices and start being proactive in creating a better culture within country music," crafted studies that changed the game, in terms of exposing the twenty-year decline for women's airplay and the depths to which those numbers fell. Keith Hill's comments, in part, mobilized them to action.

"This is the biggest bunch of BULL**** I have ever heard," Miranda tweeted in response. "I am gonna do everything in my power to support and promote female singer/songwriters in country music. Always." Margo Price wore her YOU SAY TOMATO, I SAY FUCK YOU shirt.

Keith Hill took most of the blame, but it was *Country Aircheck* that posted this logic without so much as a question, as if printing explicit evidence of the genre's rumored sexism wasn't anything to lose sleep over or editorialize in any way. It was Gary Overton, CEO of Sony Nashville, who said that if you weren't on country radio, you didn't exist—another sad truth that nobody was supposed to be saying out loud, especially not the head of one of the most important labels in the entire town. It would have been one thing if Gary Overton had said that this sheer fact was problematic, but instead he presented it as if it was etched in the stone of the industry, an immovable fact they simply could do nothing about.

There could only ever be one "tomato"—so who got to be *it*? Kelleigh Bannen, who was on a label that shared a parent company with Mickey's and Kacey's labels, remembers being told point-blank at events with her peers that only one of them was ever going to have a chance at radio, that there could simply only be one. It meant that they were conditioned to be competitors and not allies, constantly fighting for that one spot—and it meant that for women artists, writing good songs wasn't enough.

"I remember being on the phone in my backyard with one of my radio reps," recalled Kelleigh, who had a string of excellent—and radio-friendly—singles like "Sorry on the Rocks" that sadly never gained much traction on the airwaves before she eventually parted ways with her label. "And he said, 'Which girl are you? Lindsay Ell is the guitar girl. Jana Kramer is the used-to-be-on-TV girl. Which are you?'" Kelleigh didn't know how to respond—she didn't see herself as any one thing. She remembered being at CRS with Mickey and Kacey and watching them get standing ovations from the programmers who never intended to play their songs. "I was able to overlook the problematic thinking a little," Kelleigh said, "because I just wanted the dream so bad. But the reason Kacey always was able to play by her own rules was because she wasn't trying to play by the regular rules. She embraced what made her different."

Outing the "tomato" secret didn't somehow change things anyway—no radio programmers were adding women into the mix out of the goodness of their own hearts to prove everyone wrong, and label promo teams weren't aggressively trying to boost the women on their rosters, the few they had, and that's because they did follow the exact rules that Keith Hill had mentioned, down to software that did it for them. Any efforts came mostly from outside the industry structures, like with the work of WOMAN Nashville; the community songwriter night led by Caitlyn Smith, Heather Morgan, and Mags Duval called The Girls of Nashville; and the Song Suffragettes, led by the artist Kalie Shorr and a man named Todd Cassetty. Kalie had come to Nashville from Maine in 2013 and did the tours to record labels to hear the familiar refrain: We already have too many women on the roster. The idea of Song Suffragettes was just to help women get that leg up and give them an alternate route to success. Nothing changed after the "secret" was said out loud, because the secret was always normal operating procedure.

Dr. Jada Watson, a musicologist at the University of Ottawa, had been studying these trends intently. A Canadian who fell in love with American country music through the radio, she used to tape the countdown as a girl so she could teach herself to play the songs on the piano. "I was lucky to have grown up in the 1990s when there were women on the charts," Dr. Watson said. It didn't take long as a scholar of the genre and data analyst to realize that her young daughter probably wouldn't have the same opportunity. Dr. Watson was disgusted when she heard Keith Hill's comments, or any of the old excuses that hung around town, like "Women don't like to listen to women." And she also eventually understood that for country music to make any progress, it needed the data to prove what had always been assumed— that women received dismal airplay—and also that, compared to Black artists, that minimal airplay was generous. She embarked on several studies that would give power through numbers, including a breakthrough one in partnership with WOMAN Nashville, focusing specifically on *Billboard*'s Country Airplay. In addition, Tracy Gershon, Leslie Fram, and their friend Beverly Keel launched the organization Change the Conversation just months before Keith Hill's comments, to "fight gender inequality in the music industry by providing support, education, and community for female artists and executives."

They convened at Beverly Keel's house to come up with the idea, after a few initial chats at spots around town—forty or so of them. Tracy had been trying to get an artist, Natalie Stovall, a record deal, but every label was saying the same thing: *We already have signed enough "females."* It was managers and publicists, standing up and telling exactly what they had come up against, the odds that felt too hard to overcome, the publishers who couldn't get a woman in the writer's room, the attitude they received for speaking up. "Everyone told their story," Leslie said.

Beverly Keel's brick house was tucked away in West Nashville. Keel was a journalist, and it had been her father, also a reporter, who had coined the term "Elvis the Pelvis." It was at his funeral on Good Friday, on her eighteenth birthday, when she met a woman named Ruth Ann Leach, now Ruth Ann Harnisch, who was one of the first female anchors in Nashville and went on to not only have a flourishing broadcast career but a philanthropic one. She gave Beverly the bug, a passion that took her to Middle Tennessee State University, to Columbia for journalism school, and then back to Nashville, where she worked at a variety of publications, *People* among them.

"I always had to fight against the hay bale image," she says. "They would want to put a yee haw in a headline about the CMA Awards. They were condescending. There was a story about Mindy McCready, who says she was beaten by her partner and it was serious. And they were like, 'Oh, that's like a country song!' No, this is a serious violent act. You can't belittle and demean it."

Beverly had steadily been pissing off people in radio—so much so that after she had written a few editorials about the lack of women in country airplay for the *Tennessean*, she received direct rebuttals in the trade *Country Aircheck*, which felt the need to defend themselves and the industry it has a parasite-host relationship with.

A gathering had been planned based on a series of emails among Leslie, Tracy, and Beverly. "Tracy was clear this was not a bitch session," Beverly said. They knew they had to toe the line between criticism and being nice enough not to piss anyone off too much—gentle disrupters, still able to be allowed to participate just enough (they'd later be criticized for treading that line too closely). Tracy, perhaps, carried the least amount of shits of anyone, as she had been trying to launch Natalie Stovall, an excellent fiddle player and a great singer and songwriter, too, but no one was biting. She fired off a note to her friends.

"I just shopped Natalie Stovall
Here were the comments from three big labels:

1. *we are no longer signing women . . . not Natalie—just women. no women.*
2. *Its too hard to find songs for women*
3. *No one is writing hits for women . . .*
4. *She's a blonde—we already have a blonde (actually that was left over from another shopping experience but threw it in because it makes for good talk)*
5. *and now the labels are all proud of themselves becuz all have just signed A woman. one. thats the quota.*

also, a big business manager, who is a woman also told me she did not want to represent women.

Sad, but true. We eat our own.

"It was around 2015," Mickey said, "when I realized this shit sucks."

Somehow, amid all of this, Mickey was supposed to break through—break through, while ignoring the fact that women were the tomatoes in the salad of men, and Black women weren't even invited to the salad bar to begin with. But she was trying, and the label had finally put the smallest bit of oomph behind her single, "Better Than You Left Me," which was on, yet again, a four-song EP. The song was a soaring midtempo ballad that checked all the boxes, but how was Mickey supposed to see success, though, if even Miranda or an up-and-coming white female artist couldn't break through to country radio? It seemed an impossible, unfair standard, completely built to fail. And the white girls, in the wake of Tomato-gate, were busy fighting for themselves. There was no "Change the Conversation" for Black women, and while pushing for more inclusion for women was an important cause, it wasn't the same thing as country's deeply embedded racism, and sometimes it ended up doing more harm than good.

Some worried that the focus of all of it was way too dependent on solving the "problem" of women while ignoring other marginalized groups, especially BIPOC and queer artists. "I think there were opportunities to broaden, not change the conversation," Kelly McCartney said. "And they were missed, left and right."

"The year 2015 has been Mickey Guyton's year," wrote professor and country music thought leader Dr. Charles Hughes in the *Washington Post*. Everyone wanted it to be true—hoped, deep in their hearts, that it was true. Even Gayle King, on *CBS This Morning*, wanted it to be true. "I walked out of that interview and said, It's only a matter of time," Gayle said years later, interviewing Mickey in 2020. "Better Than You Left Me" did have a historic add week, meaning that radio stations signed on to play it initially. But without the promo behind it to push it constantly in the face of lazy programmers, it never cracked the top 40.

For all the talk about women in country music and tomatoes, Mickey had been trying to do what she could to get her career off the ground. She had been working and writing furiously, and headed out to open for Brad Paisley with Justin Moore. She had played SXSW, opening for Willie Nelson and Keith Urban at an iTunes Music Festival special event. She was nervous beyond belief—two icons of hers from different sides of the spectrum—and "fought away tears of joy as she left the stage," wrote Larry Heath, a reporter there for the show.

"She was wonderful, commanding the stage and getting a lot of support from the crowd—where lots of her friends and family seemed to be, all while trying not to let the magnitude of the show get to her," Larry recalled later. "And shows don't get much bigger: Supporting Willie Nelson, on Willie Nelson Blvd in the then still fairly new ACL Live at the Moody Theater. With hometown fans for both. Lesser performers may have not been up to the task, especially that early in their career, but she certainly was."

The tour seemed to expose the worst in the country fan base. Mickey heard the n-word one day doing an after-show signing, and that wasn't as surprising as the reaction she got when she told those around her what had happened. "We don't want to talk about it now," they told her. "But we will, one of these days." She routinely had to play as Confederate flags adorned shirts and hats appeared in the audience, under the guise of "southern pride."

In general, life on tour was anything but great. It was always a "pissing contest" on the bus, and Mickey's all-male band wasn't helping. At one point she got tonsillitis and had to miss a gig, and no one bothered to ask how she was feeling—they were mostly mad they were going to be short a check. Another time, she said, her bass player, seeing her try to load the bus with an armful of suitcases, just shrugged at her struggling instead of helping. All the while, she was living in a two-bedroom apartment in Nashville with three women, her boyfriend and future husband, Grant, still in Los Angeles.

"Mickey Guyton's voice is stunning," said Dr. Diane Pecknold in 2015, then associate professor of women's and gender studies at the University of Louisville, and an expert on the history of Black artists in country music. "But she may face an extra burden just because the form of femininity that's getting the most attention in mainstream country today is that sort of tough-talking, sassy, deliberately trashy country girl, and that's a tough act for an African-American woman to pull off without triggering racist stereotypes—think Miranda Lambert, or the version of Carrie Underwood who swings the Louisville Slugger."

The label and radio thought Mickey would "work" best if she were to remain neutral. Definitely not angry—angry would be a disaster. Anger and rage were only emotions and postures available to white women, and even then, they didn't always yield rewards. Her EP was called *Unbreakable*, but she was feeling anything but.

Other than being perfect for country radio—"Better Than You Left Me" was more conventionally country than Maren and Kacey— Mickey spoke openly about her faith, and her approach was nearly as mainstream as you could get. She wasn't singing about girls kissing girls, and her church was in an actual church. There was no reason that country shouldn't embrace her: she was playing by all the rules, only to discover that it doesn't matter if you're trying to play a game you'll simply never qualify for. Ultimately the excellent single "Burning House" by the artist Cam ended up taking the "female" slot of the moment, through no fault of Cam's own, and Mickey's single disappeared.

That fall, she was added to the Next Women of Country class, and debuted "Better Than You Left Me" at the annual showcase event. "Mickey may have been unfamiliar to many people in the room, but she appears to be poised for a breakthrough in 2015 when her debut album will be released on Capitol Nashville," a reporter wrote in a recap. "Although she offered a beautiful, controlled vocal performance, overpowering emotions got the best of her at the end of the song when she was reduced to tears."

Mickey took consolation in her friends, like fellow artists Leah Turner and Maggie Rose. Leah, a Californian whose father was a champion rodeo star and mother a first-generation Mexican American, came to Tennessee in 2014 and was quickly signed to Columbia Nashville, despite constantly hearing "We don't really *do* women" from labels around town. This kind of thing was foreign for Leah: growing up on the ranch, she didn't see much of a dividing line between men and women. "Cowboys, cowgirls, they were doing all the same stuff," she said. "I can ride the crap out of a horse and rope and do this and do that, and it never dawned on me. It was very hard for me to swallow: Why do I have to have the fruity drink? I want a beer."

Leah and Mickey met at a songwriter round and became instantly close—Leah had occasionally been urged to suppress parts of her story and keep her Mexican roots buried, all while artists like George Strait sang about tequila or "the border." It was something Mickey could relate to, but they also would spend endless nights just talking, singing, or sharing horror stories about how they could see men—or white women—around them cowering, getting uncomfortable.

"Country is fine with you as long as you don't make them uncomfortable," Leah said. "But getting uncomfortable means you're growing. I always remember when I was little and my legs were aching, and I would say to my mom, 'Why do my legs hurt so bad?' And she would say, 'Those are growing pains.' And you know, it hurts to grow. Change is uncomfortable. But guess what: I got these long legs now."

The Pacific Coast Highway, somewhere between Santa Monica and Malibu. The road stretched out along the California coastline, and Maren was driving her rental car with the radio on. It didn't matter where she was headed; it would be an intense few days with busbee writing feverishly in his backyard studio, and for what, she wasn't quite sure. Probably for her own album, but she could have just as easily passed the songs to someone else. That is, if she hadn't taken that drive.

The windows were rolled down, the salty Los Angeles air wafting in, the ocean in view, music playing. "You know," Maren thought to herself, "this is like church to me." She had an appointment to work with busbee the next day, and hadn't yet figured out a shell of an idea to take to the session like usual—a title, or a melody. It struck her: that would be the song. Her church.

She and busbee wrote it in under an hour. It contained everything Maren loved: country, a little bit of soul, a good amount of swagger, and nods to legends like Johnny Cash and Hank Williams.

Maren knew what she had with "My Church" almost instantly. No one was going to get this song; it was hers, it had to be hers. Whose else could it be? She held on to it like a precious gem, afraid to email it to anyone in case it would somehow leak, playing it only in the office for Carla Wallace and the folks at Big Yellow Dog so nothing ever left the building. Something strange had started happening, where she could envision herself singing it at awards shows and concerts, standing firmly onstage under a marquee of her own name.

It was at music festival Bonnaroo the summer before that she had met Janet Weir, her new manager, and it was Janet's idea to hold the song close and release it without label support. Janet came from the pop worlds of Los Angeles and Lilith Fair, and didn't tend to feel like she had to play by the rules of traditional Nashville because she didn't know what they were to begin with.

"We just decided that 'My Church' was the song, and we weren't going to send it to anybody," Maren said. Or do just any kind of release. Instead of pushing in vain to country radio, they'd try something different: Spotify.

The plan to start with streaming began at Pinewood Social, a place that was pure New Nashville: a bowling alley in the middle, charred broccoli appetizers and avocado toast, food designed to be photographed. It's where they sat down with Copeland Isaacson, who was in charge of country programming at Spotify. Copeland had access to the release calendars, could see what was coming along the pike, and could find the windows where they could squeeze in "My Church" for maximum impact.

"We constructed this plan," Maren said. "Pre-labels, just three of us, like, we're gonna put it out on new music Friday. And this was the pioneer days of Spotify. It was really the only streaming platform."

Other genres were making use of the new platforms to launch songs—musical virality on Spotify and YouTube had catapulted everyone from Justin Bieber to The Weeknd to fame. But mainstream country music, per usual, was still stuck in the eternal battle of sameness, creeping slowly to streaming platforms if not trying to create a reality that denied their existence for as long as humanly possible.

"There's a window," Copeland said. "There are no other major releases coming, so I can give you the banner and I can give you the playlist. But it's in two weeks. Can you do it?"

Maren and Janet looked at each other—of course they could. "We hatched this plan," Maren said. "Kate York shot the single art, we got a Squarespace website. My God, it was all very rootsy."

It came out and exploded. Labels that had passed were scrambling to understand what happened. "I just remember all the labels and the digital departments were like, What the fuck is going on? Who is this girl? And why is she racking up all these streams and why is she getting these like playlists placements?" Maren said. "Wondering why they had been trying for weeks to get their artists to the same place."

Janet and Maren started to take meetings again with labels. Suddenly the level of interest was much different, but most of them, despite Maren's unconventional emerging success—proof that there are, in fact, pathways to usurp the machine—were still stuck in the old ways of doing things. "'My Church' was already doing so well on Spotify and I was like, Wait, you're gonna make me do six months of radio tour and then ship it to radio?" Maren said. "I was like, 'No, it's already out.' And they said, 'This is not how we do things, and we know what we are doing.'"

"How we do things" had resulted in women being nearly erased from country radio over twenty short years. "How we do things" had made sure that even when women had success, it was tempered. "How we do things" had kept Mickey's career so far on the back burner that the stove had all but gone cold. "How we do things" had purged the Chicks, pushed out Rissi. "How we do things" was only working for certain kinds of people.

Things heated up with another record label, and Maren went in for one of the final meetings before a deal would be officially offered. When Maren and Janet showed up, there was an old brown eighties Mercedes parked out front—one of the songs on the EP was called

"80s Mercedes," a delectable pop song meant for rolled-down windows and summer nights.

"It said 'Congrats or welcome home' on the windshield,'" Maren said, the memory still making her laugh and then cringe. "It was not a good eighties Mercedes—it had a rip in the seat, but I got what they were doing. They showed me this big video for what they wanted to do for the music video and the rollout, and then a man from the label said, 'If you sign, here,' and hands me a set of keys." The key chain had a charm with her logo on it.

Maren grabbed Janet and ran to the bathroom. "I feel really sick right now," she said. "Am I getting bribed?"

She was flattered but extremely uncomfortable. Did they think a beat-up car would persuade her?

Things made more sense at Columbia/Sony. They didn't try to make her change what was already working, and they already had a track record with Miranda. Even though they initially pushed for the peppier "80s Mercedes" as the "ace up their sleeve" single (Maren won out in the end), they were willing to rush the music out just as she intended, rather than insisting they follow some long, drawn-out version of a traditional release plan—a sharp contrast to Mickey's path, where being "herself" was never even an early option. When they rereleased the EP after her signing, "My Church" broke a record as the song played by the greatest number of radio stations for a debut single in its impact week, with 107.

Columbia Nashville gave her the green light to release her debut album *Hero* without putting it through the traditional wringer, because she was never going to do it another way. "I didn't want to sit on it," Maren told the *New York Times*. "I didn't want to go through a year or two of development—it was already developed."

Chapter 15

HERO, MAGA, AND DADDY LESSONS

It was a sweltering night in Kansas City on Keith Urban's Ripcord World Tour, of which Maren was the first opener—behind Brett Eldredge, playing arenas as they filled up with people and the sun was only starting to go down. It was June 2, 2016, the day before her major-label debut *Hero* was released, and it was hot—sticky, steamy hot. Maren had decided to wear the same faux fur coat that she was sporting on the album cover, sweating through a set list that included a twenty-five-minute or so sampler of the album's songs. "So stupid," she said, reflecting back on the choice of clothing.

The lead-up in the past few months had been as close to a whirlwind as you could get, and by the time Maren got to the release of *Hero*, her streaming power was undeniable—by the end of 2016, "My Church" and "80s Mercedes" had a combined hundred million streams.

The album was due to come out June 3, so she had decided to stay up until midnight with Janet and her team, and have some champagne when *Hero* officially hit stores. Maren had been kind of shell-shocked from the rigor of release week, the intense promo and grind, all while embarking on her first major tour. "I was just so excited to be doing this professionally," she said. "I don't remember all the details because they were not as important then as they are now. I was just like, whatever happens, happens."

And what happened, happened fast. The album debuted at number five on the *Billboard* 200 chart—the chart that encompasses all genres, not just country (it was number one there, and the first one for Sony Music Nashville to hit that spot since Kellie Pickler, the now underappreciated *American Idol* contestant, in 2006). It kept up the astronomically high streaming rates, and secured Maren a spot in the coveted new artists program, iHeart's On the Verge, which came with automatic playlisting on country radio. The *New York Times* called it an "outstanding country music debut," and it wasn't an outlier in saying so. "There was so much fortitude and strength," Janet said. Elton John even called her to tell her how much he liked the record—he had it on vinyl.

Here was a country album, from a woman no less, with swears in the singles ("*shit!* I'd be rich!"). Here was a country album that mentioned "church" but instead hinted that it's possible to find faith elsewhere, outside of just religion or worship walls. Here was a country album by a woman that was both hopelessly fun and endlessly personal, with allusions to Johnny Cash and sex and hedonism and insecurities.

Fount had taken Maren around to play for folks in New York, and he was getting unusually enthusiastic feedback, even for the notoriously hard-to-crack (for country) coastal press. Maren's success, and her path there, was making people nervous back in Nashville—Maren wasn't so outside the mold that they could ignore her, but she was outside it enough that it was rattling the way things had been done. Did country music have to embrace streaming after all? What did this mean for terrestrial radio?

Another artist had riled up the country music institutions earlier in the year—Margo Price, who already started that sense of looming unease when her debut record, *Midwest Farmer's Daughter*, was released a few months earlier, in March, to massive acclaim. Margo sang about the working class, the people left behind, and the industry that had cast her aside and out for the better part of the decade. She didn't shy away from speaking about politics or race in a forceful and meaningful way, and she'd led the "outlaw" life fetishized in men: been to jail, suffered tremendous loss, pulled herself from poverty to career success with the belief of Jack White, whose Third Man Records finally signed her.

Margo had appeared on *Saturday Night Live* in April, in a coveted spot that even most mainstream country artists with major label support couldn't secure (Maren would play months later). Some praised the show while others deemed her as "cutting in line," a criticism that seemed strikingly similar to other female artists who had graced the show's stage, like Lana Del Rey, so diminishing to their talents. She had long given up trying to appease the suits on Music Row, or the trolls, who were never going to understand what she was trying to do without asking her to change this or that.

When *Midwest Farmer's Daughter* was released, it debuted in the top 10 on the *Billboard* Top Country Albums chart. It was the first time since the chart began in the 1960s that a solo woman's debut album did so without having appeared on the Country Songs singles chart. "Five years later, I'm still fighting and fucking the system," Margo tweeted on the album's anniversary.

Margo had no real intentions to flirt with Music Row success, or even major label success—that ship had sailed for her after they dismissed her album, first by their choice, and then by hers. But a year after "Tomato-gate," certain women—Margo, Maren, Mickey, and Kacey included—weren't particularly interested in using this newly public data to try to conform more. Women seemed to be making the most interesting art in the country mainstream, often outside the traditional rule book.

It was a warm day in Nashville when *Billboard* decided to gather those four, alongside the artists Cam and Aubrie Sellers, for a roundtable on that very topic. Cam had been gaining steam for her exquisite single "Burning House," and a quietly burgeoning role in forcing the industry to be more inclusive from the inside out—to the point it would often cause friction at her label. Aubrie, who happened to be the daughter of Lee Ann Womack, was a songwriter who had developed her own sound that she referred to as "garage country."

Journalist Jewly Hight, someone who had focused on country's eternal issues of exclusion, was chosen to lead the conversation. Margo was uncomfortable, she'd say later—she'd rarely seen a room full of so many people and handlers, and she wasn't super keen on things themed "women in music." So she started to talk about it. Apparently, her mic hadn't been on, or so she was told—no one seemed to want to discuss the simultaneous harm this over-examining of "women in country music" could be doing. Was it shining a light, or was it fetishizing? Was it leveling the score, or was it creating an environment of white feminism focused only on success for white women while those like Mickey were left on the far fringes?

"I very much felt like an outsider," Margo said later, reflecting on the experience. "I felt tons of warmth from Mickey that day and had a great conversation with her. I just felt like it was a cool thing they were trying to do but maybe a little awkward and a little stilted."

The women tried to talk anyway. "If they can't get your song off the ground, it's immediately blamed on your personality," Kacey told the group. "Or the fact that you're female, or that you didn't make a radio station program director feel important."

Margo had plenty of potent thoughts, too. "Women get labeled 'bossy' when it's like, 'Maybe I'm a leader. Maybe I just know what I want.'"

The year 2016 for Kacey had been a steady ride off the success of *Pageant Material*, her sophomore album, and the disappointments that came with it. Neither single from the LP had done well: "Biscuits" being joyfully catchy and technically perfect for the format, and "Dime Store Cowgirl" an autobiographical story of her journey that almost anyone could relate to. Behind the scenes, some radio programmers wondered why she couldn't get into rotation. "Biscuits" was playful, but it also contained the word "pissing," as if that was somehow breaking codes of decorum. Maybe "Good Ol' Boys Club" (another potent, truthful song) scared them—too much truth, even. Or maybe it was the launch party, where Kacey kicked off the celebration with drag queens at a local gay club, where she gave out tiaras as party favors. Still, the album was a commercial success and an artistic high achievement: recorded at RCA Studio A, it had gorgeous countrypolitan textures and a relaxed yet meticulous approach. Gena Johnson, the first woman to be nominated for Audio Engineer of the Year at the ACMs, in 2021, had been on deck during the recording and remembered it fondly. Kacey had brought in sashes and crowns, and even steel guitar legend Paul Franklin was wearing one when they were recording. ("It was adorable," said Gena. "She was always thinking about extra little things she could do for people.") Kacey gave everyone a Polaroid camera at the end as a parting gift. *Pageant Material* went to number one on the *Billboard* country chart when it was released in June 2015.

Gena remembered sitting backstage with Kacey after a show at the Ryman, and Kacey played her a recording of a tense conversation she'd had with the label after she'd handed in some of the record.

"It was clearly, 'Wow, women are not allowed to be anything else but an old white man's interpretation of what they need to be,'" Gena said. "That good ol' boys club—I think it's pretty obvious what that song is written about. Kacey was always very kind, but if you said something that maybe put somebody down or something she didn't believe in, she would tell you what she thought. She wouldn't be the person to just sit there and not say anything."

Her Country & Western Rhinestone review tour had been doing spectacularly well, and when she decided to record a Christmas album, *A Very Kacey Christmas*, Gena was one of her go-tos for the project. Gena had been interested in engineering from the very beginning, and was also very aware that she was probably an extreme outlier when it came to the worlds of production. "We kind of became instant friends," said Gena.

The album came with its own full-on kitsch Christmas tour, and there were dates with George Strait: touring with someone so traditionally country seemed to unleash even more left-of-center possibilities within her. Some might spend nights in arenas alongside a legendary figure like George and realize the ease that can come with staying perfectly consistent—she could sing songs like "Biscuits" for the next thirty years of her life and draw a reliable audience. But that wasn't going to be her plan.

One night Universal Records executive Stephanie Wright came to visit backstage at one of the George Strait tour stops, and Kacey was openly wondering if she should switch things up. "Do you think my fans will follow along with me?" Stephanie remembers her asking. "I said, if it's true and it's believable, then yes."

Being true was never going to be a problem for Kacey, so when she started writing the songs of *Golden Hour*, and eventually recording them in part in Sheryl Crow's barn, she didn't worry about if they were too pop or too indie or too country, because she'd never particularly done that to begin with. Instead of collaborating with Luke Laird and Shane McAnally as producers, like she had done on the last albums, she decided to work with Ian Fitchuk and Daniel Tashian, whom she had known from way back in the days of Hotel Villa. She felt she needed a fresh way to look at her own methods, still holding her relationships with Luke and Shane dear.

"Years ago, we were set up to write a song, and we ended up just talking," Daniel recalled. "And we never wrote anything, but we became friends. We would text every once in a while. She was looking for a new sound, and as soon as we started hanging out, writing together, we just really kind of clicked."

The first day in the studio Daniel had just gotten back from the beach, and he was lying on the floor on his back, strumming for hours. He had a little loop worked up, "sort of like a techno song," he said, and Kacey suggested she sing something over it—twenty minutes later they had the seeds of one of the first songs, "Oh, What a World." "We started affectionately calling her the 'axe man,' because we would have all these layers and all these tracks that we would add up, and she would come in and go, 'Wait, hang on, just turn half of that stuff off.' The album has a nice sense of clarity about it," Daniel said. "We all started to get addicted to clearing space out. Simplicity is power."

Sheryl had let them use her bucolic recording studio, and she and Kacey would often go and ride horses in between takes. Kacey had a little projector she bought at the airport, and sometimes they would project colors on the wall while she moved in front of it, singing and writing the lyrics. They took mushrooms, tried synthesizer and disco sounds, and didn't worry about if anything was country or not, or even where it landed at all.

"It just felt like kids playing," Daniel said.

"It was really important for me to bring my version of country music to a different group of people," Kacey told *Rolling Stone*. "I didn't want to leave country behind. I just wanted to look at it a different way."

America, 2017. Donald Trump had trademarked the phrase "Make America Great Again" in 2012, mostly out of disdain for his then enemy Ted Cruz. He had been using it casually in his failed bid for president the previous race, but he had been gaining steam, and support, to run again once President Obama was officially out of office in 2016 and he knew he would be running against Hillary Clinton, against whom white, misogynistic rage would be an incredibly powerful tool.

"Make America Great Again" could be a country song, really. Nostalgia, longing for the days long gone. He may not have had much of a taste for the music itself, but what Donald Trump understood, more than anything, perhaps, was how important it was to harness the power of people who felt their values were being ripped away by a "woke" future that included races other than their own, women, and queer people.

Pop wanted to look forward, and country wanted to look back. As in the days of the Chicks' expulsion from country radio, you didn't have to be a fan of the Chicks to want them off the airwaves, just like you didn't have to be a fan of Donald Trump to wear a MAGA hat: it was building against a common enemy, and that enemy wanted America to be less conservative, and much less white. And it worked. Somehow, against all predictions, Trump won the election. The morning after, on November 9, Margo Price walked into the NPR studios in Washington, D.C., to record a Tiny Desk session with tears streaming down her face: she was stunned along with the rest of the world, wearing an "Icky Trump" tee under her Western snap shirt.

Margo had been one of few country artists to speak her mind about the election—she knew she had already been deemed too dangerous by the Music Row establishment anyway, and her songs were capturing alienated fans of the genre and well beyond. "1,461 days, counting down now," Margo said after finishing her song "Four Years of Chances." One of the few other visible country artists taking public aim at Trump was the Chicks, who carried along a backdrop that included a photo of Donald Trump with sketched-on devil horns on their sold-out arena tour—it came up on the monitor behind the band during the "controversial" song "Goodbye Earl."

The tour, though, was so successful that the Chicks scored an invite back into the fray of country music: to the CMA Awards, to accompany Beyoncé for her performance of "Daddy Lessons," off her masterpiece *Lemonade*, released six months prior. The talk about "Daddy Lessons," a murder ballad–inspired song that wasn't any more or less country than Florida Georgia Line, had reached an inflection point—it couldn't be considered a country song, or in contention for country awards, so said the Grammy Awards, who deemed it ineligible. Many begged to differ. But *Lemonade* was above and beyond the artistic achievement of the year, and therefore undeniable. Even the puritanical hands at the CMA felt as though they needed to embrace it, along with the Chicks.

And here they were, as the centerpiece of the show.

"Texas!" Houston-native Beyoncé fired, surrounded by the Chicks and a massive band of players who looked nothing like the usual all-white and mostly male collection.

"Texas!" responded Natalie Maines as the audience both cheered and dissolved into stoic observance, the explosive horns and fiddles roaring. Many people in the room were aghast—"Why is that bitch even here?" someone muttered about Beyoncé. Trisha Yearwood and Kelsea Ballerini were dancing, but Alan Jackson ended up walking out. "They treated us very weird backstage," Natalie Maines told the *New York Times*. Garth Brooks, who won Entertainer of the Year, was a fan, though. "I thought it was just power—raw power," Garth told reporters backstage. "I love that it was all feminine raw power."

It wasn't just that the Chicks were back, and it wasn't just that there was a massive star present from outside the genre, not to mention one who was a Black woman—it also illuminated everything that can be good about country music and everything it tries to keep repressed all at once. "No one had a meltdown about Justin Timberlake performing with Chris Stapleton at the CMAs the year before," the writer and artist Karen Pittelman wrote in her essay, "Another Country." "The problem was not even that Beyoncé is Black, or at least, not only that Beyoncé is Black. The real problem was that, with the release of *Lemonade* and in particular the first single 'Formation,' Beyoncé had recently made a clear political statement and aligned herself with the Black Lives Matter movement. Of course, Beyoncé knew all this—is there anything Beyoncé doesn't know?—and I think that's why she positioned herself with the Dixie Chicks in her performance. There was no place in country music's construction of pro-establishment whiteness for Beyoncé's vision." Beyoncé and the Chicks were *political* women, on top of everything else.

Maren loved it, though—she was happily dancing in the audience, her hair in curls, a fan of Beyoncé since her days singing "Halo" in those Dallas-area honky-tonks. And she was up to something herself with her dynamic performance of "My Church," where she brought Nashville gospel quartet the McCrary Sisters and the Preservation Hall Jazz Band to back her up, adding rich gospel textures and booming horns. She took the award for New Artist of the Year, noting that in 2015, she'd been watching from a bar across the street at the Palm restaurant with Janet and Ryan, just as a fan. On the red carpet earlier, Maren had told Fount to make sure everyone knew the names of who she was performing with: "She wanted to make sure they were getting love, too," Fount remembered.

But the Chicks and Beyoncé, onstage with a band full of women and Black and queer players, two months before Donald Trump took office, were signaling something deeper. The performance of "Daddy Lessons" interpolated the Chicks' "Long Time Gone," using a band inspired by New Orleans second line music to further highlight how country was in constant dialogue with the Black experience. When Beyoncé called out "Texas" with the Chicks by her side, it was both an exclamation and a challenge. *"Texas!"*

Whose Texas was it gonna be, though? And whose country music?

While Maren was touring behind *Hero* and Kacey was working on *Golden Hour*, 2017 was proving to be one of the most dismal years for women in country radio—and, for those who were opposed to Trump, pretty dismal for women, period.

The little glimpse of airplay triumph came via Carly Pearce. Carly was from a small town in Kentucky and had grown up deeply immersed in both the Chicks and traditional bluegrass, coming to Nashville at nineteen and suffering more setbacks than most could count: she signed a development deal with Sony, which she was then dropped from, and had gone from promise to pariah overnight. She was playing rounds with Kacey, Brothers Osborne, and Kree all while cleaning Airbnbs.

Carly had also started working with busbee, who was eager to get involved with an artist before fame took hold of their careers. It took one spin on Sirius XM's influential country music channel The Highway to catapult her debut single, "Every Little Thing," to stardom; she signed with Big Machine and the song eventually went to number one. Carly had been in the same Next Women of Country class as Maren, and the only other woman really breaking through at the time had been Kelsea Ballerini, whose 2015 single "Love Me Like You Mean It" marked only the eleventh time that a female country artist has topped the charts with a debut song. Kelsea was a sharp writer, insistent on singing the songs she composed—their poppiness made them work on radio, but it also made it easy for Music Row, or critics, to look past her lyrical capabilities. She'd later publish a book of poetry to help show them how wrong they were.

The year 2017 was continuing to be about the disconnect: Miranda's stellar, career-defining 2016 double album *The Weight of These Wings* and Chris Stapleton's *From a Room: Volume 1* were two of the year's top sellers, while Eric Church continued to cement his reputation as the genre's foremost touring draw, concluding his sixty-two-date Holdin' My Own Tour by setting a new attendance record with two sold-out nights at Bridgestone Arena. None of these seemed to match up with trends settling on the airplay charts. One of the biggest new standouts was a song called "A Little Dive Bar in Dahlonega," from a woman out of Arkansas named Ashley McBryde. Ashley had moved to Nashville in 2006, sang with a potent honesty and storyteller heart, all while boasting arms full of tattoos and rejecting the blond binary that was usually directed toward female artists. She could write with the best of them—stories from deep in the heart and gut, delivered with unparalleled depth and punch. And there were plenty of people along the way who thought she might do that better in a pretty little dress.

"When it came to following my own little beacon, that just always came natural," Ashley said. "There would always be people later who would try to change that, mostly record executive type people, but they are the same people who wanted to put me in a fringy vest and over-the-knee chain boots. So at least I was armed with the fact that I do not wear shit like that. And from there, I also knew that anything sonically they suggested to me was probably also pretty fucking wrong, too."

Predictably, "A Little Dive Bar in Dahlonega" never pushed past the top 30—despite ranking atop lists of the best songs of the year.

Amanda Shires had been paying attention to this disconnect, so one day she picked up the phone and called Q100.3 FM—"Today's Continuous Country"—while on the road in her van. She had tuned in to the station on a whim, partly to see if the discrepancy between men and women in country airplay was as bad as she had been hearing. And it was not only bad—it was worse than she thought.

"Do you love the songs that you're playing?" Amanda asked, in a story she recounted to the *Nashville Scene*. A bandmate filmed the whole thing on their cell phone—Amanda wanted live proof of what exactly was going down. "Did you know that in eighteen songs, you played one woman that wasn't a request, and the second one it was a request? I was just wondering if you might be open to playing more women on the radio, like Kacey Musgraves or Margo Price."

The DJ was defensive—he claimed they always played women despite what he said was "a weird patch."

"Let's move this music forward," she responded. "Let's not stay in the past."

Amanda wasn't thinking too much about whether she was or wasn't in the country space properly for her own music, but she was being recognized by Americana awards for her excellent 2016 album *My Piece of Land*, and for her fiddle work alongside Jason Isbell and the 400 Unit. Country had never really attempted to claim her as their own—she wouldn't have had it that way. But the experience, along with reading about the dire circumstances for women along with the country's emerging Me Too movement, which spiraled out of activist Tarana Burke's work in the nineties, had got her thinking, as well as thinking about the future dreams of her daughter, Mercy. What if she started a group called the Highwomen, a play on the legendary and revered Highwaymen group with Willie Nelson, Johnny Cash, Kris Kristofferson, and Waylon Jennings?

She tucked the idea in her back pocket, as the climate only grew hotter: at the upcoming Grammy Awards, where Maren would be nominated for Country Solo Performance for "I Could Use a Love Song" but lose out to Chris Stapleton, men would dominate the winner pool. When asked about it afterward, the head of the Grammys, Neil Portnow, would respond in a way that sounded strikingly similar to the way country radio programmers had always explained away their discrimination: Women need to make better music. They need to *step up*.

Mickey was sick of being told to step up—her work was already good, and she knew it. But she was weary and worn down, and told Cindy Mabe as much as they sat down to have lunch at the restaurant Fin & Pearl, a seafood place attempting to be chic near the Gulch. Mickey was missing her family back home, her husband, her animals, so she'd asked Cindy—vice president of her label—to get together. And she was frustrated, way past the point of being able to tolerate another rejection, another season of promo pushes behind anyone but her.

"I have all these songs, and nobody hears them," Mickey said, playing them to Cindy in the middle of the restaurant on a pair of headphones. The place was filled with other industry executives and bachelorette groups lunching, but Mickey had never felt so alone.

Cindy listened intently. "These are really good," she said.

"I know they are," Mickey replied, exasperated at the same, enduring cycle. "But I really need something to change. What worked for Faith Hill won't work for me. It's not working for any woman, for that matter. We have to try something different."

Mickey had asked Cindy if they could organize a meeting with

Mike Dungan, head of the label, to see if they could figure out some kind of game plan or way forward.

"You look taller," Mike said to Mickey as she walked in on the day of the meeting. She had been taking diet pills to get skinnier, "really fucking skinny," the way she thought a woman in country music had to look to play the game, and she was drinking too much to dull the stress and pain. It was wearing on her, exhausting her. She couldn't do it anymore. Even someone noticing—albeit indirectly—wasn't helping. She felt smaller than ever, in more ways than one.

"Well," Mickey said, "I'm pretty sure I haven't grown since I was fifteen."

Mickey sat down and started playing songs for Mike and the assembled group: like "Sister," and other things she had been working on with Canadian artist-writer Victoria Banks and other songwriters that felt good, that felt like her. Working with Victoria had been transformative, like a light went on: here was someone who understood the kind of nuanced, feminine perspective she wanted to get across and, a luxury that doesn't always happen when writing with men, started off the songwriting in her specific key.

Mickey noticed Mike looking out the window after they were done. "There's just no room for pop on country radio," he said.

She stopped him right there. There was plenty of room for pop on country radio—actually, there was more room for pop on country radio than there was country on country radio, as long as the singers were white. There was even room for "hick-hop," an amalgam of country and rap, if the singers were white men. And Mickey, anyway, was *country*.

"As a Black woman, and hearing the songs you have put out, countless male artists on this label, you can never say the word 'pop' around me ever again," Mickey told him. "Mike, I love you. You know I do. I respect you. But you are not my audience. I'm not writing songs for you. My audience is gay men. They are Black women. They are women. They are any marginalized groups of people. That is who I am writing for."

Chapter 16

TO LOOK AT COUNTRY A DIFFERENT WAY

In the daytime, the Adventure Science Center museum in Nashville is usually filled with curious, snot-nosed children running wild, touching glowing orbs, and climbing up the mammoth and twisting play structure in the middle that kids sometimes get lost in, leading the parents to have to call their names on the loudspeaker (worry not, they are always found).

But on this particular night in March 2018, it was filled with media, industry folks, and Kacey's friends and family for a *Golden Hour* listening party. This was not a usual Nashville premiere: usual Nashville premieres fall under the guidelines of predictable and safe, with the same silver trays of tacos or cheese plates, the same buckets of sponsored booze surrounded by fast-melting ice. Kacey's parties had never been usual—the *Pageant Material* drag show debut, for one— but this event was one that was meant to allow the guest to fall into a state of deep, private listening. Because, as Kacey said, Nashville is the worst for listening parties.

The central event was in the planetarium, where there were two shifts: Kacey's friends and family in the second one, and media and industry folks first. Kacey wore a black skirt, demure, almost appropriate for a funeral, saying goodbye to the way her career had been thus far.

The show started and the room fell silent, everyone tucking away their phones and leaning back and watching the celestial world above their heads, swirling planets and flower shapes, all the colors in the rainbow to songs about love and humanity and happiness and wonder. Everyone walked out stunned, some wiping tears from their cheeks. The year 2018 had been an exhausting and often heartbreaking one thus far—the month prior to the release of *Golden Hour*, an active shooter had taken the lives of seventeen school employees and children in Parkland, Florida, but prompted no further action when it came to gun control. Donald Trump continued being more divisive than ever, and music needed to heal. *Golden Hour* felt like a salve on all those wounds.

It was an ugly year for country music, too: Mike Huckabee, the radically conservative and homophobic former governor of Arkansas, was appointed to the CMA Foundation board and swiftly forced to step down after rightful pressure from Kacey's manager, Jason Owen, and others. Route 91 was still having painful reverberations, with artists and families searching for healing while others tried in vain to convince their fans that it was responsible and important to talk about gun control and the genre's role in gun culture. *Golden Hour* was a bit of lightness in it all, all while the mass shootings never seemed to stop and country music often cozied up with the NRA.

The connection that country music needed to have with its fans had become more important than ever—much of white America was growing increasingly angry and alienated, and suddenly, country music found itself smack inside an evolving "culture war" where politics were infused in everything. *Rolling Stone* even ran an opinion piece by Joseph Hudak called "Why It's Time for Country Stars to Speak Up About Trump." "The vast majority of country artists who opposed Trump's ideology—and we know you are out there—remain silent," he wrote. "But it's no longer a reasonable excuse to say that country artists are stuck in the stranglehold of radio, or that speaking out means a guaranteed Dixie Chicks–style blacklisting."

When *Golden Hour* came out on March 30, the critical adoration was almost instant—it was nearly impossible not to fall in love with the record that was built out of love for her then husband, Ruston Kelly, but also the idea of love itself, and the ways it can save you and give you hope for existence. Everyone except country radio—they didn't seem to have much interest in playing "Butterflies" or "Space Cowboy," and Kacey didn't have much interest in trying to make them. At that point, it had proven to be a waste of time, emotional space, and promotional dollars. She didn't need it, the album landed at number four on the *Billboard* chart, and she traveled to Europe, UK's C2C Festival, and Japan. She had broken every rule that a country star was supposed to follow—not mischievously, but by following her arrow—and instead of career disaster, like most on Music Row had warned, it led to her becoming country's true international star of the time.

"Another year, another album of Kacey Musgraves that is inspiring all kinds of feelings in me," Maren tweeted. "You always remind me that you should never water down your art to appease others. Kacey, you're the quintessential Texas badass."

Maren was being her own kind of quintessential Texas badass, collaborating with EDM producer Zedd on "The Middle." Many different artists, huge pop stars from Bebe Rexha to Demi Lovato, had auditioned to be on the track—but Maren's voice, Zedd thought, was just the strongest: he hadn't even heard her country work before. Debuted during the Grammy Awards, "The Middle" took off and became a worldwide hit—it was an earworm beyond all earworms, and suddenly Maren was a pop star, too. It's since been streamed one billion plus times on Spotify.

They recorded her takes for "The Middle" on a rainy day at the Hutton, a Nashville hotel that was one of the first luxury stays to pop up as the city transformed. The hotel had a recording studio, and Maren laid down her vocals in twenty takes over the course of two hours. "It was one of the fastest sessions I've ever done," Zedd told *Billboard*. "I'm known for recording a singer until there's basically no more voice left—to be safe, so that I never have to ask somebody to come back."

Making "The Middle" was always going to piss off anyone concerned about those genre walls. Which kind of proved its own point: "The Middle" was never marketed as anything close to country music short of including a country star. It was not debuted on country awards shows, pushed to country radio or country playlists. Still, there was an anger that Maren even dared. Was it even worth trying to be country? What was the payback?

"When I did 'The Middle,' I was definitely accused of carpetbagging," she told *Vulture*. "It's funny, because we have such short memories. [Dolly Parton] was accused of the same thing in the late seventies. There's this amazing interview with Barbara Walters that she does, and Barbara's very pointedly asking Dolly, 'A lot of people think that you're abandoning country music and you're going pop.' That was the headline everywhere: 'Dolly Goes Pop.' And not saying I'm anywhere as big as Dolly was, even back then, but her answer was so perfect because she said, 'I'm not about abandoning anything; I'm about bringing Dolly Parton to the world.' And so, that's what I'm doing."

Even though Maren had started to work on *Girl*, which would become her second album, the songs of *Hero* were still having an impact—the ballad "I Could Use a Love Song" was her first number one record, a song that was birthed by a casual round of early drinks at Losers Bar near Music Row, and from Maren's own admission that the album didn't have a track about love in that conventional way. Laura Veltz, a venerated songwriter as well as close and frequent collaborator, composed the track with Maren and Jimmy Robbins.

Thanks to the success of "I Could Use a Love Song" and "The Middle," Maren's audience was growing larger than ever. And now that audience included Brandi Carlile, who had gotten hold of Maren's record and decided to write her a letter. Brandi has sent a lot of letters in her life—to President Barack Obama, to old friends and new artists, to political leaders and suffering kids in war-torn countries. She often wrote them from her idyllic cabin outside Seattle, the cabin she purchased at the beginning of her career and hasn't abandoned since. This letter, however, was addressed to Maren Morris, whom she had not yet even had the chance to meet.

Packaged with a copy of her new record, *By the Way, I Forgive You*, it read that she was thankful that her daughters—Evangeline and Elijah—were going to grow up in a world where a woman like Maren existed in country music. "I had just read an interview that Maren had done," Brandi said. "And I was like, Holy shit. It's really smart. Like, really smart. She's ten years younger than me, but can have me in a total state of rethinking a lot of different situations. So I sent her a letter, and she actually wrote back, asking me for advice with something that had to do with sexism. We started communicating based on this mutual respect for each other intellectually, which led to a cool friendship, because that was the foundation of it."

Brandi was not a country artist by traditional definitions, whatever those are, but the genre had been a critical part of her upbringing in the Pacific Northwest, and where she got her start, belting songs like Tanya Tucker's "Delta Dawn" at talent competitions. But as she realized that country music might not have much of a place for a queer woman like her, she left it mostly in the rearview. Though classic country harmonies virtually built the way she sings with her bandmates, Tim and Phil Hanseroth, she grew to nurture a place for misfits and rebels, where children of country music who felt like the genre had betrayed the person who they grew to be, or the person they always were, could thrive.

"Brandi Carlile: Country Without the Corn," read a headline in 2005—hinting both to the perceived corniness of the genre that often turned others away and to the rurality of it that didn't feel open to some, no matter where they came from. She had figured out that she was Americana before Americana figured out that it was her.

But after working with producer Dave Cobb on her 2017 album *Cover Stories*, which was a tribute to her debut album *The Story*, she decided to make an album in Nashville with Cobb and Shooter

Jennings, son of country outlaws Waylon Jennings and Jessi Colter. The result, *By the Way, I Forgive You*, was a huge success, commercially and artistically. It was nominated for Album of the Year at the Grammy Awards, and she took home three trophies.

It's not that Brandi was unknown in Nashville—far from it. Her song "The Story" had become a massive hit across all spectrums (covered, eventually, by none other than LeAnn Rimes). Her song "Same Old You" was cut by Miranda Lambert for *Four the Record*, and in 2011 she made an appearance at the Opry. She was ahead of the Americana rebirth that launched post–Mumford and Sons, and in some ways, she was ahead of the cracking open of country that would go on to welcome voices like Kacey's. She had crossed paths with Kacey, too, on the roots music cruise *Cayamo* in 2017. Maren had been aboard the ship as well, and Brandi and Kacey sang a cover of John Prine's "Angel from Montgomery."

By the Way, I Forgive You catapulted her to the status of misfit country icon, beloved by everyone from Dierks Bentley to up-and-coming songwriters on the small East Nashville stages.

"I remember her feeling back then that country was a world she really wanted to be in, but didn't feel like she could," said Tracy Gershon, who had known Brandi for many years. "She always thought of herself as a country singer in a weird way. But just didn't see a way in."

But suddenly, Brandi felt like she'd never had more of a place in country music—at least from the outside, and at least from people who cared to make space for her. Maren had already been trying to help facilitate the bridge over that divide. After she got Brandi's letter, she called her up and asked her to collaborate on a song for *Girl* called "Common."

Brandi's profile couldn't have been bigger—Grammy Awards, cross-genre collaborations. New opportunities beyond her wildest dreams. And that's when Amanda Shires came to her with an idea she'd hatched back in 2016.

One day, hanging out at a show at the Basement, Amanda pulled Brandi aside.

"I want to start a group, and we are going to call it the High-women," Amanda said.

Riffing off the original Highwaymen, Amanda thought the High-women could be an ever-evolving supergroup to try to challenge the country music institutions head-on—they would tell women's stories, they would court country radio, nearly daring it to play their songs. Brandi was in, and soon Maren was, too. Natalie Hemby would come later, making it a quartet, with Yola and Sheryl Crow joining in for moments along the way.

The Highwomen weren't the first women's country supergroup, of course. Dolly Parton, Emmylou Harris, and Linda Ronstadt broke the mold as the Trio, and Dolly later also teamed up with Loretta Lynn and Tammy Wynette to form the Honky Tonk Angels. The Pistol Annies were no less groundbreaking—Miranda bringing along her then relatively unknown friends was downright revolutionary. That had always been what Miranda was up to anyway, recording Gillian Welch songs and sneaking out to beloved indie songwriter John Moreland's concerts, and this was slipping her best buddies into a mainstream conversation and a mainstream scale. Their third album *Interstate Gospel* came out in 2018 as well, and it was a triumphant record about divorce and freedom.

That same year, another supergroup was formed: Our Native Daughters. Though they never aspired to mainstream country airplay, they aimed to do something even more important, which was to help correct the historical record when it comes to the origins of country music itself and its silencing and stifling of the genre's foundational Black stories. Comprising Rhiannon Giddens, Leyla McCalla (both from the pioneering Black string band Carolina Chocolate Drops), Amythyst Kiah, and Allison Russell, it sought to recast narratives from a Black female perspective. "I see this album as a part of a larger movement to reclaim the black female history of this country," Rhiannon wrote in the liner notes of the album, *Songs of Our Native Daughters*. "Black women have historically had the most to lose, and have therefore been the fiercest fighters for justice."

Chapter 17

MAMA WANTS TO CHANGE THAT NASHVILLE SOUND

"Yes, I had to sing with someone with a penis to get a number one," Miranda told the *Washington Post* at the end of 2018.

In the school of saying the quiet part out loud, Miranda was doing the work in an interview heading into the CMA Awards. She had finally gotten her first number one song in years, a duet with Jason Aldean called "Drowns the Whiskey." The irony of it all was not lost on anyone, that one of the most successful and critically acclaimed artists was having to "piggyback" on a popular, though much less vocally talented, singer like Aldean to get something that actually resonated on country radio. Even Carrie Underwood was having difficulty getting songs to the top of the chart. It's no wonder that some of them would start experimenting outside of the format altogether.

"Pair country radio's reticence to even play songs by women—an honest heresy when you think about guys in any other genre daring to declare the same—with its secret sexual-harassment problem, and the hell these singers catch from genre purists for angling for shine from collaborations outside Music Row (while men like Sam Hunt and Florida Georgia Line rack up country airplay number ones for playing the Travis Tritt right above the Tupac), and you get an impasse," the insightful *New York* magazine critic Craig Jenkins wrote about *Golden Hour* at the time. "Nashville wants its women to stay loyal but refuses to pay it forward."

That last phrase couldn't have nailed the concept better. Women were experimenting and pushing the boundaries of the genre, sonically and lyrically, because following the rules didn't seem to offer any reward—artistically, or on the airwaves. But then they were getting scolded for somehow defying the genre that gave them crumbs to begin with.

Maren had explored this in a piece for Lena Dunham's (of *Girls* fame) now defunct *Lenny Letter*. "The frustration I've had with the perspective of women in country music (who, until recently, were severely lacking in numbers) is that you either have to sing about being scorned by a lover or sing about thinking a boy is cute and wanting him to notice you," she wrote. "That's about as edgy as you can get. On top of having to make songs that are down the middle and noncontroversial, there are the aesthetic pressures for a woman to be pretty and sexy but not sexual or have desires beyond winning a guy's affections. . . . I love country music. In fact, we've had an ongoing relationship for quite some time. We can piss each other off because we make each other really look in the mirror and hold us accountable, and it's because we care. There will be distance, divide, love, and harmony (sometimes exclusively and sometimes all at the same time), but as long as there's respect and we allow each other to continue growing, we can move into the future in a really inspiring way. Truthfully, three chords and more."

It wasn't really about whether or not women got played on country radio, or at least not only that. As Maren explained, it was also the subject matter they were confined to, the clothes they were told to wear. Miranda's exquisite "Vice," about the immediate pleasure and sustained loneliness that emerges from seeking solace in one-night stands, didn't make a sizable impact on the airwaves. It was unapologetically sexual in its honesty—picking tossed-off shoes from the floor as she departs a stranger's bed. Maren was both singing and talking about sex, too, choosing her clothes without worrying if she was showing too much skin or not leaving enough to the puritanical imagination. When she spoke to *Playboy*, she talked explicitly about female desire: "I would say that if you're in a relationship and that person isn't going down on you on the regular, dump them," she said. "If it doesn't happen enough early on, you know what you're getting for the rest of it. A selfish lover is a no-go from the get-go."

She didn't care if she was "slut-shamed" for it—she wasn't going to shut up and sing.

Dr. Jada Watson was cringing. In town for CRS from Canada, she had ducked into a session called "Beer: Thirty" (with free beer from Cold River Records, a label that was in an ongoing lawsuit against artist Katie Armiger, who alleged it pushed her to over-sexualize her act and aggressively flirt with program directors), which had been billed as an open forum where issues of gender and diversity might come up for discussion. The meeting room at the Omni Hotel was filled with programmers ready to air grievances over a drink when the topic of one of country music's biggest stories popped up: Kacey Musgraves, days earlier, had won four awards at the Grammys, including the most coveted prize of Album of the Year for *Golden Hour*. In Nashville, it was all people could talk about and analyze—was country radio somehow missing out by not claiming Kacey more as one of their own? Were they doing their radio audience wrong by not playing her songs?

At the Grammys, Kacey had done what she always did when she accepted awards: hustled her co-conspiring team onstage. This time, it was Ian and Daniel, who flanked her when she took the Best Country Album and then the biggest award of all, beating out the likes of Post Malone, Drake, and Cardi B. In a red chiffon dress and with a bit of Texan oomph in her ponytail, she said with a shrug, "I would have nothing without songs."

The country radio programmers gathered at CRS, however, seemed to view Kacey differently: as an elephant in the room they didn't quite know what to do with. They hadn't played "Space Cowboy" or "Butterflies," something they felt like they could explain away in the moment due to the label's lack of aggressive promo budget, or tempo. But now here she was, the most talked about artist of the year not just within country music but at large, and a member of one of the Grammys' most exclusive clubs—shouldn't playing the new single "Rainbow" be an easy decision now?

"We tend to like and embrace artists who are interested or want to engage with the format," session moderator Tom Hanrahan of Birmingham's 102.5 The Bull said during the forum. "My interaction [with Kacey] has been hit or miss. I promise I haven't penalized her or any other artists. But from a humanity standpoint, people like to cheer on people who seem to want to row in the same direction and have connectivity. I haven't felt a whole lot of connectivity with her, but I haven't put her in the time-out chair." Dr. Watson couldn't believe what she was hearing—but, then again, she wasn't surprised. The data had shown how inconsequential radio found the music of women to be, especially from women who don't play the game or keep their politics close to their chest.

It only got worse when another programmer claimed that Kacey "won't do the promotional things radio expects especially a woman artist to do."

What, exactly, were those things? Was that letting programmers ogle their legs without firing back, or give out their private cell phone numbers or backstage passes, or far worse? And if doing those things kept women like Carrie Underwood, even, from getting number one songs, where could Mickey possibly fall in this equation? How do you make a white man *comfortable* enough to play your songs?

Maren was going full steam ahead, despite it all, much more inspired by the success of Kacey than worried about the implications of what might happen if she strayed or said too much. *Girl* was released on

March 8, after being announced at the beginning of the year with its title track, and broke the record for the largest debut streaming week for a country album by a woman. And the title track itself was building its own little movement: "Girl" started out as a letter, but grew into something bigger—a rallying cry, a perfect summation of the moment. In the video for the song, Maren wore a shirt that said FEMINIST across the front. It was a bold move: even Dolly Parton and Loretta Lynn refuse to categorize themselves that way, and it's often as dirty a phrase in Nashville as THE CHICKS. Maren didn't care: this is how she was going to come out swinging. If she went down, she went down right, morals tucked tightly into her guitar case. "We don't want any more," Maren said in the video. "We want the same."

The song didn't even come out of a direct attempt to make some sort of statement, anyway. "It was just this motto I needed to keep in my head: Don't wear someone else's crown," she told *Vulture*. "Quit comparing yourself. It's okay to not like yourself today, but tomorrow will be different. That's what I needed to hear. And I had this gut feeling about it that maybe others would need to hear it, too. It wasn't until we were really putting the whole album together that I realized, 'Oh, wow, there are more songs that have the word "girl" in them on the [country] radio chart by men than actual women.'"

While "Girl" was its own runaway train, Maren had planned something different for one of the album's centerpieces, a love song called "The Bones." She released it first to adult contemporary radio and then serviced country—it went number one on both, and gained additional traction through a remix with pop singer Hozier, ultimately going four times platinum—and Maren became the first solo woman with a multiweek number one on country radio since 2012.

"Pop and country music's synergy lives on through Maren Morris," wrote the *New Yorker*.

Maren had a massive crossover pop hit with "The Middle," transforming from country star into global phenomenon—and she could have stayed comfortably there, expanded, swapped acoustic guitars for latex and synths and dance moves. Instead she released *Girl*, which melded genres and served as a rallying cry for women everywhere to say, or scream, that there is, in fact, space for more than one in any given room or profession, but also held her version of Nashville tight. And despite the odds for women at country radio, the title song did well on the charts, and with that, another choice: she could have leaned in hard to be what Music Row demanded, playing it safe on the edge of the mainstream with just enough spice to make it interesting. She could have capped it there. She could have stopped talking about politics or gun control or sexuality, and she certainly didn't need to join the Highwomen. She could have. She didn't.

Maren had managed to do the unthinkable—be a woman who was successful at country radio, without limiting herself creatively or applying country's bejeweled muzzle to smile and nod and never say an opinion. Rarely can any artist toe the line in both, or even want to try. But here Maren was, excelling with the flow of the tide, but on her own damn boat.

In so many ways, the Highwomen project was simply an insane thing to do for everyone involved. Maren had just released *Girl* and the single to country radio, which was no time to do anything at all that might rub the folks in the mainstream country world the wrong way; Brandi was on an upward trajectory to the sky after the Grammys; Amanda was building a genre-less niche outside of roots music with her terrific record, *To the Sunset*, and Natalie was one of the most in-demand songwriters in town. That's a whole lot of capital to risk, for everyone.

"I think a lot of people on my team probably thought I was insane to join a band right in the middle of my own album cycle and tour," Maren shared with *Rolling Stone*. She'd been backstage at the *Tonight Show* when she got a phone call invite to join the band. "But when Brandi called to ask me if I wanted to be a Highwoman, and that these were going to be the people involved, I couldn't say no. I've also been touting the same message with *Girl*; it's high time for more female perspectives in the country genre."

The Highwomen had blocked a period of time at RCA Studio to record in May 2019, and Amanda had even recruited Cait Keiffer, a local tattoo artist, to ink the band and friends with their logo.

"That's a fucking hit," Dave Cobb said after queuing up the tape for "Redesigning Women," the song the band had decided would be their debut single. "There's no excuse why this can't be on the radio." Tracy Gershon, with a fresh Highwomen tattoo, wasn't so sure. She didn't want to be a buzzkill to Dave's optimism, but she knew the stakes: she knew that unless they recruited Luke Bryan to do lead vocals and boiled Chris Powell's drumming into canned electric beats, it would probably have no life at all on country radio. But it sounded like a hit in another plane. It felt good to dream.

Jason Isbell, who played guitar on the album and cowrote "If She Ever Leaves Me" with Amanda, was perched on one of the studio's couches, cracking jokes and telling a story about a time when Drive-By Truckers singer Patterson Hood got into a fight at summer camp, and Phil and Tim Hanseroth—aka "The Twins," Brandi's longtime collaborators—were there, too. It was, by design, predominantly women, which led Tracy to deadpan at one point, "There are a few penises here, but a whole lot more balls." Jason Isbell, by this point one of the most revered songwriters in any genre, was happy to take a back seat and let the women lead as mama tried to change that Nashville sound, as he sang on his own song "White Man's World."

The group made its debut at Loretta Lynn's birthday tribute in April at the Bridgestone Arena. Everyone was there—the Pistol Annies, Kacey, Margo, Cam. Everyone, it seemed, except for Mickey. She would have been a perfect choice—Mickey loved Loretta, and had even opened for her at the Ryman in 2017. But she had been pushed out of the system so far that she didn't even seem to come to mind when it came to putting together the tribute.

Mickey had just released a song, too, called "Hold On," cowritten with Karen Kosowski and Victoria Banks. It wasn't shipped to radio, but instead written for the movie *Breakthrough*. "She was ready to try something new and take a risk on people," said Karen, who had joined Victoria as one of Mickey's closest and most trusted collaborators. "She was just so open and wanting to try stuff." But she still wasn't having her own breakthrough.

"Why is it not working for me?" she asked her husband, Grant, sitting at a bar in Los Angeles one night.

"It's because you are running away from everything that makes you different," he said.

Mickey had read a book called *Black Like Me* when she was in college, about a man who had darkened his skin with ultraviolet radiation to try to understand the Black experience. She had written the title down, not thinking that it could ever blossom into a song, or that anyone in Nashville would even give her close to enough permission to record it. At a writer's camp in the spring with Nathan Chapman, Fraser Churchill, and Emma Davidson Dillon, she brought the title with her—a camp organized by her publisher Warner Chappell, with the idea to mix writers from different disciplines and genres. And she thought about what Grant had told her: that it was time to stop running away from who she thought she should be, and start running toward who she really was.

About an hour after the group had gathered and gotten comfortable together, Mickey brought up her idea for "Black Like Me," as Fraser started strumming on the guitar, talking through the trajectory of her life: growing up as a child in Texas, moving to Nashville, what it was like to be a Black woman in an industry dominated by white men. "I wanted to tap into a soulful, rootsy feel and push the harmony a little further than your typical country song," Fraser said. "I remembered thinking a voice as effortless as Mickey's deserves a little more harmonic freedom. Maybe even a key change in the bridge."

The whole thing was finished quickly, and Mickey recorded the song right then and there. The next time Fraser watched Mickey sing "Black Like Me" live, it would be onstage at the Grammy Awards.

"All of the writing came from all of us, and I don't know, it was a 'God moment,'" she said. "It was a unity moment. It really just goes to show, if you really, truly do try to understand somebody else's perspective, you really can. Just a lot of people don't try."

In June, one festival decided to shake up the norm—a bit. The Country LakeShake Festival in Chicago booked a day comprised entirely of women, as a way to respond to the growing frustrations about representation in country music. It was, unfortunately, filled with white women only. Mickey reportedly wasn't asked to participate—and how could she have been? The industry had never let her be successful enough to have the fame that would permit her. Still, in a year with abysmal female representation on country festival bills, it was something.

"Can you see?" asked Miranda, standing side stage as Maren, in sequined hot pants, a pink sweater, and a glistening white guitar, walked out to a screaming crowd that unfolded across the grounds. It was approaching dusk, and Miranda was there to watch Maren's set alongside Cassadee Pope, Lindsay Ell, and Lauren Alaina, who all played earlier and were keeping warm with extra sweaters and extra tequila on the chillier-than-most June evening. Miranda, in tie-dye blue fringe, pleather skirt, and white cowboy boots, was set to headline shortly, but at that moment she just wanted to hang and take in the show, her hand tucked into her husband's back pocket, and make sure everyone else could see, too. She tapped her boot heel as Maren sang, one Texas artist to another.

Glancing out into the crowd at LakeShake from the side stage, it looked just like any average country festival—not the girly, pinkafied cotton candy dream that seems to deck out most "female-themed" events. Beers were being consumed, already spilling out and creating sticky paths along the concrete. American flags, midriffs, tops that said things like WORK, WINE, YOGA, REPEAT. The occasional whiff of marijuana. Troops of college-age bros in patriotic shirts toasted each other, shooting down whiskey, while others posed under the many Instagram-ready backdrops, the city of Chicago lingering behind, just over the lake. The whole idea of booking a day of entirely female artists was to prove that men wanted to be here, too—that not only did women want to hear women, but men would buckle up and come on out. And it seemed to be working. There were men here, and not just dragged by their wives or girlfriends in some sort of ploy to get them to return the next day, when Keith Urban would headline. They came for the songs.

That was a premise that Maren and Miranda had gambled on, too—both taking only women on the road this year, as did Carrie Underwood and Kacey. Kacey, in particular, was doing so while breaking out of the country music barriers: she'd recruited acts like Yola, Maggie Rogers, and indie rock's Soccer Mommy along for her post-Grammy run. Miranda's Roadside Bars and Pink Guitars Tour would embark across the country starting in September, taking Maren, Elle King, Pistol Annies, Tenille Townes, Ashley McBryde, and Caylee Hammack on the road, and Maren's headlining run began in March, right around the release of *Girl*. All were selling out easily in almost every city, in auditorium and arena dates.

"Girl" was getting so big and so powerful that Maren had started to open her shows with it, letting the audience do most of the work. LakeShake was no different, and the second that signature vamp started emanating from Maren's guitar, their voices filled the whole festival in a collective note—big, powerful, hungry, together. Maren sang some words here and there, but she mostly left it up to the crowd to take care of it. *"Everything's gonna be okay,"* they cried, she cried. In this moment, that felt true.

When Miranda finally went onstage for her set, the darkness had settled over the Chicago sky, and the entire festival grounds had filled out, lit sporadically by the glow of iPhones, eager to capture snippets of the star. Once again, the rest of the women watched side stage, yielding Solo cups and dancing, but they weren't done for the night—earlier, Lindsay Ell, Lauren Alaina, Maren, Cassadee Pope, and Angaleena Presley and Ashley Monroe from the Pistol Annies would hole up with Miranda in her trailer, nailing down the harmonies to "I Still Haven't Found What I'm Looking For" by U2. This is how Miranda wanted to close the show: with all of her friends and colleagues beside her. They hashed it out quickly with computer printouts, Ashley Monroe smoking a joint and Cassadee Pope reciting the whole thing from memory, tossing her lyrics to the side.

"We're gonna make a toast to women singing women's songs," Miranda said, calling everyone up at the end of her set, and they filtered across the stage—Lindsay Ell's highlighter-yellow shirt, Maren's glitter, Cassadee Pope in cargo pants, and Lauren Alaina in a red jumpsuit, which eventually ended up covered in the cocktail Cassadee had brought onstage. Miranda stood in the middle, singing her verse with her eyes closed, and then when they got to the end, the band dropped out: it was just the women up there, alone with their voices, in tandem.

In her trailer, Lindsay Ell breathed a sigh of relief: she wasn't used to having other women around to commiserate with. Most of the time when she played country festivals she was the only woman artist in sight, and having other female artists around wasn't just about having someone to knock back a few martinis with and borrow a blow-dryer and some lash glue. It was about a different kind of security. Normally women had to look the other way when testosterone-pumped antics took over, and often there wasn't even a designated place for women to change their clothes.

Two weeks after LakeShake Maren was back in Tennessee, winding down a back road about forty-five minutes outside of Nashville in Franklin, a popular suburb full of mansions with reclaimed barnwood walls and an all-American main street. She was headed to meet her other crew—Brandi, Natalie, and Amanda, aka the Highwomen.

On a steaming southern summer day they would make the video for "Redesigning Women," the band's first single, which they were hoping might actually get some radio play. Maren parked in the grassy field where the filming was stationed, taking a break while everyone else hung out in Brandi's bus eating BLTs made with tomatoes straight from Amanda's garden. Maren was feeling a little sick and not ready to socialize yet, and would later find out that was because she was expecting a baby boy.

"We're eatin' bacon," Natalie said, wearing her white Highwomen shirt as she helped Amanda assemble sandwiches, wiping bacon grease on her jeans. Brandi's wife, Catherine, was sitting in the back, and Brandi, as she is wont to do, was shuffling around the bus making sure everyone was getting enough of anything they needed: Mayonnaise? Sprite? A water?

"Women want to see themselves represented," Brandi said as they had their late lunch. "We just think we need to help re-illuminate that path."

In a few hours, Tanya Tucker would arrive—Tanya Mother Tucker, as she is lovingly called by her fans and almost everyone there—along with some of country music's most promising voices like Hailey Whitters, Kassi Ashton, and Cam—and the plan was to burn some shit down. Quite literally: they would be wearing fireman costumes and stacking up a bonfire, setting it ablaze. There would be plenty of wine poured, and maybe a few puffs from Tanya's vape pen.

In the days prior to the shoot, the team, eager to fill the set with up-and-coming artists, had overextended their hand: they'd asked too many people to show up, and had to do the uncomfortable task of rescinding some of the invitations. And one of them happened to be Mickey's.

"On one occasion, I left my ailing husband, who almost died from sepsis, in California just four days after his lifesaving surgery because I had been invited to be a part of a female empowerment music video," Mickey wrote in *Billboard*. "I arrived at the airport exhausted but excited. I checked my itinerary only to find that the entry had been deleted; I had been disinvited. The song was about supporting women in country, yet they disinvited the only charting African American woman in country music. Do they know? Don't they see that I support them? Do they care? Do they want to see me? The answer is no. Let that sink in."

Maren was horrified when she found out later that Mickey was talking about the Highwomen. "We were notified of this yesterday + were completely mortified that such a giant miscommunication occurred under our watch at the shoot that day & have each reached out to Mickey privately with the utmost respect & apologies," Maren tweeted. "It shouldn't have happened & isn't what we stand for."

It wasn't. But it did help make it clear how powerfully the Nashville machine squashed its Black female artists—if Mickey wasn't visible to the team of people putting on a female-centric music video, how could she ever be visible? What had already gotten in motion was a rethinking on behalf of everyone involved that maybe their interpretation of feminism could grow even more from how they first envisioned it: they didn't just need to help open the door, they needed to be out there actively fighting for everyone country music left behind. They had work to do, and the Highwomen were committed to doing the work.

"There's a lot of women doing a lot harder work than us, and a lot longer or a lot more marginalized than us. But it was a labor of love," said Brandi.

It was a fall of both empty gestures and important strides: the CMA Awards would announce in August that Dolly Parton and Reba McEntire would be taking over hosting duties from Brad Paisley to join Carrie Underwood in "celebrating women" when the show aired in November (though plenty dismissed this as lip service from an organization that has otherwise done next to nothing to further gender equality), while Carrie would simultaneously lose Entertainer of the Year to Garth Brooks at a show she was hosting. Appropriately, Jennifer Nettles showed up in a Christian Siriano pantsuit and cape with the words "Play our f*@#in records please and thank you" written on the inside. Lil Nas X and "Old Town Road" would make delightful waves, only to be rejected from the *Billboard* country charts and country radio for not having "elements of country" while songs with drum machines and snap tracks made by white men hit number one.

Brandi was busy producing Tanya Tucker's comeback record, working to correct the record on a talent that country music had squandered, all while spending the year planning for the Newport Folk Festival: she'd been asked to curate an all-women mainstage lineup, so she got busy handwriting letters to anyone and everyone she wanted to show up, which is what she'd always done when she really wanted to leave an impression. This, she thought, would be the perfect venue for the Highwomen to start sending their messages to the world, and start playing their songs. Newport had always been the sort of venue for insurgent country that they were looking for, and she knew that kind of audience would be won over and ready to listen.

But first, she had to send one particular letter, to a particular person: Dolly Parton.

Well, before Dolly Parton, it was eight shots of tequila and some Radiohead. Eight shots? Five shots? Who could know, really. A lot of tequila. Like, a lot. Ouch.

Brandi had played an explosive set at Newport Folk Festival in 2018, and ended up at one of the festival's notorious after-parties, hosted by Rhode Island's own Deer Tick, led by the talented songwriter John McCauley. Deer Tick's Newport parties were the hardest tickets of all to snag, and Brandi and Jay Sweet, producer of the festival, had found their way there after a long conversation that picked up on one he had started with Margo Price a few years earlier and had continued ever since then. Margo had told Jay that he needed to find more women to populate the stages: less white men, more of everyone else. Margo's first year, in 2016, she had come on her own dime to a small Nashville-to-Newport showcase. Jay happened to be walking by and heard her set. "This isn't my last year here," she told Jay point-blank. The next year, she ended up onstage with Kris Kristofferson. Johnny Cash had actually introduced the world to Kris at the Newport Folk Festival in 1969, just a couple of dudes sticking up and vouching for each other. Women often had to give that vouch, that public fist-bump, to themselves.

Newport was always more than a festival. Famous for being the site where Bob Dylan went electric, it has been at the forefront of the intersection between music and culture—or counterculture—since its inception, especially when it came to civil rights and activism. Jay, who became the head after leaving *Paste* magazine, had felt an allegiance to positioning it as both fulfilling that mission and driving it further. Legendary folk icon Pete Seeger, who was one of Newport Folk Festival's original board members, had instructed him as such. "Learning how to sing marching songs for civil rights for extremely wealthy, college-educated Ivy League schoolers to mix with Black blues men from the Deep South, for the Georgia Sea Island Singers to mix with Appalachian shape note singers who obviously had not had the most integrated upbringings," Jay said. "This festival has always been a conduit to not only speaking truth to power and for bucking the norm, and providing a safe haven for that to happen and to be explored and celebrated. But that hadn't happened for a long time."

"This is yours to do and build, and hopefully build it back," Pete told Jay. "Find those that are trying to speak truth to power, and those that are being their authentic selves." He also said that one of the biggest ways to do this and to make sure that Newport stayed true to its founding mission was by making sure that there was a woman or a person of color on every stage, every day. "It was just kind of the rule," Jay said. Amanda Shires, Jay remembered, had also been seminal in keeping the pressure on: applauding him when lineups looked balanced, and checking him when they did not—even pushing for Mavis Staples to close the show in 2019. She was, Jay said, "my mentor for holding me accountable," and he was already looking to her for guidance as he thought toward the next incarnation of the festival.

Newport Folk, founded by George Wein in 1959, had always booked their lineup intentionally, but it had never had an all-women set on the headlining stage. So Jay handed the keys over to Brandi on that night in 2018 to make that happen, the very night that Jay felt he watched her transform into a world-class star right in front of his eyes.

Brandi had played a monstrous headlining set earlier in the day, and they were cruising around after the show on the Newport Helicopter, the festival's thirty-four-foot boat, doing some shots with Phil Hanseroth. They were emotional—the crowd had been ravenous, and Brandi and the band had sucked up every bit of lingering energy, a respite in the midst of a toxic political climate. It got Brandi thinking about what else it all could become, because "there's a revolution happening here," she said. The world was complicated if not downright sad—Donald Trump's presidency had not only further divided the country, kids were being separated from their families at the border, and long-fought-for protections for LGBTQIA+ Americans were at risk of being rolled away. Newport couldn't change any of that, but it could use music as a model.

"Has a woman ever put together a headlining set?" Brandi asked Jay, who quickly shook his head.

"No," he said. "But we are going to do a shot, shake hands, and I am going to give you the keys so that a year from tonight, you will MC an all-female stage." Brandi was immediately on board. They set the specific rules: if men were there, like Jason Isbell or Hozier, it had to be in support of women, and everyone was going to be paid the same. "You're going to make history," he said, "and it's going to be one of the best ones I've ever been involved in in fifteen years."

After shaking hands and making it official—2019 would be Brandi's all women-headlining stage, signed and sealed with their grasped palms—she and Jay decided to celebrate their "blood oath pact" at that Deer Tick after-party back in Newport at the Newport Blues Café. They'd snaked up to the front row to watch the band at the tiny, packed club, and, between songs, the crowd started chanting out of nowhere—they'd spotted her there, and wanted more.

Brandi! Brandi! Brandi!

Brandi and Jay looked at each other. "Should I sing a song?" she asked. "What do I do?"

"Yes!" Jay responded, urging her up. They'd had enough tequila to make it all seem like a good idea, and, besides, they were on a victory lap. "And Deer Tick knows every song—they're a human jukebox. Why don't you sing 'Creep' by Radiohead?"

"Fuck yeah," Brandi said, hopping onstage and whispering into John's ear, who laughed and immediately launched into the song. Jay, in the audience, was awestruck: there was Brandi, drunk and with a band she'd never met before, screaming the words to "Creep" to a crowd that had beckoned her there, a queer woman and a singer-songwriter finally reconnecting with the country roots that she'd loved in a more significant way, on the cusp of international stardom. A red bandana wrapped around her head, her denim shirt partially unsnapped, her sunglasses hanging on her collar: "*I don't belong here,*" she hollered into the crowd. Jay got chills. No one here belonged, so together, they all did.

"I watched her transform right there in front of my eyes, screaming like a fucking rock star," Jay remembered. "And I just need to get the fuck out of this woman's way. Amanda is the blueprint person, who will put her finger between your eyes. Brandi is the one who will make you believe the dream, and when your head gets too big, Margo is the one who will kick you in the balls."

Jay woke up the next morning with an enormous hangover—and Brandi got to work planning the lineup. They brought up Dolly almost as a joke. She would make it killer, they agreed—she was motherfucking Dolly Parton. No one thought it would be possible to pull off, but Brandi started writing those letters, because the importance of Dolly wasn't just symbolic. Her place as an agent of change could not have been more clear: Dolly worship was reaching a resurgent fever pitch, with podcasts, books, and documentaries exploring her influence at every corner, including a series inspired by her songs called Dolly Parton's *Heartstrings*, her fifty-year anniversary at the Grand Ole Opry, and the Netflix film inspired by her songs, *Dumplin'*.

Over the course of the year, everything felt like it was going to either implode or explode. Egos emerged and retreated, artists canceled and rebooked. Brandi and Jay went into crisis mode and back more than once, but somehow artist after artist just kept saying yes. Jay's phone would ring with constant updates, "BC" showing up when she'd call. When the Highwomen formed at the end of 2018 and introduced themselves to the world after the new year, Amanda and Brandi knew Newport would be the perfect place for them to perform.

"It was just a rolling snowball," Jay said, "that you either allow to envelop you, and go along for the ride, or get the fuck out of the way. And it was the most powerful thing I've ever witnessed. Watching this ball of musical energy start rolling downhill after people kept putting up barricade after barricade."

There were many times when it felt like everything was going to fall apart, but never more severe than when Maren's song looked like it would head to number one just as they were rounding close to showtime; she was the first woman to hit that slot in well over a year, since Kelsea Ballerini's "Legends." Suddenly, Jay could feel her team pulling back—they wanted her to be somewhere else, he thought. That was a huge deal, and he knew it—"Girl" was exploding in country and beyond, and maybe Newport wasn't the best place for her to be, about as far from Music Row as you could find, with Maren not even as the headliner. Folks from her label were calling Jay en masse: *This could be the biggest weekend for the biggest woman in country music, and how the fuck are you telling us that she is not available?*

Everyone was pulling back, except for Maren herself, that is. She wasn't backing down or dropping out, and the Highwomen's set went off without a hitch that Friday afternoon on July 26, 2019—save for the lack of permit that the band had wanted to secure so festivalgoers could get their own "Highwomen" tattoos. In custom Manuel suits and backed by Brandi's bandmates Tim and Phil Hanseroth as well as Jason Isbell, Brandi let her nerves show. "This is our first show, y'all," she said to the crowd. "And we're fucking terrified." Newport also introduced honorary Highwoman Yola to the mix, who sang with the group on the record's title track and stunned everyone with her tremendous voice. Even Sheryl Crow showed up.

"I didn't feel like a token," Yola told Natalie Weiner of the *New York Times*. "This felt like a cross intersection of women—and in country music, of all the places where you're like, 'That's so white bro it's out of control.'"

Catherine Powell, who had become the go-to photographer for Kacey and Maren, came along to shoot the band's first live photos, and she was shocked by how many people had turned up to hear songs from a band whose record wasn't even out yet. "There were people pouring out of the tent to watch them," she remembered. "We were all buzzing."

And just as "Girl" was going to number one, Maren was congratulated by Dolly Parton herself, on the Newport stage. It was the day after the Highwomen's set, the vision that Brandi had been planning all along: The Collaboration, she called it. Yola, Amy Ray from the Indigo Girls, Sheryl, Courtney Marie Andrews, Lucy Dacus, Linda Perry, Maggie Rogers, Judy Collins, and Molly Tuttle were just a few of the women who gathered to sing together (Margo, at home with her newborn daughter, had missed the festival, but Jay considered her very much there in spirit): leading to the seminal moment of Dolly. Backstage rehearsing "Eagle When She Flies" a cappella in a circle with the Highwomen, Jason Isbell had teared up, while Natalie's hands shook. Right before they walked onstage, they all got on their knees and prayed together.

Dolly had her own yellow suit embroidered with roses, and the crowd erupted at the first sight of her: a surprise they managed to keep by shrouding Dolly in a voluminous black robe as she arrived at the property (she'd flown in on a jet she arranged and paid for herself), only her ruby-red cowboy boots peeping out of the bottom. They closed the set with everyone onstage for "9 to 5," dancing together, revelatory as hell. "Everyone had this look as if they had met fucking Snow White," Jay remembered, watching the women walk offstage afterward with their mouths agape.

Writer Suzy Exposito was left afterward with a lingering, important question. "Though this year's Newport lineup was the closest it's ever come to feminist utopia, how many more years will it take until we achieve a wider-scale semblance of gender parity in music, much less any industry in the United States?" she wrote in *Rolling Stone*. "And if the future is female, will it get any blacker, or browner, or more fluid in its expression? Will it speak languages besides English, and still play guitar?"

The band was staying at a hotel across the harbor on an island—they rode the ferry afterward in shock. "We were just all sitting at dinner being like, did that really happen?" Catherine remembered. "And then we just all drank a lot of wine." It was far different than how someone in Nashville might usually celebrate a song going number one—certainly not surrounded by "Americana" artists in day-old clothes after performing at a folk festival. But that was Maren.

"She was not on a fucking stadium tour with rhinestones and singing to people wearing cowboy hats," Jay said. "She was at by far the lowest-paying gig she's probably ever done in her career once she was discovered, not singing her own songs, not even being part of the Highwomen, which had happened the day before. But literally being a backup singer to a collection. Being part of something greater. Maren fucking Morris. Maren fucking Morris was not taking a bow or doing anything. She was standing among others, singing '9 to 5' into the same fucking microphone, in cutoff jeans, doing the makeup by herself in a fucking trailer. She could have done a festival as the headliner, but she chose not to, and to do something that was better for all women, not just her." She had walked offstage and given Jay a big hug with tears in her eyes. He couldn't believe that Maren was there, that Brandi had just spent a chunk of the biggest year of her career yet leading to this moment, that Jason Isbell had eagerly taken a spot in the back seat to help elevate those around him. He couldn't believe it, but it had all come true.

"There were ten things trending in the world," Jay continued. "It was the only thing that was musical and positive. There was a shooting at a garlic festival in California, a chemical attack in Libya. The world was trending the wrong way. The only things trending positive were Brandi Carlile, the Highwomen, Newport, and Dolly Parton's surprise set."

The impact was instantaneous. "Every single festival was like, We need to get Maren Morris," Jay said. "And we will pay the Highwomen whatever they want."

Also at Newport was Our Native Daughters, with a performance that didn't get the same kind of trending topics but set in motion something even deeper and more disruptive to the status quo. Though the Highwomen were referred to as the supergroup of the weekend, here was a foursome of one MacArthur Grant recipient (Rhiannon) and three dynamite and unique songwriters in Allison, Amythyst, and Leyla, putting the banjo at the forefront of the conversation, an instrument that came from West Africa and had come to be intentionally adopted as symbol of whiteness—an act Rhiannon had referred to as "cultural genocide."

Our Native Daughters rolled in on Sunday, the day after Dolly's set, in the wake of nonstop media coverage, and felt, as Allison put it, "a little left out of the party." Rhiannon had never played anywhere but the main stage at Newport, and she was a little taken aback as to why Our Native Daughters hadn't been given that spot. "I guess you get demoted if you bring along other Black women," she quipped.

"We pulled in with these derelict buses with the kids in various stages of meltdown," Allison remembered—the band had traveled with their young children and a Montessori teacher to help wrangle them all when the moms were onstage. "And saw this absolutely gorgeous, perfectly shiny Highwomen bus. It was just very funny." Their set, though, was transformative: six standing ovations, lots of tears, and a mostly white audience being confronted by uncomfortable truths about who exactly built their country and roots music—almost hungry, Allison thought, for what they were saying.

"Within the span of an hour, the quartet traded off on an all-embracing array of old-time songs—equal parts gut-wrenching and galvanizing—that told a four-hundred-odd-year story of black womanhood in America," Jonathan Bernstein wrote for *Rolling Stone*. "There were repeated standing ovations . . . and plenty of tears . . . , but also an endless display of joy all the while. . . . As [Amythyst] Kiah put it at the end of the set, 'This has been a spiritual experience with y'all today.'"

The quartet would join Mavis Staples later as she closed out the show, warming up beforehand in Hozier's trailer and then rehearsing in a circle with Mavis herself before heading onstage with the Preservation Hall Jazz Band, Jason Isbell, Hozier, and Phil Cook. "That's the heart of Newport," Allison says. "A festival that started racial reconciliation in this country in a sense." The Highwomen, Dolly, even a sweet duet between My Morning Jacket's Jim James and Kermit the Frog on "Rainbow Connection" captured the media zeitgeist. But Our Native Daughters, that day, were steering everyone to an even bigger conversation, and speaking truth to power.

There would be no Newport Folk Festival in 2020, but Allison would go on, in 2021, to curate her own mainstage set called "Once and Future Sounds: Roots and Revolution," after the May release of her debut solo album, *Outside Child*, which was stunning, truthful, and beautifully raw. It was a performance that seemed to tackle Suzy Exposito's question: Yola, Amythyst, Joy Oladokun, Adia Victoria, Sunny War, Celisse, Yasmin Williams, and many others all gathered to sing, with Chaka Khan as the legendary surprise guest this time.

Backstage, Yola and Chaka were chatting in German, and Brandi and Margo were just happy to be dancing in the background in supporting roles, with Brandi's Looking Out Foundation helping to foot the bill to pay the artists for their time. Jay Sweet had handed over the keys once again, this time to Allison, who created the collaboration in the spirit of folk icon Odetta, who had played the very first Newport Folk Festival. Chaka had "The Fort" jumping and dancing to "I'm Every Woman" harder than Jay had ever seen—Allison and Adia Victoria sharing a mic, grinning like schoolchildren, Brandi pointing to the crowd and hollering with joy, Allison's rainbow jumpsuit reflecting the lights as she moved.

"I was very much conscious on building what Brandi began and making sure Black women were centered on that stage that we built," Allison reflected. "Because there is no scarcity. There is no world where you only need one woman's voice. Or one Black woman's voice. It's just a fallacy. And this is what happens if you let more than one of us in. It's joyful. And it's glorious."

"I didn't say fucking YEE!"

Kacey's summer of 2019 was proving to be huge, bigger than anyone could have imagined. After *Golden Hour* and the Grammys, demand for her time exploded—from live shows to the famous Met Gala, where she dressed up as a Barbie doll, complete with bleached-blond hair and a pink Corvette. She was at Newport, too (though she declined the opportunity to appear as part of Brandi's all-women stage), and traipsed around to most of the major festivals, including Governors Ball in New York, where she celebrated Pride Month with rainbows engulfing the crowd and the stage, closing the set with, appropriately, "Rainbow." "Every month should be Pride Month," she said. At Coachella, she birthed a meme by yelling, "I didn't say fucking YEE" to the crowd, but she also, once again, birthed conservative anger.

Driven to the edge by the continuous roll of mass shootings, she said from the stage of Lollapalooza in Chicago, exasperated: *"Somebody fucking do something."*

Once again, Kacey became Fox News and conservative radio's favorite target. "I'll say this about Ms. Musgraves, she's got a mouth that would make Hank Williams, Jr. blush," wrote the wildly conservative talk show host Todd Starnes in August (for the record, Hank Jr.'s son has written songs such as "Go Fuck You" and "Punch Fight Fuck"). Kacey, who had once spoken about liking Ron Paul, was doing what so many, from artists to politicians to everyday citizens, were incapable of: evolving.

"It's sad to say, but Ms. Musgraves is part of a new wave of liberal artists who are determined to change the culture and twang of country music," Starnes continued, going on to specify three conservative white men who he hoped would preserve the genre for people like him. "Now, I don't want to unduly alarm folks. So long as we have Hank and Charlie [Daniels] and Big & Rich, I think country music will be able to weather the leftist onslaught."

If he didn't like what Kacey had to say, he certainly wasn't going to like the Highwomen, whose debut album came out in the fall of 2019 after their appearance at Newport, and the critical response was fawning—but country radio still hadn't gotten on board. So the band decided to give it one last good push, gathering at RCA Studio A on October 1, the place where the record had been made. The idea was to see if they could sway the country radio programmers to their side with a live performance, and a bit of VIP treatment. Though no one was feeling exactly optimistic about the odds, they felt that if they at least did the full-court press and extended an olive branch to country radio, they could sleep at night knowing that they tried, and tried on country radio's terms.

And they pulled out the stops—the free booze, swanky bus shuttles, and a full performance, where they played several songs including

"Redesigning Women" not once but twice, maybe to see if doing so could help seep them into the brains of the programmers who were only designed to think a certain way. Familiarity, after all, was key.

It was an emotional time for Maren and Natalie especially, as busbee had just passed away—he died after a brief and viciously fast brain cancer, and the country community was in shock, especially Maren. She'd lost a creative partner, but she'd also lost a friend. The stage was charged—they had a hard time not breaking out in tears when certain lyrics came around. Maren was also the only one in the group who couldn't so easily dismiss what would become a failed opportunity: radio barely played the song. "You have to respect me, because I do this shit for a living," Maren remembered telling her bandmembers before the event—this was her turf, even if it wasn't theirs.

Brandi felt like she had to perform a level of ass-kissing she had not entertained since she was trying to grow a small fan base and get labels to notice her in the early stages of her career. "I was expected to suck up at a level that I hadn't since I was a teenager," Brandi said, "trying to get gigs at local clubs and bars or trying to get a record deal. It made me feel like I was twenty-one years old again, and I'm a forty-year-old woman with seven or more albums out. These people, especially the men, seemed like they knew they had a serious upper hand on me in that situation. I was like, wow, 'Is this culturally the way it is here?' I was a bit traumatized by the genre."

Chapter 18

WE BELONG

I'm a new kind of outlaw
Can there be a spot for us all?
So many of us feel like outlaws
Where's real community?
All of us together
I love country music, will country music love me?
—D'orjay The Singing Shaman

A little girl in a white canopy bed in the middle of Texas was lining up her stuffed animals, one by one. They were the audience and she, ten-year-old Mickey Guyton, with grass-stained knees and a ponytail, had just won a Grammy Award, floating to the stage in a voluminous dress fit for a diva like Whitney Houston or Dolly Parton or maybe some combination of the two. It was there she would practice her acceptance speech into a hairbrush, or her "surprise" face, or how exactly she wanted to thank God and her parents.

That little girl, in tights and a skirt and red bows, would become the accompanying artwork for a song she'd write decades later, called "What Are You Gonna Tell Her?" It would finally tell her truth and simultaneously break her heart.

Mickey had landed in Nashville after a flight from Los Angeles one February morning in 2020, the day she would write that very song, and she was exhausted—a new kind of mental exhaustion that grabs your being and shakes it, overburdened and run-down. She had been to a social event in L.A. before she left, a Grammy party, and everywhere she looked the executives appeared exactly the same: white, male, white, male, repeat. Though the party was filled with female superstars, no women who looked like them, or her, were actually the ones in power, and she knew that even the most famous female singers had all had to deal with the realities of a broken system and a world that makes little rectification for its deeply embedded misogyny: What did Billie Eilish or Beyoncé, she wondered, have to put up with just to get to where they were? How did they have to bat their eyelashes to be heard?

Mickey had come to Nashville for a writing session with Victoria Banks, Emma-Lee, and Karen Kosowski. Victoria, at this point a trusted collaborator, had come from Canada to pursue a life as a songwriter and had arrived in town just in time to see the female singer boom, but she was also there to watch it fall, and watch the demand for songs written for and by women tumble with it. But she did strike up a longterm writing relationship with Mickey, and they started to talk about what she had seen at that party, and how it had stuck with her.

"Mickey had been looking around at all of these female superstars in pop music, and seeing them all surrounded by men in business suits," Victoria remembered. "And she just suddenly had this epiphany of, 'We don't own ourselves.' Even the most powerful women don't appear to own themselves, and we still have to work, we have to go through this overlay of people who are in charge of our careers, and who has a say that's greater than ours in a lot of situations. And in Nashville, that was even worse."

It hit Mickey profoundly and deeply.

"You have daughters," she said, looking at Victoria that day in the studio. "What are you going to tell your daughters? What do you tell them?"

"I have no idea," Victoria responded. Hers were two and four at that point, and Victoria had been tossing around in her head how to prepare them for the world they were about to step into.

"We started talking about that," Victoria later recalled. "I was like, they're growing up. Especially my four-year-old is starting to have her own opinions about things, and she's very confident and she sees the world as a fair place. And she sees absolutely no rhyme or reason why she shouldn't be able to do absolutely anything. I think, at some point, Do I need to tell her? Do I need to warn her that she's not going to have the same shot? Or do I just let her discover that for herself? I don't know. I don't know what I'm supposed to tell her."

"Guys, that's the song that we need to write today," Emma-Lee said. She was right.

It flew out fast centered around the piano. Mickey cried through cutting her vocals, grasping the mic stand to steady herself when she needed to: she was exhausted and emotionally drained, but stuck around in the studio to finish the song that day so they could capture the intensity that had existed in the room. It was triumphant, but as usual, Mickey assumed it would never even see the light of day—she'd written songs as potent as this before, and the label had dismissed them all, and when she had played "Black Like Me" to some friends in the industry, they seemed overwhelmed by the weight of it, or maybe their own discomfort. Mickey texted the group about the new song later, texts that would go on to be printed to posterboard and hung in the Country Music Hall of Fame. "I'm still crying," she wrote. "I just want to say thank you, seriously thank you guys for believing in me. Thank you for always saying yes to write with me. Thank you for never brushing me aside. Thank you for always considering me. Thank you for accepting me. I'm just emotional right now because it's finally happening. They finally saw me."

Two weeks later, the label called. They said that "What Are You Gonna Tell Her?" was the song that they wanted Mickey to play at the upcoming CRS Team UMG luncheon—the same event where she had debuted nearly a decade before to a standing ovation and then saw nothing take off from the programmers happy to stand and clap like seals without delivering anything for her when they returned to their desks. To the same programmers and executives who had built the walls around country music, the ones she was warning little girls about in that very song. She said yes. Above anything else, what Mickey Guyton wanted to do was sing.

The day was filled with the usual range of performances—a dude named Travis Denning with a song named "Abby," programmers munching on their free sandwiches, heavyweights like Carrie Underwood and Sam Hunt. When Mickey sang, with Karen on the piano, the room stopped, quieted. Once again, she got the entire audience on their feet clapping. She thought back a lot to 2013, and how the industry had failed her since then, and how she sometimes failed herself by not doubling down on her own story. This time, though, when she came out to sing "What Are You Gonna Tell Her?" she was fully prepared for what would happen, even if she'd never be invited back on that stage again. Andrea Williams, a journalist and activist in Nashville who spent much of 2020 writing deep and profound investigations into country music's historic and current racial biases, called it "a capital-M Moment." Some in the pews wiped back tears while others tried to avert their eyes from the truth they'd been ignoring, or kept stifled. Karen had a hard time not crying at the keys, her dyed-blue hair and glasses helping to obscure welling-up eyes.

"We both went back to the dressing room, and Emma-Lee and Victoria came back there," Karen remembered. "And we all were a bit shell-shocked. It was just this kind of crazy emotional moment where I didn't know what to say or do, I just wanted to cry my eyes out. Mickey is superhuman—I don't know how she managed to do it. I was so glad that all I had to do was play piano."

What happened next was a bitter one-two punch to any plans Mickey had for what to make of that moment: a tornado hit Nashville on March 3, tearing through the town and leaving many buildings and hearts broken, including the home Victoria Banks shared with her husband and children. COVID hit the city soon after, with some of the first cases reported popping up at a fundraiser for that very tornado. Soon, everything shut down and the world froze—and it's when things freeze that they start to finally crack.

Life in lockdown was difficult for everyone, and for musicians that was no exception. Kacey played a benefit show online, singing "Rainbow" from her house in Nashville—and kept her entire crew and staff paid by selling merch, from puzzles to socks. Maren gave birth to her baby boy a few weeks in after having to cancel her upcoming RSVP Tour, and Mickey started writing furiously over Zoom. Her performance of "What Are You Gonna Tell Her?" had started a subtle chatter at least among the media—it was never going to be played by any of those programmers who stood up from their seats at the Ryman, but it had unleashed something within her that carried more than the approval of a handful of white radio DJs.

After that performance, things felt new for Mickey. Clear. She started posting videos of other country music artists who didn't fit the white, male, or heteronormative role you'd see only on country radio: Latinx artists like Valerie Ponzio and Veronique Medrano, LGBTQIA+ artists like Harper Grae, Black artists like Brittney Spencer, Stephanie Jacques, and Reyna Roberts, a powerhouse singer with bright red hair who could beat any country vocalist in range—all different, all brilliant. And like her close friend Leah Turner, who had become intent on no longer stifling her Mexican roots and reclaiming her rightful place in the story of the genre. *Country also looks like this*, Mickey would write, posting their videos furiously to Instagram.

Beautiful albums were made and released in early quarantine. One of the best came from Hailey Whitters, a singer from Shueyville, Iowa. Iowa is not the South, but it's rural cornfields and cows and silos that stand as the only high points in the gauzy Midwest sky. Hailey grew up in the middle of one of those cornfields, with hair the color of a dried-up stalk, and had actually known both Maren and Kacey from early in her career—she once got into a fender bender with Kacey while down in Texas for a Miranda Lambert event, and a decade later joined Maren's Girl: The World Tour. Her album, *The Dream*, was a pristine work of songwriting thoroughly in her own mold.

Ashley McBryde's *Never Will* was a downright stunner and independent artists like Kelsey Waldon, Jaime Wyatt, Lauren Jenkins, Michaela Anne, and Emily Scott Robinson were giving the genre a home outside the major label system. Margo Price came out with an album coproduced by Sturgill Simpson, *That's How Rumors Get Started*, that rocked and roared. Ingrid Andress asked potent questions on her debut, *Lady Like*, which found her nominated for Best New Artist at the Grammy Awards, and Caylee Hammack proved to be a vocal and lyrical force. D'orjay The Singing Shaman's *New Kind of Outlaw* gave a rallying cry for everyone left out and left behind on its title track: *"I love country music, will country music love me?"*

And Cam's *The Otherside* showed an artist in full control of her power both sonically and personally—one of the most dynamic vocalists in the genre and an ardent truth-teller, Cam had been committed to not only making music that transcended the boundaries of country, but to pushing Music Row to become a place where everyone was not only welcomed, but actively sought out and recruited. Her band, comprising ace drummer Dre Williams and virtuosic guitarist Ellen Angelico, reflected a vision where people other than just white, straight men could be on stage.

On May 25, everything changed again—for Mickey, and for America. George Floyd, a forty-six-year-old Black man, was murdered in cold blood and plain sight by a police officer on the streets of Minneapolis. Officer Derek Chauvin knelt on Floyd's neck for just over nine minutes despite calls of struggle and pain, a gruesome act that was caught on camera by teenager Darnella Frazier.

Not many mainstream country artists went out of their way to express support for Black Lives Matter or Floyd's family, though Kacey did. "It's been hard to find the words to adequately convey how outraged and sad I am," she wrote on Twitter. "WHITE PEOPLE HAVE HAD IT SO FUCKING WRONG SINCE THE BEGINNING and I will do whatever I can I help break the DISGUSTING, damaging cycle of racism and systemic privilege causes. I will not be a bystander."

Maren joined in the sentiment, too, not only showing up for protests but working hard behind the scenes with artists like Cam to begin
to force the industry's hand to face a harsh reality: according to a study
done by Dr. Jada Watson, Black women made up .01 percent of spins
in country airplay in 2020. Maren masked up and marched for Black
Lives Matter and spoke openly about her distrust and distaste for the
current president, even appearing at a fundraiser for then presidential
candidate Joe Biden. And not as a Nashville outsider, or someone who
can take the rope given to them by a secure home in Americana or pop
or any genre where voicing one's opinions is welcomed, if not nearly
mandatory, but as someone fully engaged—happily—with Music Row
and country radio, who still banked airplay despite a world that rarely
sees any presence from female voices on the airwaves. She, Cam, and
Mickey showed up at board meetings and CMA brainstorms and
Zoom calls, even being scoffed at by prominent industry insiders (both
men and women), so intimidated and uncomfortable by their advocacy.

But Mickey—Mickey was heartbroken. She watched as peers and
"friends" stayed silent in the face of grave injustice, and she thought
about the time her own husband had been racially profiled by the
police simply for existing as himself, as a Black man with a nice car.
She'd had this feeling before, though, and it had catalyzed into song—
Mickey had written "Black Like Me" after the death of twenty-six-
year-old Botham Jean at the hands of a patrol officer who claimed she
mistook the accountant for an intruder, but clearly it could apply to
any number of lives taken by the people who are supposed to be pro-
tecting them. As protests broke out around the country, which Mickey
watched from her Los Angeles apartment, pregnant, she posted a
short clip of "Black Like Me" to Instagram without even the consent
of her label. Shortly after, Spotify called and asked for a copy that they
could slot into a playlist. They had to have it—nothing quite captured
the times and bridged across the political divide like country music,
written from the perspective of a person it was designed to work against.
They would release it on Blackout Tuesday, an industry-wide initiative

to spur action and meaningful allyship, though some never engaged much deeper than a photo of a black square on Instagram.

"We didn't even decide, it was asked," Mickey told Jonathan Bernstein at *Rolling Stone*. "Spotify came to us and asked us if they could have this song. . . . Honestly, I'm having to take CBD to calm my nerves. I'm not sleeping anymore because there's such a heavy responsibility with this song. And it's not a song to capitalize off of people's pain, because it's my pain."

"I've known Mickey Guyton since I moved to Nashville and she's always had a heart of gold and a voice with such conviction," Maren tweeted. "She released her single 'Black Like Me' recently and I hope our friends at country radio give it the airtime it deserves."

"Black Like Me" resonated instantly, climbing to number four on *Billboard*'s Digital Country Song Sales chart. With fans, that is, not radio: it made no impact on the airplay charts despite streaming numbers that rose daily. Some programmers tried to dismiss it, or Mickey, as "too pop," something that didn't seem to get in the way of their embrace of artists like Florida Georgia Line or even Maren.

"If they say that, they don't have to confront that maybe they aren't putting her forward because she's Black," Brandi Carlile said. "We can say things like 'Oh well, technically that doesn't sound like country, or that 'Black Like Me' sounds like pop. It's like an old kickstand—when we don't want to include someone, we can always say they don't sound country."

"Black Like Me" ended up nominated for best Country Solo Performance of the year at the Grammy Awards. It not only synthesized the world at the macro level, it synthesized and called attention to country music itself, a genre long past a reckoning—heightened even more by the fact that country radio refused to play it.

"The only way that I can make it in this industry is by holding the door open for other Black women, for other women and people of color and other marginalized people," Mickey told *Vogue* after learning about her nomination. "There's power in numbers, right? If you look at the country charts right now, it's almost all men, which is a huge issue for me. I just want to open doors, burn down that good old boys' town, and make it more of an inclusive genre, because so many people would love it if they were given the chance to be able to sing it."

Other institutions and artists were working to make amends for sins large and small and burn down the same good ol' white boys club, including the Chicks—though mostly, and notably, institutions outside of country music. Named after the Little Feat song "Dixie Chicken," the Chicks long felt ashamed of the connotations that came along with the antebellum roots of their name. In June 2020, just before the release of their comeback album *Gaslighter*, they announced they would be dropping the "Dixie" forever. "We want to meet this moment," they said, soon releasing a video for a new song called "March March" to make clear that they, too, supported Black Lives Matter, unabashedly and fully.

Having the Chicks back on the scene felt full circle. This time, they were completely eschewing country music, to the point that some media members inside the Nashville bubble felt as though they'd been left behind in the PR push. There were no fancy listening parties on Music Row, no media roundtables, no listening sessions for radio programmers. "We've always had to buck the system a little bit to be who we were and then once we were successful in country, then they welcomed us in and that was great, then they kicked us out," said the Chicks' Emily Strayer to NPR. "So we don't really know where we live anymore." Certainly it was not within the confines of an industry that goes to church on Sunday but had not done a minute of repenting for the sins they'd cast the Chicks' way. But the country music industry was having its hand forced, whether it liked it or not.

"It was literally the first time that we're having these conversations at this level," said Amanda Martinez, a PhD candidate in the history department at the University of California, Los Angeles, who studies race and the country music industry. "It's really the first time that the industry as a whole in Nashville has been forced to actually take it seriously. And we still have a very, very, very long way to go. But we're having these conversations, and that's exciting."

"Black Like Me" didn't just provide guidance to artists of color—it was also resonating deeply with Mickey's friend and country artist Brooke Eden, who was nervous about coming out about her relationship with her longtime girlfriend Hilary. She and Mickey had been friends since they both auditioned for *American Idol* and bonded over a straightening iron—Mickey had come to the rescue with the heat styling tool to smooth out Brooke's frizz before she went in front of the judges. *Who else would do that kind of thing?* Brooke thought. *Women are conditioned to think they need to compete, and not help each other out.*

Soon before the pandemic hit in February 2020, Mickey asked Brooke if she wanted to bake some chocolate chip cookies together and listen to some of her new songs, including "Black Like Me" and "What Are You Gonna Tell Her?" They'd kept in touch over the years on and off, but had recently run into each other at a songwriting round in town.

"Oh my God, Mickey, these songs are genre-altering," Brooke said, listening carefully to the lyrics.

"I'm just so sick of trying to blend in," Mickey replied, the cookies baking in the oven. "So sick of trying to be someone that I am not."

Mickey had known about Brooke's relationship with Hilary, but she'd always been told that coming out would be career suicide. "Girl, you have to tell your story," Mickey told her. "There is no way this genre is going to move forward if the people who can make it move forward are silent."

"You're right, but *how?*"

"Look, I'm about to put out this music that not everyone is going to like," Mickey said. "And you can, too. You almost have a responsibility to do so."

It shook her in all the right ways. Brooke knew she couldn't go on living in hiding—touring and singing her songs while worrying about slipping up on a pronoun choice—and sneaking around with Hilary was infecting every inch of her being, even causing ulcers in her stomach that sidelined her from the road. Mickey told her that she could be a voice for all the queer people who were listening to and loving country music, but who just hadn't seen themselves in it. "Maybe I need to be the queer artist that helps the artists in the generation behind me," Brooke said. "I had no other choice."

Soon, after coming out officially, she released "Got No Choice," singing and sharing her love for her girlfriend (soon fiancée) openly and proudly. Country radio wasn't playing her songs, but they were resonating: ten years after Chely Wright had told her own truth, here was another woman following in her footsteps, and while still fully part of the Music Row ecosystem. Maybe what she had to say wouldn't be accepted by the core conservative base, and maybe it didn't need to be. Maybe speaking to people like her was enough. Hunter Kelly, on his pioneering Apple Music Country radio show *Proud Radio*, certainly played her songs—he was building a community outside of terrestrial radio, as was Apple's diverse programming as a whole.

"The stakes were high, but they were high for me as a human," Brooke said. "The gates are opening and having to be open. 2020 was a year when people couldn't turn a blind eye anymore. Everyone realized that this is a different world now, and we are going to have to start looking at country music in a different way, and start creating a path for the future." Once Brooke came out, her messages on social media would be swamped with people telling their stories. People saying thank you, or confessing to her how they'd never felt like they belonged until they saw Brooke in her music video with her girlfriend, kissing and embracing and living just as they were. How they'd come out to their families and were bringing their partners home for Christmas that year.

There would be another landmark moment in country music after Brooke came out: T.J. Osborne, of the Brothers Osborne, would also sit with *Time* in February 2021 to talk openly about his life as a gay man. *Time* called it "a historic moment for the genre . . . T.J. may be the first to come out with his feet so firmly planted in both the sound and machinery of mainstream country, in the full bloom of his career." The Brothers Osborne, who shared a label with Mickey and Kacey and offered up guest vocals on *Girl*, were mostly still embraced by Music Row: and by the time it got to summer, T.J. and John were onstage at the Ryman with Miley Cyrus for her Stand By You Pride Month special, singing "We Belong." Miley had recruited Mickey and Maren, too, along with Orville Peck and Little Big Town, and it was a joyous celebration that previously would have felt impossible: ending up with them all onstage dancing at the place where so many country music dreams had been both made and broken, including Mickey's twice before. Maren looked over at T.J. at one point, she wearing Pucci-print pants and he a T-shirt from one of their incredibly talented and openly gay artist friends, Fancy Hagood, and had to hold back tears: *This couldn't have happened even six months ago*, she thought. In *Rolling Stone*, Jon Freeman called 2021 the year "country music was (finally) ready to come out." "So many kids feel invited to the party again," Brooke said.

"I gotta say," Miley told the audience, in a rainbow sequin skirt, hugging the brothers close. "We do belong. All of us."

"You can hold my hand," sang Brittney Spencer. It was from the High-women song "Crowded Table," as part of a series of casual covers she'd been recording at home and posting online to keep her busy during quarantine.

Maryland-born Brittney fell in love with country music in an unusual way—through the alternative rock station on the school bus. Brittney grew up in the church, singing in choir and watching the way that women commanded their craft and their instruments while serving God. It held an unusual power, a strength and selflessness, that captured her imagination. When she turned fifteen, a friend in downtown Baltimore told her that she needed to be listening to the Chicks, so she started tuning in to CMT. And it was on that bus that she'd hear the occasional Chicks or Shania Twain song, because they were the only ones who would occasionally pop into rotation outside of the country silo.

"When I started realizing what country music was, I fell in love," she said. "I didn't have any concept of genres. It was church music or not church music. This music cut through: I loved knowing exactly what happens when you hear 'let's go girls.' Country wasn't a niche market, it was for everyone." Hearing Taylor Swift pushed her even further down this road. "She's poetic, she is from Pennsylvania, and sonically she was doing something so different."

Brittney moved to Nashville in 2013, straight into a world where both Florida Georgia Line's "Cruise" and Kacey's "Merry Go 'Round" were dominating. She went to school at MTSU, busked on street corners, and tried to find people in town who seemed to understand and want to nurture her artistic approach.

When Maren released *Hero*, it was life-changing. "I thought, 'Oh my God, there's a space for me,'" Brittney said. "It wasn't a rigid album at all, and it's so musical, not a single lyric wasted. The album was all of my worlds coming together in a single record. Maren has meant so much to my journey. Being vocal online about Black Lives Matter, gun violence. In Nashville everyone is trying to be polite but she will tell her followers to fuck off if she needs to. I so appreciated that shit."

Alone in her studio apartment in October 2020, Brittney had been tinkering around with a few cover songs—everything from Justin Bieber to the Highwomen. She'd always been a fan of Natalie Hemby's writing in particular, and recorded her own spin on "Crowded Table," which Natalie had written with Brandi and the incredible and influential singer-songwriter Lori McKenna, and then threw it up on her Twitter account, not thinking much of what might happen next. Instead, she woke to frantic texts from her friends and family, asking her if they had seen Amanda Shires's tweet: she'd shared Brittney's video, and soon, so did Maren and Natalie. Not long after, Amanda would invite her to come out to her and Jason Isbell's home studio to write with the couple and end up on the Highwomen's next song, not to mention numerous gigs opening for Jason and singing on both his and Amanda's next projects. "The biggest gift in all of this is that they just saw me as a person who is creative," she said. And Amanda was driving the Highwomen to be what it was always intended to be from the start: a collective that raises everyone up. *Everyone.* The next time the Highwomen would appear onstage in 2021, at a festival in California, Brittney would be singing with them, having practiced the songs on the flight with Natalie. "It was never about just four white women," Amanda said. "I want to expand it, have other voices and other stories and people who identify as women."

That wasn't the last time Brittney's phone would ring off the hook. Maren had shown up at the CMA Awards on November 11, with several nominations. It was her first big outing since the pandemic began, and she was feeling a bit uneasy about the whole thing—but she knew she was going to have a captive audience should she have the chance to make an acceptance speech. When her name was called for Female Vocalist of the Year, in a category with Miranda Lambert among them, she hugged Ryan and made her way to the stage in a shimmering floor-length dress as her infant son, Hayes, slept at home. After choking down tears, she took a deep breath and spoke.

"There are some names in my mind that I want to give recognition to because I'm just a fan of their music and they're as country as it gets, and I just want them to know how much we love them back," Maren said. "Linda Martell, Yola, Mickey Guyton, Rissi Palmer, Brittney Spencer, Rhiannon Giddens. There are so many amazing Black women that pioneered and continue to pioneer this genre, and I know they're going to come after me, they've come before me, but you've made this genre so, so beautiful. I hope you know that we see you. Thank you for making me so inspired as a singer in this genre."

Rissi Palmer had paused the CMA Awards so she could take a shower before Maren took the stage, and she was brushing her teeth when her phone started to buzz. Vigorously. "I just saw the speech and was left breathless," she said. Rissi had recently launched her Apple radio show *Color Me Country*, and it was taking off. Named after Linda

Martell's album of the same name, it was giving a platform where one was never going to appear if left up to the white men at record labels and white men at radio stations, as Mickey put it in a transformative roundtable with Rissi, Brittney, Miko Marks, and Reyna Roberts in the *New York Times*. "[Maren] chose a platform and a moment and chose to use it as an ally," Allison Russell said. "Careers jumpstarted—Maren just namechecking Brittney Spencer to millions of people. She mainstreamed the conversation."

Maren, meanwhile, wasn't done speaking. There were times during the months of 2020 that she thought about leaving Nashville altogether, which only heightened after country star Morgan Wallen was caught on camera saying a racial slur in early 2021. "I was like, 'Fuck this place,'" Maren said. "But then I was like, if I leave, everything will stay exactly the same. I thought, I need to stay in the ring and get the shit kicked out of me a little longer. And it's going to help more people than how I'm hurting right now. There's obviously so much work to be done, but I think I'm willing to have the hard conversations and also identify myself as part of the problem to get to a better spot because I don't want to leave Nashville or country music."

So instead of leaving Music Row or country radio, she thought she'd make it better than she found it, from the inside out. She started writing again, and came up with something different—a new song, called "Better Than We Found It."

"Better Than We Found It" was direct: the video tells the story of an immigrant impacted by Trump's desire to rescind DACA (Deferred Action for Childhood Arrivals), of Daniel Hambrick, a Nashville man murdered by police, who barely moved the needle in the national media—just another innocent Black man, shot with no justice served—and images of young activists. Maren called the song a protest song explicitly, lest anyone try to confuse her message or dilute its meaning.

In the video, Maren's singing from inside a church—she was urging her fans of faith to understand that fighting for Black Lives and equality should be an issue under God, something well within the realm of worship on a Sunday morning. Maybe these days, her world-view has shifted. Her church wasn't just music anymore, but where it can take her and what it can change.

It wasn't an instant ticket to a better world—one look around at Nashville's writing rooms or sessions, still predominantly white and male, would tell anyone that. One look at country radio, which did not play "Black Like Me," would absolutely tell you that. "Better Than We Found It" wasn't Maren declaring victory. It was her making a pledge to the future, and her pledge to understand and change how when we talk about gender parity in country music, too often Black women are left out of that conversation.

"I don't know how it got like this," Maren says in the letter to her son that was read in voiceover at the end of the video. That line carried the weight of every all-white lineup that passed without comment, every Black director glossed over in favor of the good ol' boy who is buddies with the label, every person who had been quiet while injustice and inequality raged like a tornado that far too many sat out, staying as comfortable as possible. If the last twenty years had been about making room for (mostly white) women, the next twenty years could be about making room for everyone else: Black women, queer people, Latinx artists, nonbinary, disabled, and indigenous musicians. Anyone who felt left out and wanted in: it was their country, too.

Mickey woke up on March 14, 2021, in her apartment and glanced out over the Los Angeles skyline. It was just like any other morning, with one specific difference: she would brush her teeth, feed her month-old baby, Grayson, have breakfast, and then start getting ready to go to the Grammy Awards. And not just as a guest, as a nominee, after receiving the news back in November that she had always dreamed about: a nod for "Black Like Me," the first Black solo female to ever be in the category. Ever. She was getting more and more used to being the first: the first solo Black woman to perform at the ACM Awards the previous September, singing "What Are You Going to Tell Her" with Keith Urban backing her up on piano—an event she'd go on to host with Keith the following year as the first Black woman to do so. She was determined to not only be the first but also not the last.

At the Grammys, Mickey sobbed through rehearsal and gathered herself together in time for the red carpet, where she wore a light peach dress with a sheer overlay covered in sequin pastel-colored butterflies that conjured up Dolly Parton.

Brittney Spencer watched from home. "I don't know that there is a Brittney Spencer, whatever the fuck that means, without Mickey Guyton," Brittney said. "I don't see it. She told the truth that not many people wanted to hear and she did it in the most brilliant, exquisite way. She was bold enough to tell the truth. People don't always want the truth, but it's the job of an artist to keep going, and to keep telling the truth."

Just a year ago, Kacey had come to the Grammys and, like the Chicks before her, burst doors open for women and whoever didn't quite fit into whatever the acceptable version of country music was or how to behave within it. And in 2021, the women were representing the genre were all Texan: Miranda, singing "Bluebird," a gorgeous ode to keeping the faith even when times get tough that had, despite the odds, become a number one country single. Maren, appearing alongside John Mayer and singing "The Bones," somehow combining rock and country and pop into a sound that was simply hers alone. And Mickey, in a floor-length gold dress, made history singing "Black Like Me" on the Grammy stage, Karen backing her up on piano.

Mickey didn't win an award that night, but what she gave to country music mattered more. "I realize that not only am I walking through those doors as a Black woman," she said backstage, "I need to hold the door open for many other Black, brown, LGBTQIA+ artists that have the same dreams." And she meant it. "It's so cool to be in this part of country music," Brooke Eden said, who watched from home and sobbed. "Where Black people and Brown people and queer people can feel comfortable at a country concert and feel comfortable listening to the music and feel like they see themselves in it. It's crazy that for so long it was just not that. It feels like a whole different world."

There were no big after-parties or celebrations that year after the Grammy Awards: Mickey went home to her family, and Karen to her hotel with her husband, where they ate some take-out sushi and watched TV. They'd wake up and keep working the next morning on another first: Mickey's first album, *Remember Her Name*. Ten years, and more, in the making. Finally.

Mercy was dancing with everything she had. The six-year-old daughter of Jason Isbell and Amanda Shires, the little girl who had inspired the Highwomen, was jumping up and down sidestage with a pair of pink headphones over her ears and a pink mask on her face, up past her bedtime. It was October 17, 2021, a little under a month since Mickey's album, *Remember Her Name*, had finally been released to the world. And here Mickey was, back at the Ryman after she had debuted "What Are You Gonna Tell Her?" at CRS, with Karen at the piano once again and Victoria and Emma-Lee up in the pews, screaming and clapping with everything they had. Jason had asked Mickey to open the show, one of seven Black female artists he'd tapped to do the same for his Ryman residency, including Brittney Spencer, Amythyst Kiah, Allison Russell, Joy Oladokun, Shemekia Copeland, and Adia Victoria. Jason was a Highwoman, after all, and he was going to bring more and more people along for the ride. A crowded table, really.

Brittney, having performed the night prior, was up in the crowd watching Mickey, too—she'd become a veteran on the road with Jason by now, and could barely walk through the Ryman without getting recognized or passing by a new fan. Margo Price would join Jason and Adia Victoria a few nights later on her song "You Was Born to Die," a brilliant reclamation of the blues—and Margo, who'd sold out three nights at the Ryman on her own in 2018, had no problem playing backup singer to put her friend center stage.

For many in the audience, it was one of the first times they'd been back to see live music after the past year and a half of pause. There were nervous hugs and celebratory drinks in plastic cups. There were masked faces. There were long-lost hellos. There were vaccine cards stashed into purses and COVID protocols.

Remember Her Name was Mickey's story—every drop of it so far. The song she wished she could have heard when she was driving to Atlanta to have her hair smoothed and straightened so she could look like the white country starlets, called "Love My Hair." The one that started it all, "Better Than You Left Me." The one for her husband, the one for her friends. The one for the party, the one for the patriots. The one, "Black Like Me," that got her a Grammy nomination. The one that brought her full circle: "What Are You Gonna Tell Her?"

Mickey, in a black dress cinched with a belt, would open up her set with that very song. This time, though, she had something different to tell her, something different to say. "When I stepped on this stage at Country Radio Seminar week in front of a bunch of radio guys, singing about the marginalization of women," Mickey said, "I thought in that moment my career would be over, and I was perfectly okay with leaving it on this stage. But what ended up happening was the exact opposite." They wouldn't ever play her songs much on country radio, if at all, but it was nowhere near the end. She was here. But not trying to woo those programmers anymore, crunching on their free lunches, a marionette song and dance.

She ended her set on a song called "All American," asking everyone to raise their iPhones high with their flashlights on, illuminating the Ryman seats into a ring of twinkling stars. This was country music, somehow. This was country music, thankfully. It may not have been the country music that you know—or that you think you know.

But it was.

It is.

AFTERWORD

"Play our f*@#in records please and thank you"
—Jennifer Nettles

A decade ago, I packed up the entire contents of my life, all 450 square feet of it crammed into my apartment on Ridge Street in Manhattan, and moved, despite the confusion of many friends and acquaintances, to Nashville, Tennessee. It was a few months before the town went from nothing more than a dot on a map—in their eyes, not in reality—to the "It City" as dubbed by the *New York Times* in an article that changed nearly everything for the place. Outside of my brother, who plays the banjo and loves old-time and bluegrass music, most people in my orbit couldn't possibly understand why I wanted to move to the South, based only on assumptions they had made about it from movies or books, and not from a careful understanding of the complexities that existed on our side of the Mason-Dixon Line. I was a Jewish girl from New York City, and I was supposed to stay exactly where I was, where it made more sense. But I had gone for a visit to Tennessee in 2011 and fallen in love—I had never experienced a town with so much good music in unlikely places, and so much free parking.

Arriving in Nashville felt like landing in a place I had only concocted in my dreams, an imaginary musical summer camp—I cringe to admit something so rose-colored now, but it was the truth to me then. In my first week as a resident a wonderful woman named Traci

Thomas, who is Jason Isbell's manager, took me to a small storefront on the east side of town where Nikki Lane, an alternative country artist with many tattoos and even more give-no-shits, had assembled a vintage shop and makeshift creative space: a band from Norway was playing out front. We hopped in Traci's car across the river to see another musician, this time a songwriter from Canada named Lindi Ortega, playing inside a leather goods store.

My first house in Nashville was yellow and old, old enough that the floorboards routinely broke, pipes burst in the front yard, and the kitchen flooded (not to mention the family of possums that lived in the attic and the stray cat that did not make it out alive). But it was also within walking distance from a place called Mad Donna's, where you could see world-class songwriters almost any night of the week before it closed down as the neighborhood went from slowly gentrifying to warp-speed gentrification on steroids. The bartender, Terry, would sling shots while an unknown Margo Price would play a set to a crowd of ten or twenty, sometimes mostly comprising friends just to show a little support. Other nights I would sit outside on the screened porch and spin Caitlin Rose's record on a turquoise portable Crosley.

I didn't grow up with country radio other than in the back of my father's car (he loved Shania Twain and Clint Black), doing the divorced kid shuffle from house to house, so it didn't inform me and I can't pretend to know a childhood that I did not. I grew up listening to A Tribe Called Quest, Liz Phair, and the Grateful Dead on my yellow boombox, singing to the Indigo Girls or Fiona Apple, or copying Bob Dylan lyrics into a notebook so I could study them—not because I had any designs to ever be a musician or songwriter, but because I didn't. I knew I liked words and stories, and country music, when I discovered it, seemed to tell those stories best of all.

I also knew I loved Texas, and Texan culture. My dad moved to Austin when I was about ten, which happened to be around the same time that I, like many of my peers, had become a fervent horse girl. My mom would reluctantly put me on a plane from New York and I'd spend my summer breaks, while my dad worked, at a ranch along the lake shoveling horseshit, scraping the sweat off the ponies, and riding in the grass. I didn't like the possibly venomous creatures that lurked around so much, but I did grow to love the Lone Star State, and also came to understand that it was a special place, a country in and of itself like everyone always said it was. I handled things for myself that I never thought I could at that horse ranch. Texas does that to you.

My first year in Nashville was generally a magical time full of live music, too much money spent at Grimey's records, and fast drives along slow roads. But as I started working as a reporter in town, I noticed a lot of things—there was always something about the dynamic that I just couldn't put my finger on. There was an invisible wall I couldn't touch, the way publicists circled around their clients, sitting with their back to the booth to listen in on our conversations. One time, while interviewing a famous pop star and a country duo she had collaborated with, the publicist even pretended to leave the room for our talk as I'd requested, but then lingered at the back when I wasn't looking. What could she possibly have been so afraid of, so intent to protect? And when the CMA Awards tried to prevent the media from asking questions on the red carpet about the horrific Route 91 Harvest festival shooting, as they did one year, what was the goal then?

Once I started digging and understanding more deeply the way that country music treats anyone who has a say in something that didn't conform to the status quo, I couldn't get enough of the rule break-ers. The Chicks, for speaking up against the Iraq War, something I'd paid close attention to back in 2003 while living in downtown New York and being dusted in soot and smoke for weeks after watching 9/11 unfold outside my window—and I still didn't think dropping bombs on innocent children was the answer. To LeAnn Rimes, who was such a musical pioneer but had been cast aside strangely for an affair that led to a happy marriage, a sin we've forgiven in men many times over. Chely Wright, who came out in 2010, the first out lesbian country singer. Miranda Lambert, who built a massive career without ever catering to what a superstar was supposed to do. Dolly Parton, of course, who has been country music's conscience by investing in childhood literacy and speaking openly about equal rights for all, along with writing some of the greatest songs of all time—not to mention helping fund the COVID-19 vaccine.

Jack Kerouac said the only ones for him were the mad ones, and I felt that way about country music. The rule breakers, the trailblazers. You're programmed to believe that these are mostly men—"the outlaws"—but I started to find myself fascinated with the genre's women, and enraged when I realized that catching one of their songs on the radio or atop a festival bill was like spotting a shooting star.

There are certain moments of my career that I will probably never forget: being in the studio with the Highwomen as they recorded part of their debut album, or giving Margo Price a ride home from an interview in 2015, when she had sold her car to fund her breakthrough album *Midwest Farmer's Daughter*, or seeing Kacey play Christmas songs to a teeny group at a record store that included me and my little Jewish son, or crying while watching Yola in a brewery next to my friend Sarah, who always carries tissues for these sorts of things. I certainly won't forget the morning that a piece I had spent over six months researching and reporting, about the culture of sexual harassment experienced by women in country music for *Rolling Stone*, went live and how I turned to my husband in the kitchen and asked him how he felt about packing up his bags and moving to a new city. I wondered if we'd be run out of town—so far, so good, but there's still time, I guess.

But mostly I spent the better part of a decade both angry and delighted, following these women from the early stages of their careers to massive international success. I remember the first time I heard Maren Morris in 2012, with her song "Loose Change." I couldn't really believe how good it was—it had elements of everything rootsy that I loved, a rock-and-roll swagger, a little Sheryl Crow and a little Dolly and infinite catchiness. Over the years I have interviewed her several times, and she was my first in-person interview after the pandemic for this book, beginning our chat by showing off a few photos of her beautiful baby boy.

The first time I met Kacey was at Gojo Ethiopian restaurant in Nashville in 2013. Her debut album, *Same Trailer Different Park*, was about to come out, and I couldn't stop listening to it—I'd grown up in cities and not rural Texas, but I felt like I heard myself in that record anyway. We talked a lot about her steadfast support for the queer community, and I will never forget her telling me with stoic, serious eyes that she'd rather have a few thousand fans for being true to herself than a few million for being who she wasn't. She now has millions of them, and without ever once wavering.

Mickey came to me courtesy of my old editor at *Rolling Stone Country*, Beville Dunkerley. Beville was a huge admirer of Mickey's, and I became one, too—I ignorantly assumed that she would, quite naturally, become the town's next massive star, at Carrie Underwood's level. I soon realized that yes, while things were difficult for women, white women could be trailblazers and still succeed on their own terms, if not on country radio. Mickey did everything to play the game right, and the industry's deep and pervasive racism still wouldn't let her in. And now, her debut album, *Remember Her Name*, over a decade in the making, has changed the landscape of country music forever. You may have seen her take one of the biggest stages of all, even, in 2022: singing "The Star-Spangled Banner" at the Super Bowl.

Mickey, Kacey, and Maren, along with so many of the other women in this book, from the Chicks to Brandi Carlile to Margo Price, succeeded despite everything laid ahead of them—and not just that, they succeeded on exactly their own terms. It was never easy, but it was always worth it. Just like writing this book, as I did in the middle of a pandemic with two children under seven to care for. Not easy, but worth it.

"It all ends well and in a better place," Maren told me over a glass of wine as we sat down to discuss this book. "But it just takes some hard knocks to get there."

AUTHOR'S NOTE

The stories, quotes, details, and information in this book stem from a decade of working as an on-the-ground reporter and journalist in Nashville and from extensive new interviews and research, as well as my previously published work. For this book specifically, I conducted new interviews with Maren Morris, Mickey Guyton, Brandi Carlile, Amanda Shires, Patty Griffin, Margo Price, Dr. Tressie McMillan Cottom, LeAnn Rimes, Jay Sweet, Carly Pearce, Shane McAnally, Brittney Spencer, Charlie Worsham, Brandy Clark, Rissi Palmer, Kate York, Madi Diaz, Ashley McBryde, Mindy Smith, Tracy Gershon, Radney Foster, Gena Johnson, Natalie Hemby, Beth Laird, Janet Weir, Hunter Kelly, Luke Laird, Kelly McCartney, Chris Payne, Carlo Rotella, Kree Harrison, Elice Cuff, Fount Lynch, Leslie Fram, Monte Robison, Daniel Tashian, Josh Abbott, Catherine Powell, Mike Grimes, Stephanie Wright, Courtney Jaye, Chely Wright, Perez Hilton, Hailey Whitters, Kalie Shorr, John Strohm, Abe Stoklasa, Staci Kirpach, Lauren Tingle, RJ Curtis, Dr. Jada Watson, Jules Wortman, Karen Kosowski, Taylor Tatsch, Dan Layus, Beverly Keel, Mitch Lazorko, Ty Herndon, Lilly Hiatt, Julian Raymond, Victoria Banks, Tommy Alverson, Amanda Martinez, Leah Turner, Lloyd Maines, Patrick Bolek, Van Darien, Kelleigh Bannen, David Macias, Fraser Churchill, Jessica Harp, Allison Russell, and more, as well as the late John DeFoore, who passed away while this book was being edited. I am so grateful I had the privilege of speaking with him. His passion radiated through the phone, and his contribution to the lives of the women on these pages is never to be underestimated.

The archives at the Country Music Hall of Fame were also so helpful: thank you especially to Kathleen Campbell for letting me browse your collections in the middle of a pandemic, and for taking all the necessary precautions to make it safe and comfortable.

I referenced many books as well in the writing process—these are some I found useful even if they are not quoted here, and I recommend them for further reading: *Rednecks and Bluenecks: The Politics of Country Music* by Chris Willman; *Woman Walk the Line: How the Women in Country Music Changed Our Lives*, edited by Holly Gleason; *Finding Her Voice: The Saga of Women in Country Music* by Mary A. Bufwack and Robert K. Oermann; *Like Me: Confessions of a Heartland Country Singer* by Chely Wright; *Broken Horses* by Brandi Carlile; *From This Moment On* by Shania Twain; *Segregating Sound: Inventing Folk and Pop Music in the Age of Jim Crow* by Karl Hagstrom Miller; *The Selling Sound: The Rise of the Country Music Industry* by Diane Pecknold; *Rednecks, Queers, and Country Music* by Dr. Nadine Hubbs; *Creating Country Music: Fabricating Authenticity* by Richard A. Peterson; *She Come By It Natural: Dolly Parton and the Women Who Lived Her Songs* by Sarah Smarsh; *The First Collection of Criticism by a Living Female Rock Critic* by Jessica Hopper; *Women Who Rock: Bessie to Beyoncé, Girl Groups to Riot Grrrl* by Evelyn McDonnell; *Songbooks: The Literature of American Popular Music* by Eric Weisbard; *I'd Fight the World: A Political History of Old-Time, Hillbilly, and Country Music* by By Peter La Chapelle, and *White Feminism: From the Suffragettes to Influencers and Who They Leave Behind* by Koa Beck, among so many texts that have been embedded into my brain over the years. I also recommend and referenced the podcasts *Color Me Country* with Rissi Palmer and scores of wonderful Apple Country podcasts, as well as *Cocaine & Rhinestones* by Tyler Mahan Coe and *Salute the Songbird* by Maggie Rose.

I'm not sure who to thank for Newspapers.com, but, as they say here in the South, bless your heart. And I mean that in the nondismissive way.

The following are further breakdowns of sources and research for each chapter.

CHAPTER 1

This chapter was written with several stories from the *Tyler Morning Telegraph* (reported by Jonathan Perry, thank you for catching those priceless moments with the Two Bits), *Fort Worth Star-Telegram*, *Country Aircheck*, the *FADER*, C-SPAN, and the Associated Press, as well as through deep research into events around the Bush-Gore election. It was informed by original interviews with Dr. Tressie McMillan Cottom, Chely Wright, Brandi Carlile, Staci Kirpach, and others, and a paragraph is adapted from a story I wrote for *Rolling Stone* called "How Shania Twain Empowered an Unlikely Group of Artists." I attended the Bridgestone concert referenced at the beginning of the chapter, and it was as transformative as I hope it reads here.

CHAPTER 2

Articles from the *Fort Worth Star-Telegram* once again anchored these pages, along with research in outlets such as the *Dallas Observer*, the *New York Times*, and CMT. Original interviews with Maren Morris, Tommy Alverson, LeAnn Rimes, Amanda Shires, and Mickey Guyton were core to this chapter, and sections relating to LeAnn Rimes appeared previously, albeit in a slightly different form, in an article I wrote for *Rolling Stone* called "LeAnn Rimes' 'Blue': How the Album Paved the Way for Women in Country."

CHAPTER 3

Reporting in the *Los Angeles Times*, *Time*, the *Guardian*, *Rolling Stone*, World Radio History, and *R&R* magazine informed this chapter, as did original interviews with Lloyd Maines, Maren Morris, Mickey Guyton,

Patty Griffin, Tracy Gershon, and more. The work of Dr. Jada Watson and Dr. Lori Burns in "Resisting Exile and Asserting Musical Voice: The Dixie Chicks Are 'Not Ready to Make Nice'" was quite informative and recommended as further reading, as well as Chris Willman's book *Rednecks and Bluenecks*. Laura Ingraham's *Shut Up & Sing: How Elites from Hollywood, Politics, and the Media Are Subverting America* is also referenced, but I wouldn't recommend that one unless you like to be angry. I also referenced a piece I wrote for *Stereogum* about *O Brother, Where Art Thou?* where I worked out some of these themes and ideas in the context of the Coen brothers' film.

CHAPTER 4

Research at the Country Music Hall of Fame was core to this chapter, as well as original interviews with Maren Morris, Tracy Gershon, and Natalie Hemby. Articles from Alan Cackett, KICKS 105, the *Dallas Observer*, the *Nashville Scene*, the *New York Times*, and *Entertainment Weekly* were also key. I also found a piece by Jewly Hight on NPR about Miranda Lambert to be an informative and insightful reference, and I referred back to published interviews and conversations I had myself with Miranda for *American Songwriter*, the *Nashville Scene*, and *Rolling Stone*.

CHAPTER 5

Thank you to Maren Morris, Patrick Bolek, Mickey Guyton, RJ Curtis, and Rissi Palmer for the original interviews that shaped this chapter, as well as articles from the *Ft. Worth Start-Telegram* and Rissi's own *Color Me Country* podcast. Elaine Marsilio wrote a great profile of Maren at the time in the *Star-Telegram* that was illuminating of this point in her career. I also reference the essay "The Dolly Moment" by Dr. Tressie McMillan Cottom.

CHAPTER 6

I am so honored to have had the chance to talk to John DeFoore, who brought so much insight and grace to this chapter. The Country

Music Hall of Fame, Tracy Gershon, Maren Morris, Patty Griffin, Taylor Tatsch, and Staci Kirpach provided key interviews. I also drew from *American Songwriter*, the *Lubbock Avalanche-Journal*, the *Dallas Morning News*, *SPIN*, and Taste of Country as well as the book *Make Me a Star* by Anastasia Brown. Kacey gave a wonderful speech for *Variety* that I referenced here, and I also delved into my own work on the liner notes for Loretta Lynn's *Back to the Country* for a VinylMePlease special rerelease.

CHAPTER 7

Radney Foster, Monte Robison, Madi Diaz, Kate York, Elice Cuff, Kree Harrison, Courtney Jaye, Maren Morris, Daniel Tashian, Mindy Smith, and Charlie Worsham all provided the vibrant details and recollections that made this story come to life. My sit-down with Kacey in 2014 for *American Songwriter* was also quite informative. Particular thanks to Elice for sitting down at Ugly Mugs and reminiscing about so many funny moments, and for showing me some photos from inside the beloved and stately Hotel Villa. "I had to be Hannah Montana" quote is an outtake from a conversation I had with Kacey for *American Songwriter* in 2014.

CHAPTER 8

Beth Laird, Mike Grimes, Ben Glover, Shane McAnally, and Brandy Clark interviews were important to this chapter. Ben and Mike really helped me reconstruct a seminal early time for Kacey at the Basement and in Nashville, and I loved talking to Shane and Brandy about their formative years in this town—as individuals and together, they truly changed the game for songwriters as well as queer people in Nashville. Give them their flowers, now.

CHAPTER 9

Thanks to Josh Abbott for the story that made these pages sing alongside interviews with Chely Wright, Maren Morris, Mitch Lazorko, Taylor Tatsch, Stephanie Wright, Fount Lynch, Mickey Guyton, Julian Raymond, and Leslie Fram. I loved hearing about Mickey's progression in Los Angeles from Mickey herself and on wonderful podcasts where she has discussed this early time in her career such as *Salute the Songbird with Maggie Rose* and *Southern Living's Biscuits & Jam*. They were excellent references.

CHAPTER 10

So many people helped rebuild the moments in this chapter, including Luke Laird, Shane McAnally, and Stephanie Wright, as well as Fount Lynch, Natalie Hemby, Taylor Tatsch, and Mickey Guyton. This is a seminal chapter for me as it also lines up with when I moved to Nashville and started to witness so many of these events myself. My husband was at Kacey's first CRS show—he ran outside to tell me about it immediately, he was so struck by Kacey's performance. She became a regular feature in a little music blog I launched in town at the time, called Lockeland Springsteen. The stories here from Katie Armiger were extracted from a story I wrote for *Rolling Stone* about the culture of sexual harassment at country radio—that piece and that work drive so much of this book; it's always bubbling under the surface.

CHAPTER 11

Maren, Kate York, Mike Grimes, John Strohm, Laura Wright, Abe Stoklasa, and others provided great insight to this chapter and to this early stage in Maren's Nashville life. I reference Jody Rosen's work a lot here and his creation of the term "bro-country," as well as reporting by Grady Smith in *Entertainment Weekly*.

CHAPTER 12

Fount Lynch, Brandy Clark, Hunter Kelly, Kelly McCartney, Chris Payne, and Ty Herndon were key to this story, and I made reference to my own reporting in *Rolling Stone*. Special thanks to Fount for the several phone calls and multiple hours spent reconstructing such a great moment in Kacey's life and career. And of course, much debt to the bravery of Taylor Swift for telling her truth and her story: it changed the way the tides flowed and opened up my own eyes to a world that is all smiles on the outside, but so painfully broken, and sometimes dangerous, on the inside.

CHAPTER 13

Dan Layus, Maren Morris, Luke Laird, Shane McAnally, Kate York, Brandy Clark, and Mickey Guyton all illuminated this chapter—and I must add that "Loose Change" is the song that first made me fall in love with Maren; I remember spinning it on ReverbNation thanks to a tip from my cousin Adam. A great *Billboard* cover with Kacey and Katy Perry was informative here as well. Grateful to Mickey for texting me the demo for "Woman's World." It's such an incredible song!

CHAPTER 14

Lilly Hiatt, Maren Morris, Kree Harrison, Dr. Jada Watson, Beverly Keel, Tracy Gershon, Leslie Fram, Larry Heath, Kelleigh Bannen, Mickey Guyton, Leah Turner, Maren Morris, and Janet Weir helped set the scene through interviews for this chapter, and the work of Dr. Charles Hughes and Dr. Diane Pecknold was extremely insightful. This chapter is in memory of busbee—the impact of his work and vision cannot be measured in this town, and it is lasting, important, and so valuable. He is so terribly missed.

CHAPTER 15

Margo Price, Maren Morris, Gena Johnson, Daniel Tashian, Amanda Shires, Ashley McBryde, and Mickey Guyton informed this chapter, and I highly recommend the essay "Another Country" by Karen Pittelman, as it's so important to understand the roots of this genre and to also recognize the deep, systemic racism that permeates the culture of country music.

CHAPTER 16

I was lucky enough to attend the unforgettable album premiere that opens this chapter, and had a great conversation with Brandi Carlile and Amanda Shires that helped shape this chapter. I wrote a feature on Kacey for *Rolling Stone* that year about *Golden Hour*, and spoke to

Kacey then as she trucked along in her tour bus from town to town. I was lucky enough to hear about the Highwomen for the first time from Brandi at her home in Seattle, interviewing her for *Rolling Stone*.

CHAPTER 17

Dr. Jada Watson was core to live-reporting this CRS conversation, and I was lucky enough to be in the room to witness the Highwomen recording their debut album, as well as in Chicago for LakeShake and at the Highwomen's event at RCA Studio A—this chapter pulls from that reporting I did for *Rolling Stone*. Jay Sweet, Amanda Shires, Catherine Powell, Allison Russell, and Brandi Carlile provided crucial stories about the Newport Folk Festival. I feel very honored to get to follow Brandi, Amanda, Maren, and the Highwomen around as much as I did; it was all quite unforgettable. I'll leave the mystery of whether or not I got a Highwoman tattoo myself up in the air, though.

CHAPTER 18

Thank you to Mickey Guyton, Victoria Banks, Karen Kosowski, Maren Morris, Brittney Spencer, Brooke Eden, and Rissi Palmer for illuminating this chapter. Some of these words were previously worked out on my own Substack newsletter, about Maren's "Better Than We Found It." This was the hardest chapter to write in many ways, as it picks up right when a tornado hit my neighborhood, and then, of course, the pandemic shut the world down. I always imagined I'd write this chapter out on the road that summer, hopping from concert to concert, but instead we were all at home doing things through Zoom. I could have skipped over this time with a quick paragraph and instead picked up reporting when things opened up again, but I felt it was important to instead capture what happened when the world shut down. We were able to see so much more then—the deep injustices in this world, the importance of thrusting even harder toward progress, toward making ourselves deeply uncomfortable if we needed to. It's how we leave this world better than we found it.

ACKNOWLEDGMENTS

First and foremost, thank you to Maren, Mickey, and all of the wonderful people who generously gave me their time to help make this book happen—in the middle of a pandemic. Thank you for the conversations, for letting me pop into recording sessions or your buses or video shoots or private spaces or even your homes (hi, Brandi Carlile) for work over the years. This book was written in 2020 and 2021, but it has truly been in process for so long, and every interview or concert has been a building block to where I ended up in these pages.

Thank you to the amazing people who helped along the way with research and reads: Holly G at Black Opry, Oriane Damas, Katherine Beekman, Bronte Lebo, and Allison Hussey. Holly, you are the future of country music journalism (and the genre itself as far as I am concerned), and I am so grateful just to watch your journey as the first grantee of the Rosetta Fund. If you're reading this and want the next books on country music to be written by people who aren't just straight white men, please donate: https://www.raineydayfund.org/rosetta-fund.

Thank you to everyone who talked me down from a cliff or responded to a late-night text message panic session, especially SK, whose wisdom and friendship are so important to me. I promise to give you more than five minutes' notice next time I drag you to a Kacey Musgraves pop-up event. A big thanks to Sarah Rodman for your eye and support and for always having tissues at concerts and for catching little things in this manuscript that only your brilliant eye could. And thank you to all my Slack channel women: Alison, Caryn, Hilary, Maura, and Annie, for the support in the midst of breakdowns and excellent advice, with a little extra shout-out to Hilary for being so grounding when I felt truly lost at times. A big thank-you to my Don't Rock the Inbox partner-in-newsletter Natalie, I look forward to reading your books someday soon. A big thank-you to Jon Bernstein for your input and help, and invaluable eyes—someday we will start our Americana gossip magazine and our Country Stars in New York blog and it's going to transform lives, I just know it.

Thanks to my great editors over the years who helped inform the work that birthed this story, especially Joseph Hudak and Jon Freeman at *Rolling Stone Country*. Joe, I am grateful for your daily Slack support, and you are an important country confidant, editor, and friend. Thank you to the writers and scholars in the Nashville community and beyond, who I look up to so much, many of whom I am so lucky to call friends, including Lorie Liebig, Dr. Jada Watson, Jewly Hight, Ann Powers, Hunter Kelly, Brittney McKenna, Marcus K. Dowling, and so many more. Thank you to Patrick Rodgers for responding to my email when I first arrived in Nashville and letting me write for the *Scene*; Nashville wouldn't be nearly the same without this crucial alt-weekly. Thank you deeply to Beville Dunkerley for bringing me into the *Rolling Stone Country* world and changing the trajectory of my work. A deep thank-you to Corinne Cummings for your fact-checking, such a crucial part of this process (I added this line in after you finished, so I hope there are no factual errors in it). Thank you to anyone who ever provided childcare so I could write and work during the daylight, especially Holly Street Daycare.

To the publicists and wranglers, thank you for helping me get these interviews in crazy times, when we all were just trying to get through the day, especially Asha Goodman Trebing and Lori Christian. To Catherine Powell, your cover photo gives this book a visual life I could not have dreamed of—I am in awe of your talent. Thank you, thank you.

Thank you to my agent, Susan, for reaching out to me to get this train out of the station, I couldn't have done it without that push and I love that you know and cherish country music as much as I do. To my editor, Serena, thank you for believing in this story and understanding every thread of it, and offering so much trust and care. It also meant a lot in this process to have a fellow mother trucking alongside me; I'm truly not sure what I would have done without a fellow understanding parent in these complicated times! I am so grateful for you, Amy, Anita, Hannah, Sarah, Pauline, Steven, and everyone at Holt.

To my high school English teachers Saul Isaacson and Keith Kachtick, for making me believe early on that I could be okay at this writing thing. I hope you know how much it mattered to me. Thank you to Allison and Maritza for being my friends for several decades now, I'll meet you at the chatchmo someday again soon.

And last but obviously not least, to my parents and family for always supporting my dream of being a writer even when it might not have been the most practical choice, and for not thinking I was nuts to move to Nashville: my mom, dad, stepmom, and siblings Jane, Frank, Kim, Ilan (eeeeeeeeeezzzzzz!), and Hilary. Mom, thank you for being my teammate growing up through crazy cherry-pit spitting contests in gross hotels, trying on ridiculous clothes we couldn't afford, spying on Bruce Springsteen at Fred's, and so many fun nights over sushi and bad television. Dad, thank you for loving Shania Twain, for long drives talking about where the universe ends, boat rides, and Bubby & Papa. I love you both. P.S., Ilan, thanks for being the cool big brother who played banjo and fiddle, obviously I wouldn't be in Nashville writing this book if it weren't for that.

Thank you most of all to my most special little unit of Mike, Stone, and Dylan. I know it wasn't an easy process trying to deal with me writing a book in the middle of a pandemic, and I know there were times when I was distracted or busy or couldn't play Lego or watch that cartoon with you and I wish I could have. It was really hard, but I hope it shows you that it's worth doing things that matter to you, even when it feels impossible. Mike, thank you for being that rock and for the empty book display case that made me cry, but also made me feel like someone believed in me. And there's really no topping that. Thank you for talking to me that night at the Fat Black Pussycat, and for all the adventures we have had in between from New York to Paris to Los Angeles, I can't wait for whatever is in store next, even if it's just hanging out on the couch watching reruns of *Six Feet Under* for the hundredth time, I love you. RBSIBWTV. Love, little Silz.

Stone and Dylan, I am more proud of you than words can say and I love you to the end of the universe and back again. Never give up, and always be kind. I love you, and this book is for you.

PLAYLIST

This playlist travels, albeit informally, chronologically with the book. Listen along if you will, and hopefully be compelled to dig deeper.

Shania Twain, "Man! I Feel Like a Woman!"
Faith Hill, "Breathe"
Dolly Parton, "Jolene"
Kitty Wells, "It Wasn't God Who Made Honky Tonk Angels"
Loretta Lynn, "Coal Miner's Daughter"
Patsy Cline, "I Fall to Pieces"
Bobbie Gentry, "Ode to Billie Joe" and "Fancy"
Jeannie C. Riley, "Harper Valley P.T.A."
Sammi Smith, "Help Me Make It Through the Night"
Tammy Wynette, "Stand By Your Man"
Linda Martell, "Color Him Father"
Rose Maddox, "Lonely Teardrops"
The Carter Family, "Foggy Mountain Top"
Wynonna, "No One Else on Earth"
Jamie Lin Wilson, "The Being Gone"
Freda and the Firedogs, "The Only Thing Missing Is You"
Jessi Colter, "I'm Not Lisa"
Kacey Musgraves, "Rainbow"
Yola, "Faraway Look"
Maggie Rogers, "Light On"

Chely Wright, "Single White Female"

Tanya Tucker, "Delta Dawn"

LeAnn Rimes, "Blue"

Dolly Parton, "Coat of Many Colors"

Frankie Staton, "Never Too Late"

Martina McBride, "Independence Day"

Kacey Musgraves, "Good Ol' Boys Club"

Patty Griffin, "Truth #2"

The Chicks, "Travelin' Soldier"

Miranda Lambert, "Me and Charlie Talking"

The Chicks, "Not Ready to Make Nice"

Rissi Palmer, "Country Girl"

Carrie Underwood, "Before He Cheats"

Loretta Lynn, "The Pill"

Miranda Lambert, "Dry Town"

The Wreckers, "Leave the Pieces"

Kree Harrison, "This Old Thing"

Mindy Smith, "Highs and Lows"

Taylor Swift, "Tim McGraw"

Josh Abbott Band featuring Kacey Musgraves, "Oh, Tonight"

Kacey Musgraves, "Merry Go 'Round"

The Band Perry, "If I Die Young"

Nikki Lane, "Walk of Shame"

Pistol Annies, "Hell on Heels"

Jason Isbell, "Cover Me Up"

Sturgill Simpson, "Life of Sin"

Tim McGraw, "Last Turn Home"

Mickey Guyton, "Better Than You Left Me"

Kacey Musgraves, "Follow Your Arrow"

Brandy Clark, "Stripes"

Ashley Monroe, "Weed Instead of Roses"

The Highwomen, "Loose Change"

Mickey Guyton, "Pretty Little Mustang"

Maren Morris, "My Church"

Margo Price, "Hands of Time"

Cam, "Burning House"

Kacey Musgraves, "Biscuits"

Beyoncé featuring The Chicks, "Daddy Lessons"
Carly Pearce, "Every Little Thing"
Ashley McBryde, "A Little Dive Bar in Dahlonega"
Amanda Shires, "You Are My Home"
Kacey Musgraves, "Golden Hour"
Zedd, Maren Morris, and Grey, "The Middle"
Brandi Carlile, "The Joke"
Our Native Daughters, "You're Not Alone"
Allison Russell, "Nightflyer"
Maren Morris, "Girl"
The Highwomen, "Redesigning Women"
Mickey Guyton, "Black Like Me"
Dolly Parton, "9 to 5"
Mickey Guyton, "What Are You Gonna Tell Her?"
The Chicks, "March March"
Brooke Eden, "Got No Choice"
D'orjay The Singing Shaman, "New Kind of Outlaw"
Hailey Whitters, "Ten Year Town"
Jaime Wyatt, "Neon Cross"
Lauren Jenkins, "No Saint"
Kelsey Waldon, "Anyhow"
Emily Scott Robinson, "The Dress"
The Highwomen, "Crowded Table"
Brittney Spencer, "Sober & Skinny"
Rhiannon Giddens, "Freedom Highway"
Leah Turner, "Vaquera and the Cowboy"
Miko Marks, "Ancestors"
Reyna Roberts, "Stompin' Grounds"
Maren Morris, "Better Than We Found It"

ABOUT THE AUTHOR

An award-winning journalist, **Marissa R. Moss** has written about the topic of gender inequality on the country airwaves for outlets like *Rolling Stone*, NPR, *Billboard*, *Entertainment Weekly*, and many more. Moss was the 2018 recipient of the Rolling Stone Chet Flippo Award for Excellence in Country Music Journalism, and the 2019 *Nashville Scene* Best of Nashville Best Music Reporter. She has been a guest on the *Today* show, *Entertainment Tonight*, *CBS This Morning*, NPR's *Weekend Edition*, WPLN, the *Pop Literacy* podcast, and more. She resides in Nashville, TN, with her husband and two children.